NOBODY
LEFT

CONVERSATIONS WITH FAMOUS RADICALS, PROGRESSIVES
AND CULTURAL ICONS ABOUT THE END OF DISSENT,
REVOLUTION, AND LIBERALISM IN AMERICA

MR. FISH

FANTAGRAPHICS BOOKS • SEATTLE

Special thanks to the Village Voice Media Company,
Harper's Magazine, *The Nation* and Truthdig.com for funding
my excursions into the ravaged wastelands of American
counterculturalism in search of survivors. And a very special
thanks to Gary Groth for always keeping his eyes peeled for the
decency police while I fluff the naked truth into something lewdly
formidable and entirely capable of begetting future generations.

Publisher: GARY GROTH
Editor: GARY GROTH
Designer: JUSTIN ALLAN-SPENCER
Production: CHRISTINA HWANG

Fantagraphics Books, Inc.
7563 Lake City Way NE
Seattle WA 98115
(800) 657-1100

Fantagraphics.com • Twitter: @fantagraphics • facebook.com/fantagraphics.

First Fantagraphics Books edition: June 2020
Library of Congress Control Number: 2019944931
ISBN 978-1-68396-293-9
Printed in the Republic of Korea

CONTENTS

For my friend Chris Hedges,
who was not interviewed for this book
because my internal dialogue will forever be
in conversation with his radical example

AUTHOR'S NOTE

Papa what is the moon supposed to advertise?
—Carl Sandburg, from *The People, Yes*

IN 1857 KARL MARX ASKED an important question about the stupefying effect of human ingenuity when made tangible in the face of more profound considerations involving perhaps deeper existential truths: "[I]s Achilles possible with powder and lead? Or the *Iliad* with the printing press, not to mention the printing machine? Do not the song and the saga and the muse necessarily come to an end with the printer's bar, hence do not the necessary conditions of epic poetry vanish?" In view of the book you now hold in your hand, the agency of the question remains relevant, perhaps even more so, when framed blatantly and in worrisome contempt of the modern world: Does not the exploratory wanderings of the human heart and the precise and inquisitive inspections of the wholly unknown by the intellect come to an end with modern technology and the automation of private curiosity and public authoritarianism?

(I will pause to allow my reader to remove his or her phone and to simplify the question for a Google search hoping that he or she can pursue a viable answer without succumbing to the innumerable siren songs of clickbait forever swarming the nation's concentration like the shiniest of slow-moving coins.)

Six months after I began work on this book, people started to drop dead. I was living in Southern California at the time, still working steadily as a writer and cartoonist for the Village Voice Media Company, Harper's Magazine and the Los Angeles Times, just before the mass die off of American journalism. It was 2008 and I had agreed to do a book called *One Complete Revolution* for Random House all about how progressive radicalism as an antidote to systemic complacency had finally been fully and completely coopted by commercial democracy and how marketing and the commodification of information had thusly made political and editorial art obsolete as an effective tool for social change and personal enlightenment. Ironically, though in absolute support of the broader thesis of the book I had started, *One Complete Revolution* fell victim to the financial crisis of that same year which saw massive layoffs and the wholesale slaughter of fledging

manuscripts within the publishing industry and would be tabled for another 11 years.

The original idea for *One Complete Revolution*, which was retained and expanded upon for the new iteration, was to conduct interviews with writers, artists and journalists from the middle part of the 20th Century who had for a time effectively battled back against the private wealth of the ruling corporate monarchy that, in the 1960s and early 70s, had been shaken to its core by the popularity of a newly radicalized self-advocacy movement among common citizens and minority populations. What had happened, I wanted to know as part of this sudden deradicalization of what was broadly seen as the progressive left, to end the arts community's involvement in the broader public discourse about the ambiguous connection and tenuous symbiotics that had always existed between what we pretend to be as citizens and who we are as human beings? How had our intellectual and spiritual adventurism been quashed so effectively and replaced by its docious and incurious anti-twin, the vast frontier that had once called to us with its boundless possibilities having been recast as a bleak wilderness full of diseased and unpredictable monsters? Specifically, what had happened to our collective appreciation and tolerance for alternative and independent thought?

In preparation for the investigative work I'd planned for myself, I assembled a list of potential interviewees whose names I taped to the wall next to my writing desk. Curiously, the only two public intellectuals to whom I'd briefly mentioned my book proposal to years before attaching it to an actual publishing house were Susan Sontag and George Plimpton, who had died prior to my starting. This was in 2002 at The Los Angeles Times Festival of Books and my comment to each of them came in the form of a question that was too broad to be interpreted as anything other than rhetorical: *Why are all the most effective American radicals over 65?* Neither Sontag nor Plimpton had the time to offer an answer of any substance, the brevity of a book signing line scarcely long enough to contain within it much more than faint praise and obliging salutations, which made me feel, when I finally did begin my book, as if I'd already lost two of my strongest chapters. Placing their names at the top of my list and then running a red line through them for the purpose of giving my roster a sense of urgency, I added 20 more names, the youngest of which was Neil Young at 63. Over the subsequent 18 months I'd slash additional red lines through the names of Kurt Vonnegut, Norman Mailer, George Carlin, Robert Rauschenberg and Studs Terkel, each of whom, minus Rauschenberg, I'd already been in email contact with and proposed dates for interviews. For Rauschenberg I'd been given a phone number, which had been secured by my editor at the *LA Weekly*, who knew somebody who knew somebody who knew somebody else. After dialing and letting the telephone ring for a solid minute, I hung up and promised myself I'd try again the next day, only to find out later that Rauschenberg was at home dying of heart failure when I called and had died not long after I hung up. It was then that I decided to remove my list from the wall and place it in a drawer, fearful that someone walking by my window might mistake me for an assassin of brittle and kittenish American geniuses.

Others I'd attempted to include in this book and failed to procure were Gore Vidal, Nat Hentoff, Leonard Cohen, Tom Hayden, Gloria Steinem, Donovan Leitch, Robert Crumb, Angela Davis and, as previously mentioned, Neil Young. Due to a combination of, yes, more death, scheduling difficulties, blatant disinterest and, in the case of Young, no guarantee that, according to his publicist, upon arriving at his front door with my tape recorder and notebook he wouldn't run out his backdoor and hide in the woods until nightfall, such voices remain absent from the collection, though their contributions to the argument can be found in the historic sea changes left by their participation in the culture — at least for now, the parameters of *now* shrinking exponentially as I type and the foundations upon which we should be securing our firm comprehension of existence beyond our mere reaction to its present tense being fractured and atomized by targeted obsolescence. ✳

PROLOGUE

INSTRUCTIONS FOR USE

IN POST-1950S AMERICA, an average person's concept of what might be the meaning of life was more likely than any other time in history to draw on a wide range of source material culled from a broad swath of disciplines throughout the culture. In order to understand why peace was elusive in Indochina, for example, in addition to looking to contemporary scholarship and modern reporting on the subject, one was as likely to draw on the teachings of Gandhi, Jung and McLuhan as much as on the work of Kerouac, Coltrane and Warhol. When contributing to a conversation about baseball, transcendental meditation or political assassination, insight was as likely to stem from a passage pulled from C. Wright Mills, Samuel Beckett or Susan Sontag as it was from a musical quote excised from Charles Mingus or a visual denouement remembered from Ernie Kovacs or a publicly pulled punch line from Ken Kesey and the Merry Pranksters. *MAD* magazine was in competition with the *New York Times* for truth-telling, female sexuality was the volatile and thrilling combustible MacGuffin created by combining equal parts Miller and Millett and the news analysis offered from *That Was the Week That Was* and *Rowan & Martin's Laugh-In* was often eminently more insightful than that offered from Walter Cronkite and CBS News or Bishop Sheen or mom or dad.

The truth, never capitalized, was a sloppy approximation of accumulated thoughts and feelings about singularly fleeting moments; it was *not* a rigid and uncompromising mandate from God that was so far beyond our comprehension that we'd need to spend our entire lifetimes straining, and forever failing, to lift it off our brains.

Specifically, the concept that one required a certain familiarity with a number of different points of view in order to perceive the three dimensionality of existence — that is, that one need not automatically assume that mainstream media was the most complete and reliable information source available — was verging on common knowledge and, as a child, I thrilled to the notion that I might grow up both contributing to and becoming enlightened by all the burgeoning guesswork being offered by humanity as to what it meant to be the missing link between the most compassionate apes and the most treacherous angels.

In fact, there was a definite sense while growing up in the early 1970s that, finally, after

a very deliberate and concerted effort by a dedicated group of very brave and very imaginative first generation baby boomers, all the repressive social apparatus that had found its fullest expression by the middle part of the 20th century had been unraveled by the emergence of the Counterculture and the growing popularity of a number of different literary, social and art movements, including the Beatnik movement, the Civil Rights movement, Bebop and cool jazz, abstract expressionism and action painting, protest folk, modern dance, Theatre of the Absurd, neorealism and art house films, *new* and Gonzo journalism, the Confessionalist movement among poets, the feminist movement and the *satire boom*. Never again, so sounded the promise, would Americans need to feel so pressured to believe that their civic duty to both God and country alone trumped whatever personal journey of self-discovery their natural curiosities and personal inclinations begged them to commence upon and that to succeed in life they had to subjugate themselves to the woefully narrow fairytale that the upward trajectory of Western Civilization required that everyone maintain an unquestioning allegiance to, and nonparticipation with, the bureaucratic elitism of the federal government while simultaneously maintaining an almost manic devotion to cloying patriotism, rampant materialism and the codification of racism, sexism and classism into the status quo.

Because of the Counterculture, anti-establishmentarianism could no longer legitimately be regarded by straight society simply as a *non*-belief — as nothing more than a reactionary disdain for the tenets of the dominant culture for the sole purpose of demonstrating contrarianism — but, like atheism, was correctly perceived in more contemporary terms as a viable, humanitarian philosophy unto itself, characterized by its own moral and intellectual purpose and self-perpetuation and frank usability. In other words, there was a definite sense while growing up in the early '70s that, finally, after decades of political and cultural and existential struggle, American democracy was enjoying its fullest expression and that anything — at long last! — was possible.

Regretfully, however, after spending my entire adolescence memorizing, first, all that had inspired the '60s enlightenment period — namely, the turn of the century European and Russian intellectualism as demonstrated famously by the worldwide propagation of Marxism, psychoanalysis, existentialism, individualist anarchism, modernism, Bohemianism, naturalism, realism, nihilism, agonism, futurism, decadence and absurdism — followed by a thorough examination of all the players responsible for igniting the democratizing era that ran for about 14 years known as *The Sixties*, I eventually came of age in a culture composed significantly less symbiotic parts than I'd been preparing for. Gone, suddenly, was the worldwide People's Movement that had promised to socialize empathy, communalize self-reliance, intellectualize the passions of the id and to institutionalize a radical intolerance of institutions. In its stead was something that appeared to be its opposite, exemplified by such things as the War on Drugs, the Yuppie Movement, the Meese Report, parental advisory labels, civic evangelism, Reaganomics and fashion trends that, like a network of completely perplexing diseases, sociologists are still wary to approach for close analysis for fear of contracting a truly virulent strain of Earl Solomon Burroughs, otherwise known as *Hammerrhea*.

Staring open-mouthed at 17 in my Buddy Holly glasses, chinstrap beard, espresso-stained insides, no underpants and newsprint-smudged fingertips, I wondered what had happened to the world into which I was hoping to enter so well-rehearsed. Had the idealism of the sixties been so ethereal as to have dissipated like marijuana smoke, a victim of its own weightless glee, or had it been dismantled by the super-sizing of corporate America? Had it been forever destroyed by the massive deregulation and privatization movements begun in the 1970s and early '80s? Movements that had given unprecedented amounts of power and influence to business markets which had then in turn — by being, at their philosophical centers, nothing but private anti-democratic tyrannies capable of corrupting even the most humanely driven among us (Jerry Rubin being the most famous example) with what Lewis Lapham once referred to as "enlightened selfishness" — bribed its participants, literally, away from their ideals with the most excessively narcissistic and ego-gorging of creature comforts?

Hoping to answer this question once and for all, I decided to hit the road in 2007 and ended up spending the next 11 years meeting up with many of the surviving participants and first-person observers of the mid-20th century hippie and countercultures and asking them why liberalism had died — the real hardcore Age of Aquarius meets Izzy Stone meets Huey Newton meets Mike Nichols liberalism — before I even had a chance to braid its hair, stroke its beard, share its joint, drop its acid, raise its fist, burn its bra, bless its patchouli-soaked heart, pilot its space cadet hard-on and contribute to its all-important longevity.

And this is what they told me. And this is what I ended up telling myself. ✳

MR.FISH

NOBODY LEFT

WHAT DOES IT MEAN to be *left*, anyway?

For somebody who's been both anointed and shamed by the label for the last 25 years by fans and detractors because of the pictures that I draw, you'd think I'd have some idea of what the word signifies. I don't. To me, it's a word like *faggot* or *bitch* or *nigger*, although much less cacophonous than any of those, meaning that it is a term of chummy endearment when bandied about between friends and club members and a revolting slur that begs for a bare-fisted retaliation when blasted from the sphincter of a perceived shithead. Of course, *left*, like any other word, has no real agency in the world, having, like any other word, been invented as a correlation to reality. A word, by lacking mass, has no intrinsic meaning whatsoever and therefore cannot legitimately be judged and convicted as an independent agent operating as a rogue element beyond our command and control. In fact, to argue that there exists either malice or virtue from an isolated word, *any* word, would be like attempting to condemn or revere an inert hammer because it has equal potential to create as destroy.

That said, it is my guess that the overwhelming majority of those who self-identify for reasons of conceit as left-leaning will also classify themselves as being activists after liking an Instagram post that says *My Pussy Has Teeth!* or *If God Hates Gays, Why Are We So Cute?* or *THIS PIZZA WAS BROUGHT TO YOU BY IMMIGRANTS*. These are the same people who are environmentalists because they scissor up their plastic six pack rings before sending them out into the ocean, or they use reusable shopping bags when they drive factory farmed food home in their suvs. They are the same people who, from the *right*, would be *pro-Americans* because they are uncomfortable around Hispanic people and *patriots* because they are vigorously uncritical of any war crime perpetrated by any soldier, sailor or politician claiming blind allegiance to a thin, wind-blown banner composed of slick red and white racing stripes and a rectangle that looks like outer space. Regardless of which political wing we seek shelter beneath, our virtue is almost always conceptual and seldom experiential, making our moral con-

victions largely expressions of fandom meant to signal to other people which team we root for from the sidelines and nothing else. Rather than a true demonstration of personal integrity, we are content to brand ourselves with all the claptrap of principled beliefs without testing their mettle in the real world.

To boot, how many hardcore pacifists who claim the moral position of finding violence unjustifiable under any circumstances have actually been in a warzone or a collapsed society overrun with desperate and predatory psychopaths? Likewise, how many 2nd Amendment advocates have considered the armaments available to Washington, D.C. while simultaneously insisting that their small arsenal of Glocks and AK-47s are a viable protection against a federal government turned tyrannical? My guess would be approximately as many white supremacists have fraternized with actual black, brown, red, yellow and off-white people and as many raging male homophobes have tasted cock and as many climate change deniers

who work for big business have gotten into a pool, pissed in the middle of it, made lemonade with the water and then poured a glass for their son or daughter.

In fact, most of our identities, whether we're *right* or *left*, come from the cultivated visual cues we devise for others to react to as a sort of shorthand designed to parody capability and accomplishment without forcing us to suffer the exhausting chore of actually accruing real experiences or deliberating on complicated notions of truth and beauty. It is a way of saying, without actually saying, "Look — I have a sex drive like a wet chainsaw because I have a mustache and wear sunglasses!" or, "Look — my white privilege in no way contributes to systemic racism because I can claim with absolute certainty that Samuel L. Jackson is my 4th favorite Jedi Master." Remember that nobody wears a Rolex watch simply to keep the time, just as nobody hangs a gold crucifix around his or her neck to give voice to the meek who are rumored to be inheriting the earth any day now. Most people pick their favorite players and stay off the field and let their fan jersey perpetuate the delusion that they are symbiotic with the athleticism unfolding before them. Of course, how we see ourselves is determined by how we see others seeing us, which is why we tend to concoct our identities using the most superficial and slapdash materials available to us, facades requiring no solid foundation nor adherence to any of the strict building codes expected of substantive architecture. Why nail yourself to a cross when you can piggyback your own concept of virtuousness onto somebody else who shed real blood for a real cause? It isn't even a purely intellectual decision, this boycotting of true sacrifice for the sake of ease and luxury, since the reflex to avoid pain and discomfort is hardwired into our physiologies with stronger bolts than those attaching any philosophy of life to a rewarding methodology for living.

We are more likely to delight in the grotesque irony that the Nobel Peace Prize was named for a wealthy weapons manufacturer who invented dynamite and built his fortune on war than be profoundly repelled by it. Additionally, most people will stand for "The Star-Spangled Banner" with tears in their eyes without giving a shit that Francis Scott Key was a strict anti-abolitionist and a racist lawyer who frequently argued against free speech and the protections guaranteed by the First Amendment. What's more, the overwhelming majority of those inspired by the Statue of Liberty might consider it bad taste to remind the world how the original design for the monument celebrated the end of slavery by including broken chains and shackles, all of which had to be removed (minus those hidden at Liberty's feet) because the wealthy white Americans financing the project were offended by the concept that Emancipation might be broadly recognized as a positive development and that black people freed from over 200 years of forced labor, soul-crushing servitude, rape, murder and torture was, well, meh.

And lest anybody think I'm judging such willful indifference as cowardice, I'm not. It's obvious that any effort made to question the validity of any conventional truth is really just a call to stop and think, which is to momentarily resist the crushing and unforgiving flow of the impossibly expansive and mighty mainstream. Nobody wants to do that. Not only is it hard work, but it's rude. To stand still in such a stream is to reveal the tide and to interrupt the dozing passivity of those around you who are content to float through their days with the wind in their faces and their eyes closed, their forward momentum forever being mistaken as progress with your disruption seen as an attack on propriety, civic harmony and what incurious redundancy has caressed into *normalcy*. Understand, too, that anybody trapped in a current that may or may not be polluted will always be unaware of the particulates surrounding them, whether they are bits of garbage or something as benign as fallen leaves. Remember, too, that mirrors, even when laid flat and liquified as water, will always see our head set squarely in front of us as an immovable obstruction to the figurative past and the literal future cresting the horizon. Only when a person is asked to resist the momentum of the rushing water, to anchor her feet into the slippery ground and to take a stand, will she be bombarded by whatever she's been blindly riding along with: rusty shopping carts, eviscerated diapers, dead bodies, stillborn condoms, pulverized oysters of shredded newspaper pulp, somersaulting bullet casings, brassieres, Band-Aids, wigs, wands, whatever.

Now extend that already strained metaphor to include, not just literal debris, but also psychic, emotional and conceptual debris. Imagine that you are surrounded by a myriad of assumed truths that you've adopted without vetting because you have had your eyes closed and the wind has been in your face and these assumed truths support whatever narrative you've either chosen for yourself or have been tagged with by others. You are a leftist, a rightest, a sexist, a savior, a sinner, a cynic, a king, a queen, a patsy or a fiend.

Now stand.

And if you're a cartoonist, draw. And if you're a poet, write. And if you're a singer, sing. And if you're a human being, be humane.

I guess. ✳

ON AND OFF THE RECORD
WITH GRAHAM NASH

In the end we shall have had enough of cynicism, skepticism and humbug, and we shall want to live more musically.

— Vincent Van Gogh

IT TOOK ME THREE YEARS to finally drip all the way out of college and I doubt that I would've been able to do it without headphones. That's me on the D bus at Rutgers University with hair in my face, filthy black horn-rimmed glasses and a Walkman clamped onto my head like forceps tasked with the dubious job of pulling me from the supercilious hole of cynicism that I'd been gestating in ever since leaving high school. I'm listening to a bootlegged Beatles jam called *Watching Rainbows*. John Lennon is singing, "Shoot me! Shoot me! Whatever you do you gotta kill somebody to get what you want, you gotta shoot me! You gotta shoot me! Please shoot me!" and I'm deliberately *not* standing up to

get off at my stop to go to my Tuesday afternoon class on expository writing where I'd be forced to remove my headphones and listen to a middle-aged woman in sensible shoes lecture me on how to bow at the waist and square dance politely with her syllabus. Or that's me *not* getting off the G bus to learn about third-person thesis construction because I'm listening to CSNY sing *Blackbird* at the Fillmore East in 1970, or that's me not getting off the L bus to make tree-rubbings and collaborative scrap paper collages with girls in top-siders and digital watches because Bob Dylan is telling me how, "Disillusioned words like bullets bark as human gods aim for their mark, make everything from toy guns that spark to flesh-colored Christs that glow in the dark, it's easy to see without looking too far that not much is really sacred."

I was like a lot of other kids unsuited to the minty austerity of a traditional classroom education, having graduated 12th grade with an 'A' in art and a long line of solid 'D's in *Don't give a flying fuck about anything else*. Unless the information was unmanicured and told to me internally by my own voice, preferably with a cocked eyebrow and a shit-eating grin, I wasn't learning anything. Graham Nash, according to his omnibus autobiography, *Wild Tales*, suffered the same impatience for gratuitous conformity and refused to accept the conventional spectatorship of life. "Once rock 'n' roll got under my skin, it was all over for me," he explains in his book. "Instead of listening to my lessons at school, I began doodling... Daydreams took over, and I pulled myself toward those dreams. No matter what they tried to teach me, I knew where I was headed. Nothing was going to derail my dreams." His was a life saved by saying *fuck you* to those least likely to comprehend the concept of deliberate and uncompromising self-preservation. Even as a child, Nash, knew enough about the existential toxicity of straight society's relentless demand for total acquiescence *not* to stand up and to lift the needle off the Everly Brothers 45 spinning inside his beloved Philips record player, for to do so would've resulted in him succumbing to the common trajectory of all the similarly fated lads around him: an abbreviated lifetime spent toiling in the Salford cotton mills or the coalmines of Manchester, his only reward for following the rules and coloring within the lines being a pitying Jesus on weekends, the demented satisfaction of an early death and scarcely a pot to piss in.

I met with the artist on a rooftop terrace bar overlooking New York City in September 2014 to talk about politics, radicalism, indecency, hicks and critics, Yoko Ono and what Joni Mitchell might remember about one of the most significant moments of his life. Here is a portion of our conversation.

❋ ❋ ❋

Let's begin with your book, *Wild Tales* [*A Rock & Roll Life*]. I want to talk about how the book begins and how it ends.

All right.

It begins with the sentence, "It *always* comes down to the music," and it ends with, "It *all* comes down to the music," which are two different sentiments. Phonetically, both sentences serve beautifully as bookends, but when you consider the content, one communicates a conceptual idea and the other a literal observation.

You're the only person I've spoken with who noticed that.

Well, I think it's a lovely detail. You begin by introducing an idea that, if left alone, could be interpreted as trite and so broad that it's sentimental, and you end with a nod to the weightiness of your narrative about what music is and why somebody's life might come down to it. Was that intentional?

Most of the things we do as human beings are intentional, so, to answer your question, yes. I also love to have things unfold, which happens in music all the time. You can listen to a piece of music for months and suddenly say, "Holy shit! I didn't notice that before!" *Life* is like that.

Life *is* like that, but music and art are different. With life, you give yourself the opportunity to eventually notice things that have eluded you before because life is all around you. [Life is] inescapable and happens every day, relentlessly, but art needs to be sufficiently interesting for you to *want* to look at it again and again, or, with music, to listen to it again and again, because it *is* escapable and will only become 'all around you' if [it's] shared by enough people.

Unless you're creating it yourself—*then* it's all around you, fuck everybody else, it doesn't matter what anybody thinks.

Point taken.

Have you seen the Sigmar Polke exhibition at MoMA?

No.

Go see the Sigmar Polke exhibition at MoMA. It'll blow your mind, the amount of work he produced, the range. As a new painter, myself, it absolutely blew my mind.

New painter? I feel like I've read about your art-work before — I know your photography.

Well I did two paintings when I was with Joni [Mitchell], but that was forty-odd years ago and I never did anything since — except that book I started in '74, which was just me drawing to save my own sanity. But painting, in large scale? The ones I did with Joni were little.

A reflection of how big the place was in Laurel Canyon where you painted them —

More a reflection of how big my mind was at the time.

How committed are you to these new, large scale paintings? Are you losing yourself in the process in a similar way to how you create your music and photographs?

Absolutely, but it's different. With music, apart from the writing, I'm involved with other people, whether I'm making a record or doing something live, there are always other people involved. With painting there's nobody there but me and I don't give a fuck about what other people might think about it. I don't even know what I'm doing half the time, but I'm having a great time. And there's a certain focus that I get into when I paint that is unlike anything else. I can lose myself completely and it's a wonderful feeling. I love to be invisible — I don't want to stick out. I don't want to be [David] Crosby who can't walk 10 feet without being recognized.

That's what's so sacred about being a poet, isn't it? As a poet, whether we're talking broadly or specifically, you feel an obligation to avoid disturbing the moment that you're trying to write about and to remain invisible and not influence the emotional physics of what's happening around you. It's about being a witness and not an instigator. Plus, you let your guard down when you're inside your own head — there's less bullshit when you're your only audience and it's easier to tell ugly truths.

Right.

I'd argue that that's where most protest songs come from, from allowing that private moment of real outrage to inspire the creation of a piece of art that can then be shared with the public. Do you find that with a song like [*Almost Gone*] *The Ballad of Bradley Manning*, for instance, that when you perform it live and people walk out that they are reacting out of some obligation to not publically shame the United States government, where if you played the same song to them in private they'd more likely agree with your opinion about the injustice [of Manning's torture and imprisonment]?

I'd really like to talk to the people who walked out on us during our 2006 [CSNY Freedom of Speech] tour because we criticized George Bush and we sang that song *Let's Impeach the President*. I'd like to know what they think now — "What the fuck do you think about the Bush Administration and Dick Cheney and Donald Rumsfeld and all those fuckers now, who lied us into the war and killed over a million people; what the fuck do you think about them now?" And, with all due respect, if you buy a ticket to a CSNY concert, what the fuck do you expect?

They were expecting a nostalgia show. [They] were not expecting you to behave just as you always have: as a relevant group dealing with contemporary issues.

I feel two ways about it. I respect their opinion [and] I don't need for them to agree with us. They have a right to walk out, but to walk out over *that* song — the song about the President lying? We didn't sing that song until about two and half hours into our show and that's the one that really pissed them off. None of the songs that Neil did about soldiers and how their deaths affect the family and how brave they are to go serve in a war that they might not agree with pissed them off. But to say we should get rid of George W. Bush for lying, they walk out.

I've always believed that the greatest threat to our survival is our manners and how dedicated we are to being polite.

I don't think people are polite enough!

I'm talking about the kind of politeness that prevents people from engaging in conversations about politics and religion because it's somehow inappropriate to challenge political or religious

MR. FISH

bullshit in certain settings. It's like trying to talk about politics or religion at Thanksgiving dinner. For most people it's never going to happen, because there is a time and a place to talk about Bradley Manning and that isn't it — it would be too impolite.

(*Laughing*) Got it.

Decency, in that case, is utterly *indecent* because it prevents people from engaging in some very important conversations about who we are as citizens and how we behave as human beings.

You're right — maybe those [performance] halls are our Thanksgiving table and maybe we're wrong to say what we say there —

No! That's the power of art and that's your responsibility as [artists], to provide people with an opportunity to think and feel things that polite society [seeks] to censor.

At least [those people who walked out on us] felt something, even though I disagree with them. At least they understood the point of what we were trying to say. At least they [had] opinions that they [felt] strongly about, God bless 'em.

And maybe, at least for some of them, their walking out inspired some conversation later on that went deeper than the kneejerk patriotism that told them to leave. *Why did you walk out?* "Because they said the President lied!" *Well, he did lie.* "Well, gee, I guess he did — " And that's the beginning of contemplation, which, in a way, gets us back to your book. There is a lot of emphasis placed on you and others looking for and finding harmonies together and the more [I] read the more [I realized] that your appreciation of harmony had less to do with music and more to do with camaraderie and a humanitarian yearning for how best to live a life. It's a very intimate study of how an artist thinks and feels.

Sure, [my] work is not just about what goes on at the Thanksgiving table, but also what goes on in the bedroom and it's personal. I can't speak for anybody else. I only know what I can do, or what I try to do. People are always asking me who the new protest singers are, or, more to the point, *where* the new protest singers are and I can't speak to that. Again, I only know my own passion for what I do. I am not responsible for other artists.

But you are in a position to speak to how art distribution has changed over the years, specifically how art is consumed by the culture. You have a terrific line in your book that addresses how perverse and insidious corporate [infiltration] of the industry has become, like when you compare the first Woodstock [Festival in 1969] with the 1989 version and you say that the later version was all about, "…corporations realizing that half a million people could be customers."

That's right. When you put half a million kids on a flat piece of concrete and you charge them $12 for a bottle of water, knowing full well that they'll need to buy it, that's cold.

Which, I guess, begs the question that so many people ask you about where the new protest singers are. Let me ask it: Where are the new artists, the ones who are being brought up in a world that is trying to normalize this new paradigm of corporate mega-control of everything, who should be inspiring a dissident, radicalized way of approaching the issue?

That's the point, is it radical? Is saying '*fuck, no!*' to a corporation radical? I don't think it's radical at all. I think it's just common sense.

I'm glad you said that because I've always thought that the single most important feature of your work, particularly your work with CSNY, is your attempt to subvert the traditional idea of what is and what isn't political.

Yeah.

Most people, for reasons that I mentioned before, won't engage in political conversations with strangers, usually because it's considered impolite, but also because most people don't feel smart enough to get involved. It's the same thing with sports. I know the rules of baseball, for instance, and I've played the game before, but I don't follow any particular team and I don't give a shit about stats and I don't have a stake in which team wins over another, but if you and somebody else are engaged in a discussion about the players and why one is better or worse than another based on your team loyalty or statistics or whatever I'm shut out of the conversation. It's the same with people who have party loyalties and talk about politics like it's a sport. Those people are only interesting to their friends and nothing is being debated. You [and

Crosby, Stills and Young] make the subject of politics feel safe in other peoples' mouths.

That's nice.

It's important! It's important to have an opinion about war, about whistleblowers, about the NSA, about really substantive issues that should be talked about outside of Sunday morning circle jerks.

I agree, I agree.

So, yeah, become a musician, put those politics into songs and make those songs so terrific that people will want to listen to them over and over and over again, be inspired to share them with tons of people and suddenly saying 'fuck you' to the government won't be so controversial.

That's what we do.

And speaking of controversial issues, for decades now there's been a famous debate going on between you and [Stephen] Stills about the specifics of where [CSN] first harmonized together. Stephen says that it happened at Mama Cass's house in Laurel Canyon and you say that it happened at Joni Mitchell's house down the road.

I *know* that's where it happened.

I find it plausible, though, that, according to what I've read, Stills was too intimidated to play and sing anything in front of Joni Mitchell.

And my answer to that is that when you write a song like *Helplessly Hoping* the first thing you want to do is play it for a beautiful woman because it's fucking brilliant. Why would you not want to play that song, especially if you want to get laid?

Have you talked to Joni about it? What does she remember about [that night]?

That's a good question! I've never spoken to Joni about that — maybe I should.

Call her — call her right now and find out! We could put the whole controversy to bed with one phone call.

(Nash goes through phone contacts and looks for Joni Mitchell's assistant's number. No luck.)

I'll get an answer to that question and let you know.

I'd love to find out.

Yeah, me too! I'd like to know what she remembers!

(A few days later, Graham forwarded an email from a close friend of Mitchell's which stated: Well I finally had the opportunity to ask Joni about the first time CSN sang together. She said she thought it was at her house, she remembers that there was a gasp because all of you were so surprised at the remarkable harmony you three created. She said she knows that Stephen thinks it was a Cass's house, but his memory during that time was not always an accurate recollection of what had occurred.*)*

Let's talk about the recent release of the *1974* box set, which contains music from [the CSNY] 1974 reunion tour. What I find remarkable about those recordings is how you're able to maintain that intimate Laurel Canyon feel on songs like *Our House* and *Lee Shore* and *Helpless*, despite the fact that you're playing to tens of thousands of people, while other tracks, such as *Chicago* and *Ohio* and *Black Queen*, are absolutely blistering and raw.

That's why I chose that image for the cover [of the box set]. I showed the image to Neil and told him that this is what I want to see for the cover because for me that sums it all up in a twentieth of a second. And he said, "Nah, absolutely not." And I asked him why not and he said that it looked like we were aggrandizing ourselves, that we are pumping ourselves up too much. And I said, "Okay — so we didn't do that. We didn't do that for 31 shows, we didn't play to 80 thousand people — that's a Photoshop?" And he said, "You have a point."

The other thing that is captured perfectly by the recordings is — when do you think the 1960s really ended?

Nineteen-seventy ... *four.*

Precisely.

When Nixon left.

And the Vietnam War ended, which is what also makes the [*1974*] recordings historically interesting. Very similar to Dylan's *Rolling Thunder Revue* in '75, your tour in '74 definitely signaled a shift from young idealism into something harder and world weary and ... I wouldn't necessarily say *masculine,* but —

It's definitely a coming of age sound and we were ballsy — we were a ballsy band. Take, for instance, the song by Neil, *Goodbye Dick*, which lasts a minute and a half and was only ever done once. Me and David and Stephen never heard it before he did it live in front of us. I had also written a song one morning [during the tour] for Calli Cerami, my girlfriend at the time, that I wanted to do in front of I don't know how many thousands of people and you can hear it on tape. I'm saying, "I wanna sing my song!" And Stephen's yelling, "What are the chords, Willie?!" And I'm saying, "Well, you go from D to B-flat minor, I think, and I don't know what the name of this chord is but it goes like [this]..." and we do the song. Now that's a fucking ballsy band.

That's the same spontaneity that you had when you played on the BBC *In Concert* series with David [Crosby] in 1970. It's obvious that you guys had smoked a ton of weed and came out with no set list or any idea of what you were going to do and it was brilliant.

(Laughing) You're right, you can tell from the tape that we were completely unrehearsed.

And, as a result, the immediacy and the ease of the performance could not be better.

We were very high, that's how it was.

I'd also argue that the [CSN] *Demos* record that you released in 2009 is among the best music you've ever put out for the same reason, not because you were high when you recorded them, but more because of the spontaneity and the unrehearsed quality of the songs. I think that some of the demos are better than the official versions.

There's something about demos — you can't beat them. They're usually recorded within an hour of when the song was created and there's something pure about them that can't be duplicated later. Often times there's a syndrome when you're in the studio and you're chasing the sound of the demo and there's a certain point when you say, "Fuck! We can't beat this!" And then you decide that maybe it's time to move your silly little 2-track over and overdub some drums or whatever.

I know that [John] Lennon was something of a collector of what he called "pirated" Beatle recordings, which were just bootlegs, the sort that Dylan now releases as legitimate music through his *Bootleg Series*. Did you ever get into collecting pirated recordings of your work or anybody else's?

Me and my friend, Dan Curland—who has a great vinyl record store (Mystic Disc) in Mystic, Connecticut—we do have a huge collection of bootlegs. But do I collect them to listen to? No.

Are there any plans to release more CSN demos?

Well, there are a lot more to release for sure, but at the moment, having spent the last four-and-a-half years working on [the *1974* box set], I'm kind of done with CSN music for a while. I'm working on a couple of very interesting albums right now, one with me and Crosby singing with a bunch of other people, plus there are the jazz concerts we did with Wynton Marsalis right here at Lincoln Center.

How was that experience?

At one point [while playing with Marsalis] Crosby says, "Hey, we're playing with the grownups!"—and he's seventy-two.

Wow.

Yeah, I'll never be able to finish all that I want to do—*hopefully*.

Having been around for a while now, what kind of perspective can you offer as to how the culture has changed, particularly how the younger generation deals with its role in influencing politics?

About twenty years ago I was asked to do a couple speeches at colleges and the first one was at Kent State.

And when was this exactly?

This was '85, somewhere around '85. And I asked [the students] about [the Kent State massacre] and none of them knew much about it. So I explained to them that there is a history of political change coming from universities—it came from the Sorbonne in Paris, it came from Berkeley, it came from Columbia, it came from students who were getting fucking pissed off and speaking their minds. And I said, "The fact that you're at Kent State and you don't know what I'm talking about is appalling to me!" It upset me greatly. I could understand if I was at Georgetown University, but this was fucking Kent State!

I think people at Georgetown are responsible to know what happened at Kent State, too, quite frankly. That said, whose responsibility is it to inform students of events like the shootings at Kent State—specifically of events where innocent life was lost at the hands of state power?

It's everybody's responsibility! We have to all keep reminding each other of what happened because there's such an incredible rate of forgetfulness in this country. The headlines change every day and people are expected to care just as much about Justin Bieber's fucking monkey as they do about the missing Malaysian airline—right? There's very little focus on the history of how we got to where we are.

Is it because the fractured narrative that we're fed [by the media] is preventing us from contemplating our fate and reflecting on yesterday and comprehending who we really are and where we're headed?

Absolutely—we're too busy with our Google glasses trying to get porn to give a shit about much of anything else.

Let's take a minute to talk about some of the people who were NOT in your book, starting with Pete Townshend and The Who.

I have great respect for Pete. He's an incredibly important member of this musicians' society. He's a man who tries his best to speak truth. I didn't read his autobiography, though I'd like to—I'm a fan! I liked [The Who] back before they were

The Who, when they were The High Numbers on Ready, Steady, Go! in England.

What about Leonard Cohen?

Obviously, Leonard is a great writer. There's a certain part of us all that writes to get laid, but Leonard is in a class by himself. (*Laughs*) No, but he is a brilliant poet and a very serious man and I'm happy for the amazing resurgence he's had. He never did play to the Royal Albert Hall and fill it, but he's doing that now and that's fantastic. Fuck, he's older than me!

You mention Joan Baez [in your book] but you don't talk about her music.

I've never been a great admirer of Joan. I understand her place in history and I understand her sense of purity in terms of voice, but her voice does nothing for me. I'm probably opposite to a lot of men but she just doesn't make me cry like Aretha does.

Have you ever heard her version of the Phil Ochs song *There But for Fortune*?

No.

That makes me cry.

I need to hear that, because I have great respect for her as a musician, but her voice doesn't do it for me. Send it to me.

Brian Wilson.

I've never met Brian. I have the ultimate respect for him. I think the man is a genius, an absolute fucking genius. I'm sorry that he got waylaid there when he did, but I can understand how a person might collapse under the pressure of being a genius and all your peers knowing that you're a fucking genius. He's written some of the greatest songs in the world, most when he was just a kid.

You mentioned in your book how, when you first came to New York, you hit a bunch of record stores in the Village and picked up some Lenny Bruce records.

Yeah.

Did you ever have any interaction with Bruce?

Nope.

Never saw him perform?

I never saw him perform, no. I think David [Crosby] did, a couple of times. But to be crucified for saying the word 'fuck' and talking about tits and ass and rocking the boat is tragic.

His biggest mistake was thinking that the 1st Amendment had functionality.

Justice doesn't really exist.

Where were you when John Lennon was going through his immigration troubles in the mid '70s? I ask because you became an American citizen without a hassle and Lennon spent years fighting Nixon and the FBI—

And John Mitchell, right. No, I didn't have any interactions with John when he came to the States. All my dealings with him were in England. He was an interesting guy. He always had this underlying anger and, oddly enough, an underlying insecurity about who he was.

I know that Crosby spent some time with him during his famous Lost Weekend in LA—did he keep in touch with him? I know that he hated Yoko.

Well, in many ways, Crosby's stupid. How can you hate Yoko? She saved [Lennon's] life and he really loved her. How can you hate Yoko Ono, that's just a silly thing to do. You can disagree with her and not like her music, but hate? That's way too strong a word. She blew my mind—I saw her about ten years ago. I was at some Grammy event here in New York and she and I were at the same table and she looked over at me and said, "Thanks for the ride."

What does that mean?

When [The Beatles] were doing *Sgt. Pepper* John had to stay to do overdubs and she wanted to go home so I drove her home. So when she said 'thanks for the ride' I knew exactly what she was talking about, it was wild! After all that time! (*Laughs*) *Thanks for the ride.*

So, just to bring us full circle, let me ask you this. If, like you say, 'It all comes down to the music,' are you confident that we've taught our children well the right chords to play and the right harmonies to share and the right combination of humility and courage to be able to sing together?

My son, Jackson, runs a blog called Superforest and in one of the articles that he wrote he talks about something that I'd forgotten about. When he was about 12-years-old I took him to the movies and we went to take a piss right before the movie and the bathroom was just disgusting so I cleaned it. He never forgot that. In other words, the only teaching that we can do is to lead by example.

And there's lots and lots of shit to clean up — *always*.

Right on. ✳

EMPATHY FOR THE DEVIL

I FIRST SAW THE MASSIVE SPREAD of twinkling lights that is Los Angeles at night from the San Gabriel Mountains in the early 1990s while visiting from Philadelphia. It was stunningly beautiful and made me think of a phone interview that I'd heard on CNN a year earlier just after New Year's during the Gulf War.

The images that were being telecast during the interview were those of nighttime warfare, the sort that made every television set in America appear as if it was a murky green fish tank full of randomly ejaculated sparks and vague flashes of percussive light almost too dim to see. Saddam Hussein by that time had already lost his air force and had begun to run out of Scud missiles, which, as projectiles, were never any more precise or destructive than far-flung empty hot water heaters, and there was little doubt, particularly in countries not being fed the CNN feed, that some brutally excessive and wholly unnecessary slaughter of Iraqi soldiers and civilians was being perpetrated in the desert.

The interviewee was a 10-year-old Israeli girl who was being asked her opinion about how well the U.S.-led coalition forces were faring in their bombing campaign — a loaded question to be sure, particularly because a 10-year-old girl might not be trusted to honestly answer the question "Did you brush your teeth?" without a corroborating fondling of her toothbrush's bristles to test for wetness; forget about asking her to elaborate on something as outlandishly subjective as a war. Thus, it was not a question in search of a real answer. Instead, it was an attempt by a news corporation to give its viewers the same thrill at holiday time that radio listeners got to experience in the 1940s while listening to Edward R. Murrow tell them how the GIs were sacrificing their own innocence and pleasant dispositions and apple-cheeked virginity to the noble barbarity of butchering all the fascist monsters who wanted to devour America's children, grandchildren, puppies and kittens.

The girl answered the question by saying, "I heard an American pilot who was dropping bombs on Baghdad at night say that it looked beautiful, like a Christmas tree. I don't think I'll ever understand Americans."

Sitting in the dark woods above the L.A. basin a year after that interview, with the scent of pine and damp roots and cold earth permeating my clothes, I wondered what super-sparkly destructiveness I was looking at down below and I questioned the sanity of my elation. Sure, I knew that there was a difference between me looking down at Tinseltown from a wooded mountaintop in Southern California and a U.S. fighter pilot exploding the soft gooey insides of Iraqis from an F-15 Eagle, but the difference was by no means significant enough to make what was startlingly similar inconsequential; the similarity, of course, being that both my and the pilot's physiologies were completely interchangeable in their reaction to what each had experienced.

Both said "neato" and asked that we not turn away, declaring that there was poetry in what we had witnessed.

Ever since then I've wondered how anybody can ever really feel morally superior to anybody else, even when comparing himself to those who might find beauty in the rocket's red glare as it vaporizes those whose only retaliation against annihilation is to stain the soles of the conqueror's shoes. With that in mind, I've also extended my mystification to the question of whether or not anybody can truly be classified as evil. Kurt Vonnegut has famously claimed that there are no villains in the human species, nor are there heroes. It was his belief that only those circumstances born from the intellectual and emotional inadequacies of humankind should be seen as being either good or bad — and, then, not even as *good* or *bad*, but rather as fortunate and unfortunate.

Can this be right?

In early September of 2010 I went to Yasgur's farm, the site of the 1969 Woodstock Festival, to douche Glenn Beck out of my brain. Earlier, after several days of watching and rewatching the televised footage of the Fox News nimrod pacing back and forth in front of the Lincoln Memorial and spouting off, like an Archie Bunker who had been properly Eliza Doolittled, about how it was time for all the white, racist, heterosexual, gun- and tea-toting Jesus freaks in Middle America to reclaim their former glory as repressive and paranoid snobs unembarrassed by their infantile urge to flaunt their prejudices and petty hatreds in public, the coiled slime inside my skull had become fetid and stinky and in need of the hard vinegar stream of some bleeding-heart, communal optimism.

Remembering a conversation that I'd had with my brother several weeks earlier, I knew that three of the most notorious bleeding-heart communal optimists known to Jann Wenner were scheduled to perform at the Pavilion Stage at the Bethel Woods Center for the Arts, just several hundred feet from the pile of rocks marking where the original Woodstock stage stood some 41 years earlier; those bleeding-heart communal optimists being David Crosby, Graham Nash and Stephen Stills, the Peter, Paul and Mary of the Folk You! Generation. With only lawn seats available for purchase, I decided to send an e-mail to Graham Nash, whom I'd interviewed several months earlier and with whom I'd enjoyed some correspondence, to ask if he could get me a ticket that might put me closer to the stage. Seventy-two hours later, I was walking down a grassy hillside from overflow parking at the Bethel Woods Center for the Arts, with the inspiring tang of marijuana smoke in the air and the deeply satisfying vision of young

and old hippies and bedraggled Vietnam vets and their wives and girlfriends and kids, everybody congregating around their cars and minivans and warming their conversations over small hibachis and beer coolers and Bic lighters.

"QO?" muttered a barefoot teenager sitting cross-legged on a Mexican blanket who, with the long hair and beard, might've been Jesus Christ had his lips, ears, nipples and nose not contained enough piercings to make me think that he was much more like a fish that, by being festooned with so many hooks, had been mutilated by the questionable good luck of having escaped the frying pan.

"Huh?" I said, stopping to look down and notice that he was surrounded by rows and rows of what was either homemade jewelry or Slim Jims that had been fellated into thin reeds and used to lasso whatever he could find at the bottom of his grandmother's junk drawer.

"Quarter ounce?" he asked, grinning and squinting into the sun that was setting behind my head. "Thirty bob?"

"What?" I said.

"Thirty bob, governor?" he said, no doubt attempting to turn his little drug deal into something quaint and literary and time-honored.

"Oh, no thanks," I said, smiling and walking away. Shielding my eyes and looking in the direction of the Pavilion Stage, I figured that I had about half a mile to go before I reached the will-call window, so I busied myself by trying to remember exactly how much a quarter ounce of pot was and whether 30 bucks was even a fair asking price. I remembered back to my freshman year at college and the time when I went with my older brother to buy some cocaine in North Philly. I thought about how I felt as if we were ascending the innards of a cuckoo clock upon climbing the wooden stairwell in the drug dealer's apartment house, which was dark and ramshackle and full of cobwebs. Then there was the drug dealer himself, living all alone in the top room, precisely where I imagined the clock's cuckoo would reside, all bug-eyed and sweating, his insides seemingly full of baby spiders all looking for a way out, the job of going cuckoo every half-hour enough to prevent him from ever relaxing, much less sitting down and catching his breath. "Your brother tells me that you're a writer," he said, worrying the grubby hem of his T-shirt with his yellow fingers, his red hair and freckles making him look like an explo-

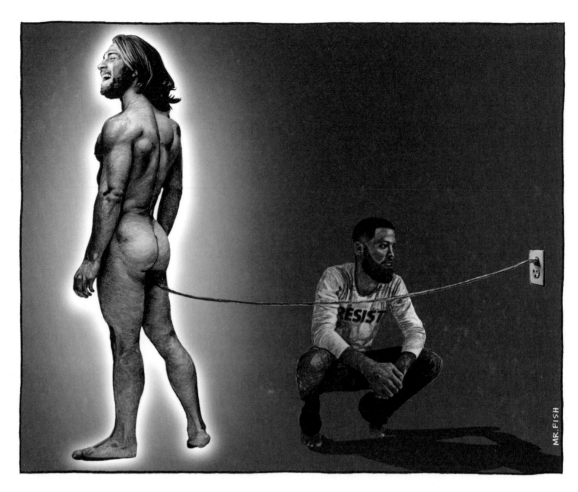

sion in mid-blast. I half-shrugged and agreed. "I am, too!" he said. "I got something that I want you to read. It's a reworking of "Freewill" by Rush. I rewrote it in Elizabethan English and it's a little long, practically fills a whole notebook, but it's awesome — let me get it!" He went to get it and I picked up the tiny pile of crushed twenty-dollar bills that I saw on his dresser and shoved them into my pocket, figuring that dealing coke might be against the law but combining Rush with Elizabethan English was an abomination against both God and nature and something that nobody should be allowed to give away for free.

I thought about the drug dealer's scale and how my brother looked that afternoon hunched over it like a chemist. Then I thought about all the scales that all drug dealers everywhere use. I considered the ounce as a unit of mass and I wondered if when a drug dealer says that something "weighs an ounce" he's referring to the drugs that are being weighed or the mechanism that registers the weight. Sure, I figured, an ounce requires the corroboration of a scale to qualify its

legitimacy, but if all scales have slightly different calibrations — and they do! — then where does the truth reside, in the ounce or in the device used to qualify the ounce as an ounce?

That said, is an ounce an ounce because it is deemed to be an ounce by a scale or is it an ounce because an ounce is a hard-core truism that we use our minutely varying scales to roughly approximate? Can the truth even be approximated or is the truth true only when it is absolute? If the truth can be approximated, then it cannot be a fact, but rather it must be an opinion, and if the truth is a matter of opinion then morality can have no legitimacy as a foundation upon which humankind can determine right from wrong. Thus, human values are as arbitrary as favorite colors and because no one has a favorite color called *whitepinkredorange-brownyellowgraygreencyanblueviolet*, the twin classifications of *hero* and *villain* must at one time or another fall to each of us with at least tangential justification, whether we're driving like an asshole down the highway or trying to balance a budget or trying to keep a crown on our head or dropping bombs on so-called enemies on a battlefield or forgiving the devastation of the environment because we can be thrilled by a trillion twinkling electric lights that stretch to the horizon.

After 20 more minutes of walking at Bethel Woods I settled into my seat, barely 15 feet from the stage, feeling less like somebody who was there to have Glenn Beck and his *Nur für Deutsche*-type Honor Rally flushed from his short-term memory and more like somebody who had exploited the very same hierarchical social structure that Beck and his chums typically celebrated as enlightened living, the In-GOP-We-Trust coins remaining unspent and copulating in their trousers, their noses thrust into the air with the tips edging that much closer to the air-conditioned ass of God™ himself. I had tapped into a system that rewarded privilege and relegated everybody else to the slow line, and because I had access to the celebrity of Graham Nash — celebrity being just another word for *royalty* — I was able to enter the event free of charge and glide past all the cheap seats and half-pirouette into my chair like Elton John at a royal wedding. It didn't matter that my favorite color was light blue foil and that I never comb my hair and seldom wear underpants and that I can't keep my fingers out of my nose and make no secret of my disdain for practically everything that the dominant culture stands for: I was no more moral than anybody else. Only arrogance and conceit will ever tell you any different.

And then, when the old lady in front of me, during Stephen Stills' guitar solo for "Love the One You're With," lost her teeth because she was doing the Hammer so hard and people needed to use the light from their cell phones, mine included, to find them, I didn't care that I was just another face in the crowd because I knew that at least in a crowd, every once in a while, everybody will lift his or her feet together and peer into the darkness to find a single person's filthy smile.✳

PAUL WONDERING WHEN SOMEBODY IS GOING TO INVENT A DEMOCRACY APP THAT WILL MAKE GIVING A SHIT ABOUT THE COUNTRY EASY AND CONVENIENT

MR.FISH

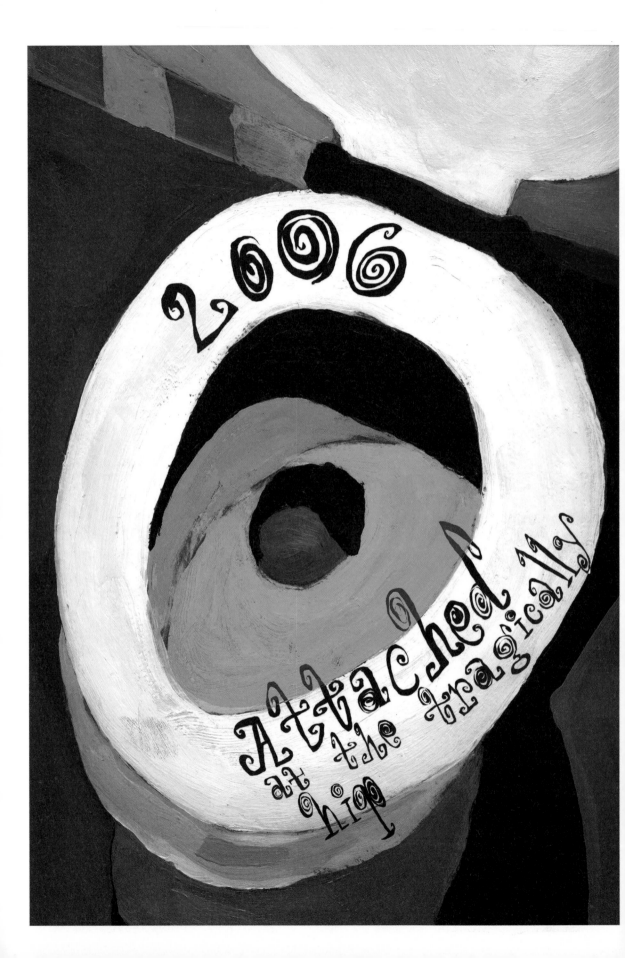

IT WAS 8:08 P.M. ON OCTOBER 7TH in Los Angeles, California, and there I was, standing in front of my bathroom mirror, watching myself outlive John Lennon.

I'd been preparing for the moment ever since I was 17, six years after Lennon was murdered and right around the time I was headed off to college seriously pissed off that my generation didn't have a bloody, unjust war to protest against, nor a draft to dodge, nor a culturally viable excuse to engage in an enormous amount of anonymous and unprotected sex with braless, straight-haired girls with names like Windy and Ryvre and Feelfree. Rather than growing my hair for peace and reeking of some glorious combination of patchouli, thrift store mothballs and Peace Corps dung bricks, I was bullied, by the cultural amnesia that had Binaca-blasted the 1960s out of the public consciousness, perhaps forever, into cutting my hair super short so that there would be no mistaking my disdain for Geddy Lee, Nikki Sixx and Shadoe Stevens — not exactly the most gratifying act of political dissent and public outrage but one I embraced with all the seriousness of any young 1980s, anti-Reagan revolutionary convinced that doomsday was just as likely to arrive carrying a shitty Yamaha keytar and wearing leg warmers and rainbow suspenders as it was to goose-step through the confetti-filled streets with perfect abs, an infectious smile and Communion wafers in its stool. So, the idea that one day I would actually reach the age that Lennon was when he was gunned down outside his New York City apartment building — a tragedy slightly softened by my belief that 40 was the retirement age for any public intellectual wishing to avoid crapping up his reputation with too much grace, whether he was murdered or allowed to live on — made me wonder how it would feel to have finished my life's work as a great artist at 40 and gotten everybody in the world to know my name.

I always thought the whole story would've been better if God rested after the first day instead of the seventh. It certainly would've made Him seem a lot smarter.

How do you mean?

Think about it. Who creates a universe of pure light and then steps back and says, "Hey, I know what would make this even better - frisbee golf, Ryan Seacrest, gonorrhea and Yoo-hoo?"

It never made sense to me.

Well, I guess if we were going to go by the Bible, man was created on the 6th day 6,000 years ago, which means I wasn't an accident.

You can't go by what you read in the Bible.

It was written by people who used to throw rocks at the moon. Carbon dating alone proves that the most accurate part of Genesis is the punctuation.

And yet people are putting their left hand on the fucking thing everyday and swearing to tell the truth.

Why not just jerk off the bailiff instead and swear to not get sticky?

Wait a minute - we never finished my thing about not being immortal.

I thought we were done with that.

No - we never really got started.

Well, you know what Kurt Vonnegut said.

What.

We are here on Earth to fart around and don't let anybody tell you different.

I don't want to fart around! I want to have a serious conversation about life and death!

You mean my deliberately distracting conversation about Ryan Seacrest and pescatarians didn't help?

You didn't say anything about pescatarians.

I didn't?

No.

Do you even know what a pescatarian is?

Sure - it's a vegetarian who eats fish.

No - it's a carnivore who doesn't eat animals with eyebrows.

I thought it had more to do with omega-3 fatty acids.

Nope, it's the eyebrows. If beagles had gills there'd be no sushi.

That sounds like something you pulled out of a fortune cookie.

You can put anything in a fortune cookie and it suddenly sounds more insightful than it really is - you ever notice that?

I never thought about it.

Listen to this: LEFT LANE MUST TURN LEFT. See what I mean?

I could've done without the racist accent.

A zebra is really a gray pony that isn't vibrating fast enough to appear gray.

On second thought, I miss the accent.

I can imagine the Dalai Lama at the China King opening his fortune cookie and reading YOUR MOM BLEW ME LAST NIGHT to a packed room of followers and everybody squinting and nodding like fucking Jedi. People make me sick.

Wait a minute - you did it again!

Did what?

You're distracting me away from my outrage!

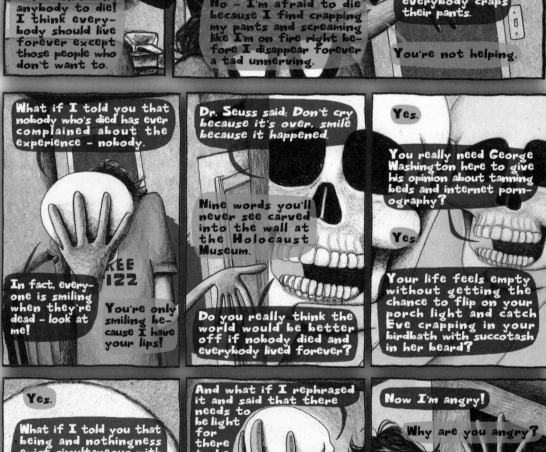

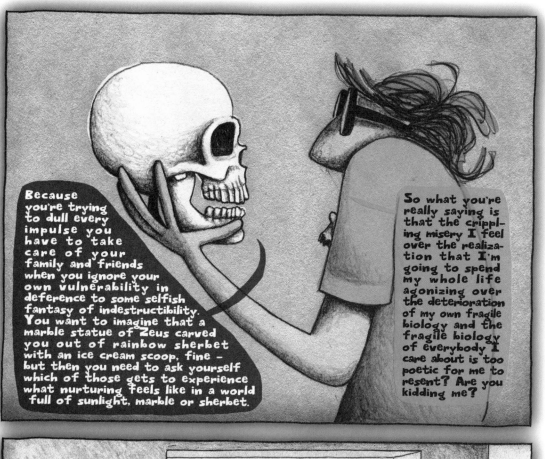

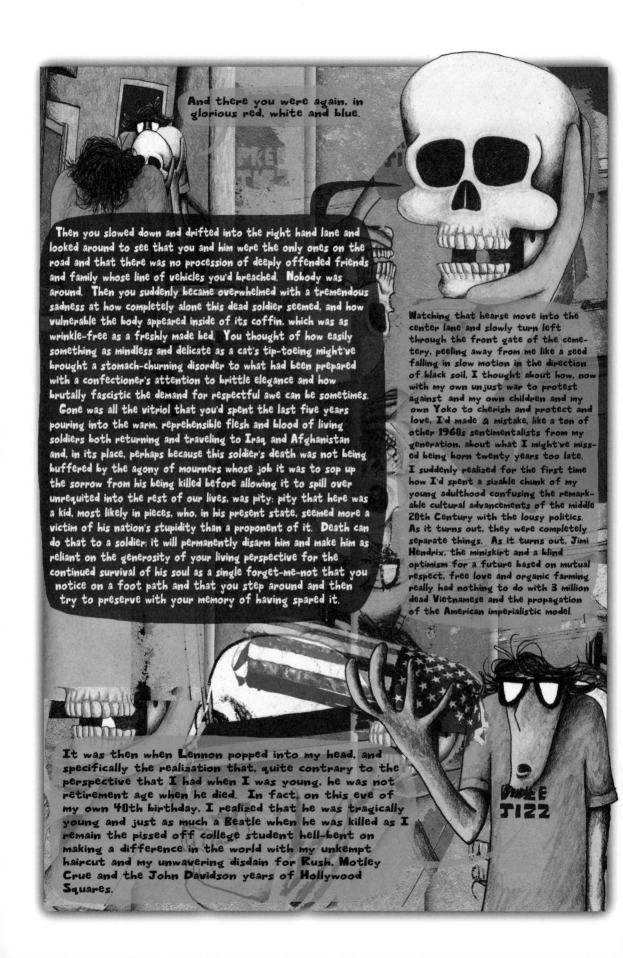

And there you were again, in glorious red, white and blue.

Then you slowed down and drifted into the right hand lane and looked around to see that you and him were the only ones on the road and that there was no procession of deeply offended friends and family whose line of vehicles you'd breached. Nobody was around. Then you suddenly became overwhelmed with a tremendous sadness at how completely alone this dead soldier seemed, and how vulnerable the body appeared inside of its coffin, which was as wrinkle-free as a freshly made bed. You thought of how easily something as mindless and delicate as a cat's tip-toeing might've brought a stomach-churning disorder to what had been prepared with a confectioner's attention to brittle elegance and how brutally fascistic the demand for respectful awe can be sometimes.

Gone was all the vitriol that you'd spent the last five years pouring into the warm, reprehensible flesh and blood of living soldiers both returning and traveling to Iraq and Afghanistan and, in its place, perhaps because this soldier's death was not being buffered by the agony of mourners whose job it was to sop up the sorrow from his being killed before allowing it to spill over unrequited into the rest of our lives, was pity; pity that here was a kid, most likely in pieces, who, in his present state, seemed more a victim of his nation's stupidity than a proponent of it. Death can do that to a soldier; it will permanently disarm him and make him as reliant on the generosity of your living perspective for the continued survival of his soul as a single forget-me-not that you notice on a foot path and that you step around and then try to preserve with your memory of having spared it.

Watching that hearse move into the center lane and slowly turn left through the front gate of the cemetery, peeling away from me like a seed falling in slow motion in the direction of black soil, I thought about how, now with my own unjust war to protest against and my own children and my own Yoko to cherish and protect and love, I'd made a mistake, like a ton of other 1960s sentimentalists from my generation, about what I might've missed being born twenty years too late. I suddenly realized for the first time how I'd spent a sizable chunk of my young adulthood confusing the remarkable cultural advancements of the middle 20th Century with the lousy politics. As it turns out, they were completely separate things. As it turns out, Jimi Hendrix, the miniskirt and a blind optimism for a future based on mutual respect, free love and organic farming really had nothing to do with 3 million dead Vietnamese and the propagation of the American imperialistic model.

It was then when Lennon popped into my head, and specifically the realization that, quite contrary to the perspective that I had when I was young, he was not retirement age when he died. In fact, on this eve of my own 40th birthday, I realized that he was tragically young and just as much a Beatle when he was killed as I remain the pissed off college student hell-bent on making a difference in the world with my unkempt haircut and my unwavering disdain for Rush, Motley Crue and the John Davidson years of Hollywood Squares.

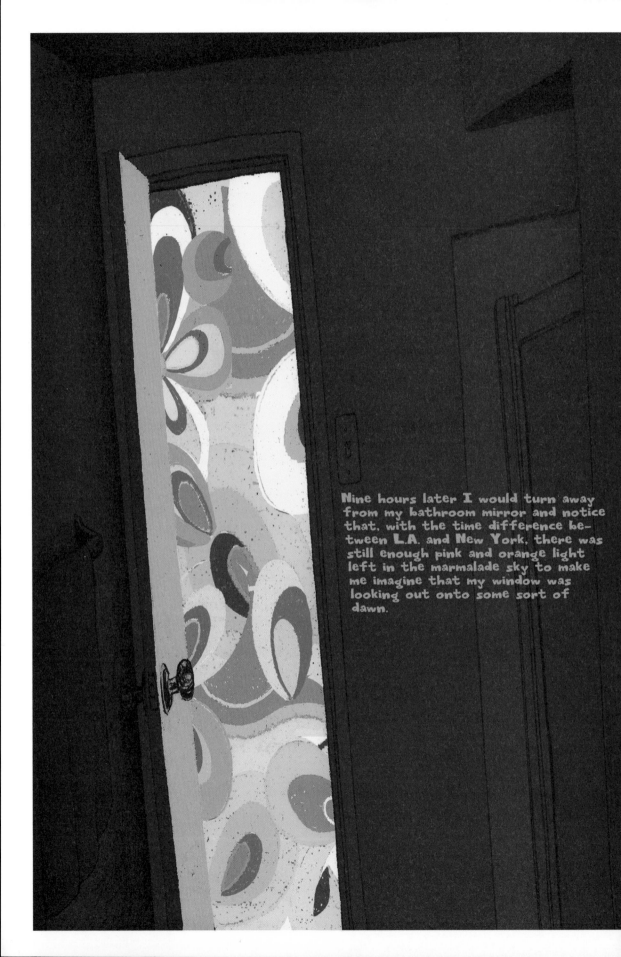

Nine hours later I would turn away from my bathroom mirror and notice that, with the time difference between L.A. and New York, there was still enough pink and orange light left in the marmalade sky to make me imagine that my window was looking out onto some sort of dawn.

FOR CHISTOPHER HITCHENS

HE APPEARED EQUALLY CAPABLE of pissing into your grandmother's fish tank as beating you at chess; the Angus Young of quasi-omniscient political journo-intellectualism, looking as if he had been assembled hastily by sausage makers hoping to fill a suit with all the succulent impropriety of vitriolic meats made sane by delectability. Well aware that the shortest distance between birth and death is a very *straight line*, his reputation was that of a man prone to the rich experiences offered by staggering. And, contrary to the caricature so lavishly and lovingly rendered by friends and foes alike that painted him as either a reliable guard *or* attack dog, one with a ferocious mouth that showed no mercy, Christopher Hitchens was not a wild animal, much to both my relief and dismay.

It was like meeting a clown outside of his makeup, away from the hysteria of his profession, who appears lovely and handsome and noble, if only because he isn't trapped in a spotlight at the center of a ludicrous pie fight.

In fact, having recently won the 2007 National Magazine Award for "Columns and Commentary" for his outstanding work for Vanity Fair, not to mention the surprising popularity of his then-new book, "God Is Not Great: How Religion Poisons Everything," which reached No. 4 on Amazon's best-seller list even before its official release date, there was something both cheerful and elegant and, dare I say, sober about Hitchens when I met him at dusk sitting alone on a squat sofa in the posh outside reception area of his Beverly Hills hotel. In his rumpled trademark suit the color of Caucasian neutrality, a camouflage for anything but, he had just arrived in town to do the 2007 Los Angeles Times Festival of Books, which I would see him do 16 hours after interviewing him and, much to the shock of everybody in attendance and in sharp contradiction to the outstanding premise of his book of there being no deistic magic in the universe, he performed the jaw-dropping miracle of receiving more applause and admiration than anybody else on his panel, the equivalent of walking on whiskey at a venue that typically booed him. One felt that the air he drew through his ever-present Rothmans Blue cigarette while he walked from the crowded ballroom to the signing area afterward was the lightest it had been in quite a long while. It was amazing. Christopher Hitchens, crucified more times by old friends and new enemies than all the velvetized Jesuses in Tijuana combined, had been born again.

"M. Poisson," he said when we first met, in response to my gregarious hello, using the French version of the name that I attach to the bottom of my cartoons.

"Sir Hitchens," I said, resisting the temptation to make a joke to myself about what rose-colored version of doomsday he must have been seeing through the rose-colored retinas I was all too happy to notice, his roguish reputation gleefully revealed to be picture perfect.

He stood, we shook hands. "Do you want to get a drink from the bar before you sit down?" he asked, making me feel like the guest and him the host in my own hometown.

"Sure," I said, looking at the coffee table separating us both and seeing a pack of cigarettes, a cup of espresso and a wine glass the size of an inverted bell jar containing just enough red wine — a *dead Jesus*, we used to call it — to tease a postage stamp.

"Do get the Coppola," he insisted, a name that I was unable to recall 90 seconds later while standing at the hotel bar, having not made the connection to the famous film director's winery. Had the connection been made, it would have most certainly turned me off, as I had lost my taste for any celebrity-named foodstuff in the summer of '75 when I ate enough Bobby Clarke Peanut Butter to caulk a chimney. Instead, I asked the bartender for a glass of cabernet that had a name I'd have a hard time spelling, that didn't sound too much like an Italian sports car or a brand of designer jeans or something that a moneyed Napa Valley hippie might find delightfully sardonic — no Barefoot wine, nor Mad Housewife. His choice cost me 18 bucks, whatever the fuck it was.

"Did you get the Coppola?" Hitchens wanted to know when I returned.

"Yes," I said, setting my gigantic glass of *whatthefuck* down and turning on my tape recorder.

✸ ✸ ✸

MR. FISH

Let's talk about the title of your new book first, "God Is Not Great: How Religion Poisons Everything." There's nothing obtuse about it, is there? In fact, I can't imagine anybody buying the book and then being offended because they didn't know what they were getting.

No, which is the point. A lot of people have been waiting for something like this for a long time, this push back to religious bullying and stupidity. The title came to me in the shower, which is where most of my ideas come to me. That's why I'm so clean.

Do you care that such a blatant title might limit its readership to mostly those who need no convincing of your argument? Is it really going to change anybody's mind?

I *do* think it will change minds, precisely that.

Why do you think so?

Because I think there are a lot of minds that are not so much in a solid form of dogma. The book isn't just about saying *to hell with you and your foolish faith*. I think it's probably useful to have at least some knowledge of the other side, empathy even.

Can a person be spiritual without being religious?

I suppose so. Everybody, whether they're laying a brick wall with a trowel or shearing a sheep, has experienced the transcendent, that's one thing. It's quite another to believe that the universe is directed towards you. The holy texts do actually say what they say and they do mandate a lot of incredible stupidity. I'm rather proud of the chapter [I wrote] about Dr. King. Many people, at least ostensibly, have been motivated to do grand, good things by faith, but why is that necessary? You don't need the supernatural to be in favor of abolishing the condition of slavery, for instance, whereas you do need the Bible to keep slavery going so long. Subjectively, do I really know whether Dr. King was a believer or not? I don't. Did he actually think that the story of the Exodus was true? If so, he contradicted it at every turn

because he did not promise black Americans that they could kill everyone who disagreed with them.

It could be argued that the threat to humanity posed by religion pales in comparison to the threat posed by science and technology — napalm didn't come out of the Vatican, it came out of the chemistry department of Harvard University. One could feasibly make the point that at least God doesn't require 30 billion barrels of oil a year to keep his halo glowing.

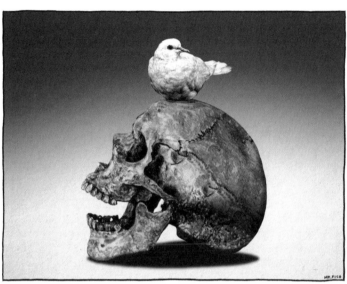

No, but then if you look at what could be very frightening you would have scientific knowledge plagiarized by unscientific people who have contempt for both science and reason. That's now been made possible by our global internationalized civilization. Surely, to most people, that's the most scary thought; in combination is apocalyptic technique in the hands of messianic forces. Let's be honest about it, there is an advantage to the rational mind as opposed to the fanatical one — the fanatical one is not very good at science and, so far, this advantage has played out in our favor.

Still, does science bear no responsibility when they create, essentially, a doomsday machine and then say it should only be used for peaceful purposes?

I would think it was a bad thing if the species was destroyed by an apocalyptic weapon, but I can't

WHICH VERSION OF ADAM MIGHT'VE BETTER PREPARED US FOR A FUTURE WHERE AUTHORITY WILL ALWAYS TRY TO GET THE LAST WORD ON OUR MORAL INDEPENDENCE AND PERSONAL AUTONOMY?

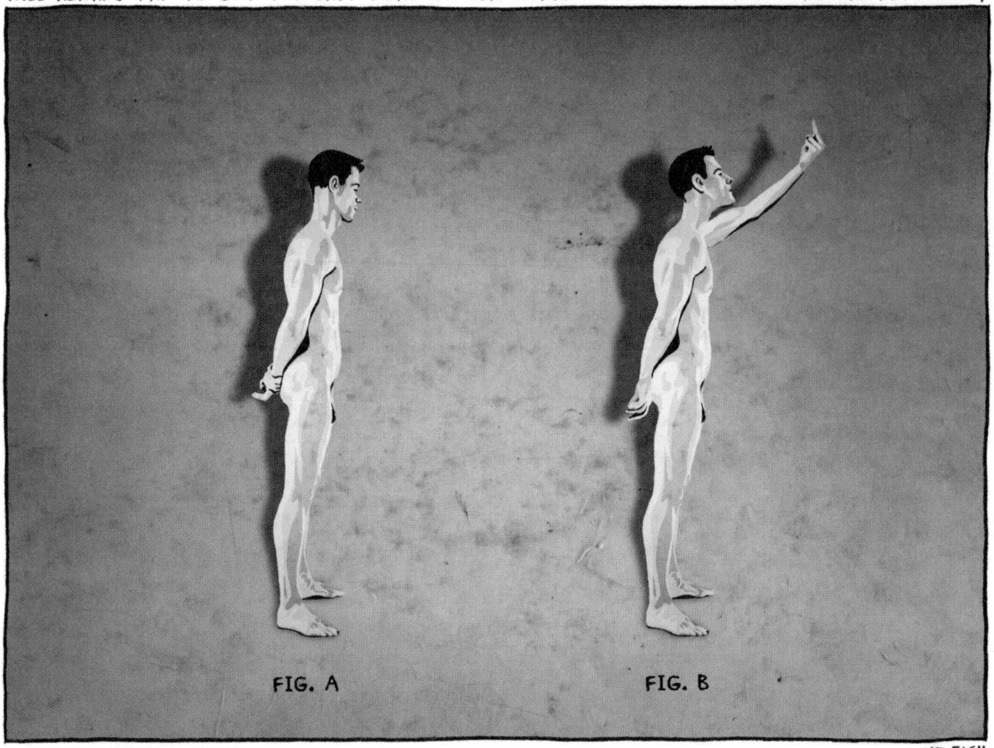

FIG. A   FIG. B

MR.FISH

see how any religious believer would think it was such a bad thing. To them it's not a tragedy, it can't be. They've repeatedly said so. And, sure, a secular power with a nuclear weapon could make the mistake [of ending the world] and several times nearly has. Nothing stops that. The idea that we could die as a species is obviously very high. The fact that we've survived this very brief time is rather surprising. It would be ironic if it were something that arose from our intelligence that got rid of us.

Maybe intelligence is the wrong word.

Well, we've been used to that ever since nuclear physics was discovered. This kind of thing seems to be common sense, our tenure on this planet is very fragile—goddamn. By the way, in my view, in case I didn't make this clear enough in the book—which, actually, I think I didn't—outgrowing the supernatural and the superstitious is not sufficient for emancipating the human race. It's only the beginning. All our big discoveries and big arguments are ahead of us, but the one that has to be subtracted is the fanatical one that prays for the end of time.

Most of the religious people I know are not religious because they're adhering to some ancient, antiquated text or because they're afraid of spending eternity burning in hell if they misbehave. Do you think that religion, for some people, simply fulfills the same purpose that fiction and literature might for you or I, [as a way to quantify] ideas of right and wrong?

That's why I say, in many ways, that [the question of religious inquiry] is a literary question; it's about ethics and the origin of ethics and the best way in which they're expressed is a dilemma—ethical dilemmas are in literature and myth, yeah, sure. The difference is that I can step outside of it and as soon as you can see it from the outside you can see that it's man-made. Being man-made isn't the worst thing. It's just you can't then make it into a transcendent law that everyone must obey. And that's what I object to and that's what has to stop.

There's a basic question that I seldom see included in this discussion and that is the question of the viability of human consciousness itself, and whether or not it perceives reality or just per-

ceives itself perceiving reality. In other words, can consciousness even perceive the truth or does it only interpret a version of the truth relative to a person's mood, opinion, ideology, [et cetera]?

No school of philosophy has ever solved this question of whether being determines consciousness or the other way around. It may be a false antithesis. Here's what I do know, those who claim that they do know this are bound to be wrong. The argument is not equal between us and the supernaturalists. They don't just claim to know there is a supernatural that can be miraculous as a designer, they don't just claim to know that, which is more than they can know. No one can know that. I admit that I can't. They say, 'No, no you can! Not only that, you can know God's mind. Not only that, you can know what he wants you to do about food and sex.' If we start by excluding those who say there's no point in the argument, who say they already know the truth, if we drop them then we may get some progress. Then we're left with an argument among grown-ups.

Do you find that an argument against the existence of God is not unlike an argument against the existence of obscenity? Or, how about this — this is the equation: There's a difference between a cent and a penny. The cent is the imaginary value of the penny, it isn't real, yet when we see the penny we see the cent because we've made them interchangeable. The cent is what we react to, but [we] have to believe it exists first.

I think I know what you're saying — go on.

We've developed this habit of using the incontrovertibility of physical reality to give incontrovertibility to our imaginations, therefore, we're capable of making our imaginations seem real, so God can seem real. You can see it when you look at the words "cunt" and "vagina." Both words refer to the same exact thing, yet one is considered obscene. The difference between the words cunt and vagina is imaginary.

I know what you mean. However, cunt is a hate word.

But it was invented to be such.

It's true that obscenity is a matter of taste and in the eye of the beholder. The real objection to obscenity, in my opinion, is the result of our makeup, specifically that the urinary/genitry/excretory is mixed up. That's what makes children laugh and whistle and grin. If that were not the case, we'd be a lot better off, perhaps. Obscenity comes from grime. *"Free education is a gift to the poor, it raises them out of the gutter. It teaches the*

"Alright - how many of these fucking things do I have to dye for your sins?"

girls to write cock on the door and the boys to write cunt on the shutter." It's the relationship between the spiritual and urinary, that's where obscenity comes from.

That's my point, is obscenity — or God — something we can even have a rational conversation about if we've only been conditioned to react to it? Is consciousness an evolutionary flaw?

That's what I say in my first quotation in the book:

> *"Oh, wearisome condition of humanity*
> *Born under one law, to another bound;*
> *Vanity begot, and yet forbidden vanity,*
> *Created sick, commanded to be sound."*
> — Fulke Greville, "Mustapha"

The situation is we're mammals, we leak and we excrete and then we're told to forget about that or to deny it. Religion is totalitarian because it demands the impossible. [Like religion], obscenity shuts you down. The secular argument, or the liberal argument, is to, as much as possible, remove taboos so things do not become unmentionable; to let some air into the discussion. I'm old now — I remember when D.H. Lawrence's "Lady Chatterley" was banned because the government thought that once you ban the book you can get people to stop thinking about these things. And I remember thinking that's a mistake, a very obvious mistake. You probably increase the chances of [people] thinking about these things.

Which reminds me of my favorite Lenny Bruce quote.

What's that?

Knowledge of syphilis is not instruction to get it.

[Chuckles] It was easy to argue this kind of thing in the '60s, against censorship, against bans on homosexuality, et cetera. Now you do run into people who say, *then why would you forbid pedophilia? Would the same standards hold for this? Or snuff movies? Or third trimester abortions?* This argument takes place among rationalists and humanists and sociologists. We don't say that if you allow [these things] we would be comfortable with obscenity. I do think there are lots of things you don't have to be taught. Most people don't

have to be taught not to eat dead human beings, let alone to kill them in order to eat them. You don't have to drill this into children. You don't have to drill it into children that if one of their parents wants to go to bed with them that they should go and stay at the neighbor's for the night, you don't have to. You could say that that's an argument for a creator with a benevolent view but then you'd have a huge rational argument about why we are programmed to kill and torture and so on. It does show that morality precedes religion, that ethics precedes religion, not the other way around.

Still, I wonder if our survival as a species is something we can *will* given a consciousness that is able to make its imagination seem real?

We can't stand far enough outside of our dilemma to think it completely through. It's like the mind/body distinction. There may not be a distinction. The mind is clever enough to consider the distinction, but it's not clever enough to get far enough outside the body to arbitrate it.

And that's the rub.

We don't know that we're not dreaming. Look, we can't resolve these things today. Here's what I insist on: Those who say they know are out of the argument and should be treated with less respect. We are having, even here in this lobby with the traffic, here in L.A., we're already having quite a high-level discussion, about things that are fairly imponderable to combat, up against a phalanx of people who say *what's the point in having this discussion? We already know the answer. What's the point of struggling and arguing and researching?* This is what I find hateful.

Some people might accuse you of asking everybody to be comfortable living in a godless universe that is completely indifferent to them. How do you imagine people will go about satisfying their own sense of purpose?

Obviously, it's not possible for people to do that all of the time, but it is possible for them not to draw any conclusions from their belief that the universe is all about them. If a huge rusted fridge fell through the ceiling and obliterated you without warning, I would think *well, that was lucky.*

Presuming that the fridge was directed at neither of us, it's not lucky at all. But I would not be human if I didn't think it was a bit of luck. This is why religion can't be beaten, because it does derive from all these forms of selfishness, self-centeredness, fantasy and so on. Fine, I concede to that, but then why do people keep saying that I have to respect it? I don't have to respect any belief, nor do you, that a rusted fridge that killed you and didn't kill me was a piece of luck. You do not have to respect that. You can recognize it and see where it comes from. You can analyze it, you can even sympathize with it. You can't really say that I insist also that you respect it.

There is in religion, however, some practical application. Take, for instance, the very radical notion that the meek have some intrinsic value. African-Americans, just to take an obvious example, were told for centuries that they were something much less than human, so for them to have access to a Bible that tells them that they are significant, that white society doesn't determine their worth, is, well, significant. For them it was a belief system that acknowledged, and still does in large part, that they were human beings that were being mistreated. Respecting that aspect of religion doesn't demand that you also kowtow to superstition.

Of course, of course, I see what you're saying. Since there's no justice in this world, there better be some justice on offer in the next. Again, you can see where it comes from, fine. It's the same when Karen Armstrong [author of "The Great Transformation: The Beginning of Our Religious Traditions"] writes about Islam. Arabs were being teased by Jews and Christians, "You haven't had a prophet yet." Well, they were going to get one, weren't they? Then you have the Archangel Gabriel appear to some fucking peasant merchant who can't read, exactly borrowed from the [Judeo-Christian] faith. Yes, of course I understand that, but it's too much to ask me to believe it. It's too much to ask me to respect it. It's too much like I would be, too much like myself. I can't respect something that follows my own wish fulfillment. I don't. The last time I prayed was for an erection. Don't ask me if I got it or not — who cares?

Having had just enough Sunday school to know the story of Lot's wife and how to recognize an unhealthy temptation when I heard one, I struggled hard to keep my eyes above c-level and asked Hitchens a final question about whose existence was easier to disprove, Henry Kissinger's or God's. He laughed and said that it was the same process for eviscerating each high-profile Jew in print and that, essentially, the quantitative differences between nonexistent entities was not measurable, being the difference between the hole in a very old bagel and the hole in a relatively recent one.

When he stood to say goodbye three hours after we began our conversation, I did not stand to shake his hand, not because I was trying to be disrespectful, but rather because I figured a greater disrespect might have been expressed had I fallen down on him. I was drunk. Waiting until I was sure he was a safe distance away, I stood slowly, stacking my vertebrae like hermit crabs beneath a bowling bowl, and zigzagged outside and took a moment to look up at the stars and to recall something that Mark Twain had said: "*Go to heaven for the climate, hell for the company.*" "And back and forth," I thought to myself, amending the sentiment, "if you have any interest in learning anything about anything."

Four years later, on the morning of Dec. 16, 2011, I poured myself a glass of red wine and went to the window and toasted the same stars that, although I couldn't see them through the freshly dawned day, I knew were still there. ✳

❈ ❈ ❈

MR.FISH

THE CON

"LOU FERRIGNO IS A FUCKING ASSHOLE, that's what I'm taking home with me from the 2007 Comic-Con, a fucking ass *hole*!"

The speaker was a forty-something year old adolescent, freckled, strawberry-blond hair, bald and sweating bullets, his pale skin appearing fair enough to sunburn inside the pop of a flashbulb. He was referring to the musclebound deaf actor who was famous not so much for his acting but more for his willingness to have his bovinity spraypainted green. He threw down his plastic bag of comic books and collapsed into his cafeteria chair. "The fucking opposite of Jonathan Harris (Dr. Smith from *Lost in Space*), I swear to fucking Christ! The *opposite!*" His 300-pound friend absorbed the fury of the rant with a shrug and sat down and cracked open a Diet Coke. He drank it through the pink slit in his beard.

"*Lou Ferrigno*?" I said, sitting opposite them at one of the communal lunch tables set up just beyond the snack bar in the main exhibition hall at the San Diego Convention Center, home, for almost forty years, of the Comic-Con International. I was relaxing with a Vitamin Water and looking over some notes that I'd written up on a napkin pinned to my knee from the pressure of my pen point during my two-and-half hour drive from Los Angeles for a panel I was on about editorial cartooning. A dainty pair of Asian women sat quietly next to me making origami swans out of junk flyers.

"Yeah," said the guy. "He's charging twenty-fucking-dollars for a Polaroid! He's an asshole."

"He's *here*?" I asked.

"Yeah, [the] motherfucker."

"You should've told him that you'd give him *forty* dollars if he could say *Egg McMuffin* legibly."

"Right," said the Hulk-hater, laughing suddenly and mopping his head with his naked palm, "or sixty dollars if he could turn back into *what's-his-fucking-name*, Bill Bixby — "

"And talk about *My Favorite Martian*," said his friend.

"Or *The Courtship of Eddie's* fucking-*Father*."

I'd gotten to the Convention Center two hours earlier, having walked in behind a rotund Captain America whose costume was a one piece that tied in the back like a hospital gown, and was offered a free *Smallville* tote bag that was truly immense; large enough, I imagined, to smuggle the carrier's inner child into the great hall where it could be released amid the many booths bursting with toys, anime, collectibles, books, comix, video games, figurines, movie chotzchke, TV memorabilia and twenty dollar Polaroids, its eyes like pinwheels, its appetite for bright plastic and flashing lights and deaf C-list celebrities manic and grotesque and insatiable. I declined the tote bag. My costume? *Dignity*. And looking around I half expected to be hounded all day by convention attendees blown away by the uniqueness of my disguise, demanding that I share the sewing pattern with them.

Inside the crush of people, which the Comic-Con officials would put at 125,000 by the end of the weekend, a new record, that had swept me along with them for the quarter mile from the parking garage that morning, I'd overhead a middle aged man dressed as some sort of space lizard in a blue Speedo and green leotard say enthusiastically to another middle aged man who was dressed in a silver body stocking, boots and star spangled cape, "My wife thinks I'm nuts, but I tell her that it's just me stepping out of the closet once a year — give me a break!" I turned to look at his outfit, which most certainly seemed as if it had

been put on inside a closet; a *dark* closet, I figured, that had to spill directly out onto the sidewalk, for anybody willing to cram himself into a Speedo that small would be unable to move through a house where he might catch a glimpse of himself reflected in a mirror, a window or even the chrome of the toaster.

"Right on," said the other guy. I turned back around to the sound of a high-five being clapped through gloved hands.

And when everybody cheered at a Wookie riding by in the backseat of one of the many rickshaw bicycles I'd noticed shuttling conventioneers everywhere around town, their applause inspiring him to stand up and to do a Tarzan yell and to pound his chest triumphantly, my annoyance at both his shortness and his bravado quickly spread to a deeper annoyance with myself for being angry at the character crossover: *Chewy, even if he was 5' 4," wouldn't act like Johnny Weissmuller, not even with a gun to his head, you lousy cocksuckers!* I savored my rage, repeating the thought over and over again against my will (robinson), until my concentration was broken by the sight of the male Princess Leia riding next to the chest-thumping buffoon. Properly bosomed and as demur as royalty, he wore a goatee and real cinnamon buns on either side of his head, raisons and all.

Two hours later, during the Q & A portion of my panel, a woman asked me, after seeing ten of my angriest cartoons projected on a screen the size of a dead sail, if I was afraid of the U.S. government. I looked past her at the helmeted storm trooper in the very last row rummaging through his shopping bag and remembered my favorite Leo Tolstoy quote from *War and Peace*: "Whatever question arose, a swarm of these drones, without having finished their buzzing on a previous theme, flew over to the new one and by their hum drowned and obscured the voices of those who were disputing honestly."

"No," I said, "not exactly." ✳

THE CARTOONIST FACING THE TRUTH OF CONTEMPORARY AMERICAN POLITICS HEAD ON

MR.FISH

WHY I MISS NORMAN MAILER

MR.FISH

I THOUGHT THAT I'D DONE EVERYTHING I was supposed to do. This was back in the springtime of 2007, about seven months before Norman Mailer died. I'd sent an e-mail to the address in the newspaper and made a reservation to see him talk about what would be his last novel, "The Castle in the Forest," at the Writers Guild Theater in Beverly Hills, but I never got a confirmation e-mail back. I couldn't even get anybody on the telephone. For four days I tried. It pissed me off.

"Writers Guild," I grumbled to myself, listening to the telephone ring off the hook at the theater at 1:30 in the afternoon, six hours from when the event was scheduled to start. "What is a *writers guild* doing in Hollywood, anyway?" I asked myself. "What is a writer in Hollywood?" I knew what a writer was on the East Coast: He is a smoker, works on a typewriter and is an enormous failure; he is a sandwich maker who cries easily and can quote Nabokov and Algren and Eliot. The West Coast version of a writer is a 50-year-old fat guy in white sneakers who wrote a couple "X-Files" episodes 13 years ago and knows the name Faulkner only as a screen credit on some old Bogart movies.

As the phone continued to ring, I imagined the 50-year-old fat guy asleep beneath a torn "Dark Side of the Moon" poster somewhere in Westwood, his bed loaded with cats, nothing but dirty cereal bowls in the sink, his comic book collection archived in a stack of dusty boxes in the closet and ready to be sold if things get really bad, like if he all of a sudden got a girlfriend. I slammed down the receiver and called Book Soup, the retailer that was sponsoring the event. They told me to take a hike, that they were connected to what was happening at the Writers Guild only as booksellers, not as seat warmers.

Seat warmers. I wanted to kill somebody.

I got in the car and zigzagged my way from Pasadena for an hour and a half through rush-hour traffic until I got to Beverly Hills, the whole time trying to listen to a public library CD of Mailer reading, with his wife, his book about the Kennedy assassination, "Oswald's Tale." Parking, I was happy to turn the car off, the trading off of passages between Norman and the Mrs. having never amounted to much more than the dullest Sonny and Cher routine ever recorded.

The theater had the beginnings of a sizable crowd swirling around the lobby when I got there. Luckily, nobody was under 70 and practically everybody was a woman, so the swirling was dainty, like dandelion spores, not the least bit treacherous. Seeing the only other dude in the room, a youngster of about 65, sitting all by himself at a brown cafeteria table with a list of names and a cash box, I steeled myself against what I assumed was about to happen by sweating out my ass.

"Name?" said the man, cheerfully, as I approached.

"Booth," I said, clenching my jaw.

"*Booth,*" he said, moving his pen down the row of names on his clipboard. "Ah, here we are, *Booth,*" he said, stopping at the name Booth, Melissa, his insatiable need to be both cheerful and accommodating blinding him to the specific purpose of his task. He made a check mark and said, "Twenty dollars." With perspiration running down my legs to meet my socks, I handed him a pair of wet 10-dollar bills and found my seat, paranoid that it was only a matter of time before Melissa Booth found the back of my head with her cane. I made myself as small as I could in my chair, not an easy feat with so much osteoporosis in the room.

At last, after 45 minutes of waiting, from the rear of the auditorium came Norman Mailer. He walked slowly using two canes, his knees as brittle as cookies, his body matronly and small, his brow furrowed, his tremendous ears both containing hearing aids, his eyes as fierce as little knives. The applause followed him the full length of the room and all the way up to the stage before it stopped abruptly, as if the noise might disrupt his concentration just enough on the stairs to send him toppling. Squeaky thuds from the rubber tips of his canes hoisted him uneasily into the glare of the C-SPAN television lights, his frailty bringing some measure of sorrow to the moment. He collapsed into his chair just as David Ulin, book critic for the L.A. Times, sat down opposite him and readied his notes. An introduction was read

clumsily from a podium while a glass of red wine was delivered surreptitiously to Mailer and hidden behind a short vase of flowers on the small table separating him from his host. The author was then handed an immense microphone that he held in his lap like a dead flashlight, and he waited for the interview to begin. I felt gloomy about what the next hour might bring.

Then Mailer spoke. Then the night was glorious.

There's a story about Mark Twain going to visit James McNeill Whistler in his art studio and approaching one of the painter's canvases resting on an easel. Leaning in to examine the detail of the work, Twain reaches out a finger to touch the face of the painting before being stopped by Whistler who shouts, "Wait! The paint is still wet!"

"That's OK," Twain says reassuringly, "I'm wearing gloves."

It is one of the earliest examples of artistic celebrity trumping art, something that Mailer would, some 60 years later, master better than anybody else in his generation — elevating, in fact, the notion that the ego of a writer, when inflated with massive amounts of hot air, may be capable of carrying him to heights so great that he is required to look down to observe the culture of his time. And while such a perspective might, at first, seem an unforgivably arrogant position from which to comment on a society made tiny by such a lofty point of view and panoramic range of vision, it was the humanity of Mailer's brain and the fallibility of his all too human eyes and the contradictions in his heart that made the artistry of his observations divinely lacking in condescension. In fact, he maximized the reach of his sympathies by offering their emollience to saints and sinners alike, something that no God wishing to subjugate those beneath him with the jurisprudence of a codification of their souls would ever do.

"He may have been a fool," Mailer once suggested as a suitable epitaph for himself, "but he certainly did his best and that can't be said of all fools."

Certainly, many would say that Mailer's massive ego was precisely what ruined him as an artist. True, he appeared sometimes not to entirely trust the ability of his audience to understand his writing without excessive coaching. Oftentimes his work seemed as if it were being presented to a reader pre-chewed; that is, so rigorously vivisected that those readers not repulsed by having to slog through the innards of whatever he's overwritten — which is typically full of plot points that are revealed slowly, from the inside out, and with greatest aplomb for the stench and creepy sinewy-ness of the whole exercise — might still wish that *they* were the ones doing the chewing and subsequent tasting of the material. It's the difference between being handed an entrée at a restaurant and being left alone to eat versus being brought back into the kitchen to have the cook explain why each ingredient he's cooking with needs to be appreciated — *a lot*. And then there's the help in the preparation. And the cleanup. And then the picking through the excrement days later to see that, in fact, each ingredient was properly digested and nourishing to the right bones.

The question is: Is that art of terrific depth or is it just the expression of a mammoth insecurity that forces a writer to continuously talk over his reader's shoulder because he doesn't want anybody to notice how thinly his characters are rendered or how idiotic the scenarios that inspire them to act one way or another are when they are left unadorned with an author's incessant commentary?

Of course, suggesting an answer would belie the whole point in asking the question.

One thing that is undeniable, though, is how seriously Mailer took his responsibilities as a novelist — responsibilities that are indeed profound. He knew how pitifully incompetent and morally bankrupt *real* reality was when compared with fiction, and yet he always did his best to outfit his ideas with strings that would prevent anything resembling escapism from suggesting that the brutal truths of existence should be fled. He understood better than most how fiction, by simulating reality, was able to harbor all the emotional significance and inspiration offered by real reality with

one rather remarkable difference: unlike *real* reality, fictitious reality was both editable and portable. The fictitious Manhattan of 1951, for instance, as gray as a pewter ashtray and cold as the bottom of a wishing well, can be experienced anywhere in the world by anybody with a library card. Likewise, if you've never enjoyed the rare pleasure of jerking off into a hissing frying pan or pissing into the uterus of a cackling fishmonger's wife, nor did you plan on ever having the gumption to enjoy such rare pleasures using your own fluids, you can always pick up something by Charles Bukowski or Henry Miller. *Real* reality is never that generous. Real reality is immutable; it's nothing but the prop closet and the set upon which we stage our fiction.

Fictitious reality can also do something that real reality couldn't do in a million years: suggest that the universe is not indifferent to the existence of human beings. In fact, fictitious reality remains the only version of reality that,

MR.FISH

by being both editable and portable, people are able to conduct controlled experiments upon as a way of figuring out how to conduct their real lives in real reality in a way that maximizes the unsubstantiated fantasy that what they think and what they do has some meaning other than simply being more cosmic balderdash. Fictitious reality provides human beings with the only reality that offers them anything like justification for their continued survival as a species. It is literally the lie of sanity.

But perhaps Mailer's greatest achievement was his invention of something I'll call *theophysics* in fiction, which might be defined as a detailed study of how the spiritual dimension (assuming there is such a thing) might coexist with the corporeal dimension, both sharing and affecting the same exact reality without being entirely aware of the other's presence or purpose. I imagine that it's not dissimilar to how plants and animals coexist. Despite the fact that a fruit-bearing plant possesses a completely different type of *awareness* of the world than a rabbit or a deer and that neither is, therefore, capable of having anything resembling sympathy for the other's suffering or empathy for the other's quest for comfort and joy, both, by being able to experience each other's existence through interdependent cycles of sustenance and reproduction, still have an obvious influence on each other's behavior. Likewise with humanity, there most certainly must be a number of super- and substructures of reality in the universe that are completely incomprehensible to human beings, yet they are still an influence on how humanity behaves, or, in the case of Mailer's work, misbehaves.

"God," he once said, "like us, suffers the ambition to make a destiny more extraordinary than was conceived for Him — yes, God is like me, only more so."

And now God is dead. And we are left with the remarkably profound gift of nothing being any better or worse as a result.

The final question from the audience in 2007 came from a woman in her 50s who said that she was writing a play about Marilyn Monroe and wondered if Mailer had any insights into the deceased superstar that might help her finish. Ugh. Mailer looked at her impatiently and asked if she'd read his book on Monroe. She had. "I have no other insights to offer other than those in the book," he said, "although I do have an anecdote I can share with you." He then proceeded to tell how he and Arthur Miller actually lived in the same brownstone in the 1950s and how they'd met nearly every day at the mailboxes downstairs. In all the years that they shared the same address, Miller never once offered to introduce him to Marilyn. "He knew that I'd try to steal her if I ever met her," said Mailer, "and there's nothing that eats at a thief more than being prevented from committing his crime."

Standing up to leave, with real satisfaction in my chest, I imagined Melissa Booth sitting at a nearby bus stop trying to ball her arthritic hand into a fist, wondering who the fuck had stolen her night out at the theater and why there was so much evil in the world. ✳

EVERY OTHER TUESDAY
WITH MORT

MR. FISH

THE FIRST TIME I MET MORT SAHL *was in the spring of 2007, a month before he turned 80 and two months before he and I started hanging out every other Tuesday to diagnose what we believed was either the disease of modern politics or the lobotomizing cure for the pesky annoyances of Enlightenment thinking. I had been asked by the* LA Weekly *to interview him and to find out why so many comedians considered him to be the Ardipithecus of all the baboons currently claiming the moniker of social satirist. This is what I said:*

Inventor of American standup commentary, surrogate older brother to Lenny Bruce and George Carlin, forgotten uncle to Richard Pryor and Bill Hicks, revered godfather to Bill Maher and Jon Stewart and — before he decided to sacrifice the sharpness of his wit exclusively to the cutting of George Bush's free gubment cheese — Dennis Miller, Mort Sahl squinted in the pristine, almost minty Bel Air sunshine while sitting outside a crowded Starbucks, the Halliburton of caffeine, and asked, "What's wrong with America?"

Dressing as always like a 1950s grad student, in a yellow V-neck sweater, black loafers and khaki slacks, Sahl still has that outraged intelligence in his eyes, only now they're surrounded by delicately engraved, 80-year-old laugh lines. It's a visual irony that makes his question hilarious in the most tragic sense of the word, as if he were a doctor looking down at a head lying before him on a tray and asking it, "Do you ever experience headaches?"

With no apparent mellowing of his disdain for political dishonesty and the cultural malaise that sustains it, he seemed to take no solace in having been right about so many things so much of the time and usually decades before everyone else. In 1960, for instance, he warned the audience at San Francisco's *hungry i* that Israel was becoming something of a nationalistic bully in the Middle East. In 1963, he told Paul Krassner, editor in chief of *The Realist* magazine, that the Kennedy administration was "generally in agreement with the Republicans" and that it was "suddenly possible to be a Democrat and Republican at the same time." Sound familiar?

Being reminded of the latter quote, Sahl laughed and attempted to clarify the point by making a distinction between how liberalism manifests itself among everyday people versus those who become part of the power elite. Of those lefties uncorrupted by plutocratic ideals in the highest seats of government, he said, "It's almost as if there was a summit meeting and America was divided and the fascists got banking and world power and the liberals settled for music and movies and then they tried to pretend that music and movies had real political power."

He stood to remove his sweater, the sinking sun being a little too generous with its Hollywood reputation for any real human being to tolerate. "Maybe the whole exercise of liberalism," he said, settling back into his chair, "is to be noble publicly and to lose gracefully and to be the oppressed majority." Meanwhile, at a nearby table an heiress who was skinny enough to X-ray with a flashlight held a tiny, vibrating Chihuahua puppy in the palm of her hand and nuzzled it mercilessly with itty-bitty moans.

"I get a lot of flack whenever I take on the liberals," Sahl said, setting his loafer into the crotch of the iron table and hoisting his $5 paper cup of coffee, "because I think they're way too self-satisfying. That's why I can't look upon them as any kind of savior. I keep hearing, 'The Democrats are in trouble!' *In trouble?* They've been in trouble since 1965, and what do they do about it? They just keep going to those meetings at Stanley Sheinbaum's house to talk about electing more women into Congress."

Despite the joyful confidence with which Sahl injected his absurdist buoyancy into the existential dread surrounding him, there was one subject that brought a wistfulness to his face, and that was his alignment, 40 years ago, with Jim Garrison, the Democratic district attorney of Orleans Parish, Louisiana, who is best known for his investigations into the Kennedy assassination during the 1960s. Because of Sahl's close ties to the Kennedy White House and his public condemnation of the findings issued by the Warren Commission, Garrison made him a deputized member of the D.A.'s team assembled to expose the supposed cover-up of the real facts covertly surrounding the murder. Sahl then attempted to parlay the investigation and the controversial subject of conspiracy into his act, reading from the Warren Report and wondering aloud if the U.S. government might not be populated by homicidal maniacs. (Sound familiar?)

"When the murderers [of our social democracy] came along and people started talking about my paranoia, that was very disappointing," he said. "I thought it was going to be like the movies. I thought I was going to run the rustlers out of town and the rancher would say to me, 'Maybe you can stay here and be my straw boss and marry my daughter.' And I'd say, 'Sorry, I got to be riding on to the next town.' But this town never got cured. I'm still here — and vastly outnumbered!"

Asked about his infamous friendships with Ronald Reagan, Alexander Haig and George H.W. Bush and whether such alliances compromised his reputation as a radical truth teller, he said, "I've written for a lot of politicians — the Republicans are the only ones who pay me!" He laughed hard. "It all comes down to whether or not you're honest with yourself. A lot of people have no intellectual capacity and operate on this instinctual masculine fatalism. Right-wing guys are honest about who they are and liberals are honest about what they wish we all could be — that's not being honest with yourself. If I talk to people today about John Wayne, for instance, and I mention *The Sea Chase* and James Warner Bellah or somebody they don't like politically, they won't acknowledge their art; they don't like that they wrote that Americans aren't sorry for themselves and aren't sentimental about Indians, which leads us to the question that everybody dreads, which is: can we forgive our failings?

"Nowadays, you open up what's supposed to be a left-wing newspaper and you get a cartoon of Dick Cheney with his fly open. Bush is supposed to be the bad guy and you're supposed to be morally superior, and this is what you do? Come on! When all you do is label the opposition as the enemy, you run the risk of becoming sophomoric in your understanding of the world."

Politely declining a roaming Starbucks barista's offer of a hideously sweet hors d'oeuvre, he stood to leave. As Sahl walked away, literally into the sunset, his shoulders weary with the weight of knowing that a lifetime of truth seeking had come to this, it's hard not to wonder, as James Thurber did in 1958, if "perhaps Mort Sahl is the answer."

❊ ❊ ❊

The last time I saw Mort Sahl was in the summer of 2008, just before he separated from his wife and moved, brokenhearted, to a friend's guest house in Northern California, where, like the wine corked, crated and shipped from the vineyards surrounding him, his depth and complexity would slowly become only meaningful to a fistful of connoisseurs who would keep him in their basements, beneath the ground like Lazarus, and only take him out as a miraculous blessing to share with their dearest and most cherished friends. This is how I talked about our last meeting together for Truthdig:

If legendary comedian Mort Sahl felled his one-millionth diseased tree of cultural lethargy and political disingenuousness in the vast and ever-expanding forest of American megalomania and Wikipedia wasn't there to acknowledge it, would anybody know to give a crap?

Doubtful.

To quote Ambrose Bierce, an inventor is "a person who makes an ingenious arrangement of wheels, levers and springs, and believes it civilization."

So then what does it mean to our concept of civilization when our primary source of information gathering, the Internet, informs us through its preeminent encyclopedia, Wikipedia, that Mort Sahl deserves an entry that is roughly the same size as those for Miracle Whip and Joe Piscopo and only half the size of the entries for flatulence and hard-boiled eggs?

This, after all, is *Mort Sahl*, the Hugh Hefner of political satire and social commentary.

If journalism is the first draft of history, he has proven with his public eviscerations of the national news for 50 years (and counting) to be one of history's most invaluable and dedicated proofreaders. It means that civilization is more or less anything we do and the monkeys don't. In other words, if evolution were really the process of our retaining only those characteristics most useful to the betterment of the species and the disregarding of all that is useless and nonsensical, then there would never have been the emergence of the Atomic Age, "Godfather III," a Caucasian Jesus, breech-loading weaponry, compassionate conservatism or the pubic toupee.

In fact, it has been argued that any conclusion we make about the world comes to us at the moment when we get tired of thinking.

Tired of thinking several Tuesdays ago, I sought out the company of somebody who I knew would be willing to do some thinking for me; somebody who had previously, both in person and on LP, taken hold of the other end of the piano, so to speak, and helped me move it into a brighter room. A real honestagoodness player whose music drifting out my window made me considerably more beautiful to the world.

Sitting at Fabrocini's Italian restaurant in Bel Air, I try to wipe what turns out to be an existential fog from my glasses with the hem of my T-shirt while ordering a spinach salad and a triple espresso from a beleaguered waiter. Sitting across from me is Mort Sahl, whose eyes are as bright as freshly sharpened pencils and whose eyebrows are perpetually knitted as if life were an impossibly itchy sweater that needed to be unraveled and turned back into yarn and returned to the sheep. He drinks water and glances through the New York Times.

❊ ❊ ❊

I was listening to your 1960 recording "Mort Sahl at the Hungry i" on my way over here and I was stuck by how, when you were talking about the FBI infiltrating protests at college campuses and posing as students in order to disrupt what might otherwise be orderly gatherings, the audience seemed shocked and unsure as to whether or not you were joking.

Sure, I remember.

It was fascinating because nowadays, with agencies like the NSA, everybody automatically assumes that they're being spied on, that we don't even have to leave our homes anymore to be infiltrated by the FBI. The shock today might be that the government *isn't* listening in on you.

You know, [General Michael] Hayden used to be NSA, now he runs the CIA — he was going to be on Larry King and all week long they ran promos during the day (impersonating Larry King), "Michael Hayden and your phone calls!" (*Laughs*) I bet, I'm sure.

See, that's what I mean — that's such a great joke, a good inadvertent joke. Where is satire today? How does a satirist get work when all you have to do to create satire is report the news with a straight face?

You have to see it as a joke, that should be the first thing — you have to recognize the humor of the situation, plus you need to perceive the irony of why it's funny. Liberals see the irony, but they're too self-righteous to laugh about it. They'd rather remain serious about it because they prefer tragedy to humor.

Because tragedy has political application, while humor can't be used as a hot potato to throw in the other guy's lap. Both sides do it.

That's right. But the Democrats have to start doing something other than just to repeat over and over that they're not Republicans. They feel powerful now because they think the Republicans have painted themselves into a corner and [the Democrats] are the only ones we can vote for.

Are you at all frustrated by [Barack] Obama's recent public displays of toughness, his willingness to bomb Pakistan and Iran, etc.?

Obama is a black guy made in the lab by white guys. Again, it's about [Democratic] virtue, "We're going to nominate a black man." Look who they pick — they didn't exactly pick Paul Robeson or Malcolm X. Or it's like with Hillary Clinton. She says, "Believe me, I won't let the war go on!" What reason is there to believe her? She's running on the *entitlement* ticket. It isn't enough that we had [Bill Clinton], now we have to have

her? Has everybody forgotten that he went into Kosovo and that he bombed civilians in Yugoslavia? I mean, his presidency wasn't exactly a high time in America — maybe for the stock market. But getting back to Obama, Bill Bradley just the other day referred to him as a rock star. What kind of an appraisal is that? It's not even a good parallel — how often do rocks stars have anything to do with music, not the music industry, but *music*? It's vaudeville.

Maybe [Bradley] was exactly right, then, that Obama is good vaudeville. I mean, isn't there such a thing as the profession of "celebrity?"

Remember Ambrose Bierce? He said in his book of definitions that a celebrity is a person who's famous for being well known. And that's the extent of their influence — celebrity trial lawyers, celebrity charity givers. Do we really want a celebrity president?

There's another point to be made about spying, getting back to that for a second. When the FBI infiltrates the left, it's doing so because the power elite doesn't understand the language of dissent — dissent that is born out of victimization, right? And if that's the case, aren't we all suspect when the power elite views everybody they subjugate with suspicion for fear of revolution? It's like a butterfly collector who infiltrates a meeting of stamp collectors to understand why they prefer stamp collecting to butterfly collecting — absolutely nothing can be learned by such an exercise.

Intelligence agencies do log a lot of overtime in the area of suspicion and it does encourage them to find a lot of pigeons. But, you know, Hoover and McCarthy were never after communists. They were after nonconformists who might want to resist the fascist tendencies of big government. If you look at that whole blacklisting period, Judith Copeland was acquitted; Alger Hiss was convicted of perjury, not spying. Most of the government cases fell apart when they got to court. They were never looking for communists — they never found any. Sure, the country is in real danger of losing its soul, but it's not because of a group of dedicated nonconformists.

Right — it's conformity that is the backbone of totalitarianism, not nonconformity.

Yeah — and who are the nonconformists today? Who do they consider the leftists now? Arianna Huffington? She's on all those cable shows talking about fighting the system — it's been pretty good to her. (*Laughs*)

Well, since you were at the center of all that blacklisting stuff in the 1950s, maybe you can tell me: What exactly was so wrong with communism? I mean, forget about what the government was saying about it, it seems that a lot of intellectuals condemned it, too. If you look at the definition of communism in the dictionary —

Sounds like Jesus, doesn't it?

Yeah, I even wrote it down in my notebook because I wanted to ask you about it. It's defined as: a theory advocating elimination of private property *and* a system in which goods are owned in common and are available to all as needed.

When they couldn't sell that as a threat to capitalism, they started calling it *Godless* communism.

Which is also amazing to me — it seems that if you're looking for some hardcore evidence for what might be a political philosophy that ruins people's lives and devastates the environment, probably irrevocably, you'll find it more with capitalism than communism. What's that Upton Sinclair quote? *Fascism is capitalism plus murder.*

Capitalism needs a war always to bail it out because it can never pay for itself, I agree. You have to wonder about all that philosophically. With all the privilege of the [American political elite], the Dulles brothers, the Bushes, Sullivan and Cromwell, Brown Brothers Harriman, all that Ivy League pedigree — Fidel led the life he wanted. He did for 50 years. These other guys are like ferrets trying to keep the bank open any way they can.

And why is this not part of our public discourse? Wasn't that part of the promise made by you and the counterculture, that serious discussion about what we are as a species and what we might become should happen much more freely?

People refuse to connect the dots. Nobody will look seriously at how violent the CIA has

been — they killed Lumumba, they killed General Rene Schneider in Chile, they killed Allende, 600 attempts on Fidel. What about the kidnapping of Chavez? Why has the violent side of the agency never come up in a serious way?

People, I think, will only be interested in seeking the truth if they feel they can apply their findings. But getting back to the thing about capitalism — it's a system that's incompatible with the human equation; both are based on completely different value systems. Capitalism is based on an accumulative value system where the more capital you have, the more value you have and human beings are supposed to be a constant value system that doesn't fluctuate, everybody's right to exist being equal. But with the value of capital and accumulated wealth being what it is, it will always be able to supercede the intrinsic value of a human being and, therefore, humanity itself, which is why extinction of the species is possible, because it might make sense on paper.

Yeah, no question.

Well, where's that conversation? There are a lot of conversations about different non-economic ideologies and what their pros and cons are, but there never seems to be any conversation about economic theory and the viability of a system of government based solely on a tyranny of ascending and descending numbers.

I know what you mean. Look at clubs today — just compare the ambiance of the Hungry i with the Laugh Factory. A comedian today is anybody who can stand up and talk about nothing endlessly.

Who's to blame there, the artist or the audience? Is the artist unable to do good work or is the audience ill equipped to recognize good work when they see it?

I think the artist is only that good. I don't think it's a broker's decision to even try to meet the audience's needs. A comedian nowadays is there to accommodate the audience's materialism. They don't have anything on their minds. [A comedian] will get up there and talk for an hour about women like they're aliens, and that's his act. I was in New York and I saw Judy Gold and she was complaining that CNN runs that line of headlines at the bottom of the screen — is that really what's wrong? I just don't think there's any cultural depth perception anymore. Even the guys at "The Daily Show" aren't making fun of the worst of [political wrongdoing]. Maybe they should just do more of what the real news doesn't do. Those guys at CBS really ended [the Vietnam War] — Rather, Morley Safer and John Hart — by showing us what was going on. Everyday we hear that a bunch of American soldiers got killed, but we don't see anything. You will on Al-Jazeera.

What is it that Amy Goodman says?: CNN shows us where the missiles are launched and Al-Jazeera shows us where they land.

She's good, very impressive, although you have to wonder about Pacifica [Radio]. They play her twice a day but they got rid of Marc Cooper, who was pretty good.

So, getting back to what we were talking about: What will it take for people to demand authenticity from their existence? Do people need role models to emulate — role models that are genuine and honest and not afraid to dissent and challenge the government? I started doing cartoons because I wanted to be John Lennon, or Norman Mailer, or Kurt Vonnegut. Who is there to emulate today? I feel like I'm stuck in your past. (*Laughs*)

Role models, right. Well, the culture now mostly just asks people to settle for second or third best. The people who voted for Kennedy would never vote for Hillary Clinton. They wouldn't even let her into the convention. They knew they did something wrong when they denied Dean and embraced Kerry; they knew that wasn't truthful. And when their kids get drugged out and play ersatz black music on their iPods and act like gangbangers when they live in Bel Air, they all know that's a lie. There's not much resistance to these bourgeois notions. People don't fight it very hard.

Do they need the fight demonstrated for them to pick it up or can they teach themselves? Isn't it a kind of heroism if nobody's doing it? If it is heroism, then it has to be demonstrated by somebody to be emulated by everyone, right?

What they do to deter heroism in this country is they keep you on the defensive. It's a strategy. They try to tie you up, get you defending yourself all the time, [where you're] trying to prove you're not crazy. People just have to remember what we're all here for: to find our way home and to search for justice and romance along the way. Heroism is just learning how to listen to your better angels. ✳

A BRIEF NOTE ON DAVID SEDARIS

BY NOW IT'S IMPOSSIBLE TO KNOW for sure if David Sedaris is the most deeply gifted American humorist since Mark Twain due to his talent as a writer or as a reader. Maybe it's not a case of being one or the other, but both. Have Joan Baez pick up a guitar and sing *Blowin' in the Wind* and you're likely to nod your head in polite recognition. Have Bob Dylan pick up a guitar and sing Guthrie's *Pretty Boy Floyd* and you're sure to tap your foot. Have him pick up the same guitar and sing his own *It's Alright, Ma (I'm Only Bleeding)* and you're liable to have a different hairstyle, a pregnant sister and an aquarium full of dead fish by the time he finishes — there's a big difference. Likewise, to hear somebody other than Sedaris read *The Santaland Diaries* or *Repeat After Me* aloud would be like having a female impersonator expound endlessly upon the profoundly cathartic agony of childbirth.

Looking like a tasteful blend of Stan Laurel and Woody Allen — baggy pants and the serene face of a timid saint made beautiful by a fiendish twinkle in his eyes — Sedaris stepped out onto the stage at UCLA's Macgowan Hall Little Theater in January of 2008 and explained to the audience the reason for his visit. The program was billed as The Black Box Readings, a black box typically being defined as anything that has mysterious or unknown internal functions, and he announced that he would be workshopping, for six straight nights plus one afternoon, a handful of new stories to be published the following June. The title of the collection, *Indefinite Leave to Remain*, referrs to an immigration status granted to a person who doesn't hold the right of abode in the United Kingdom but is allowed to stay indefinitely, a status literally true for Sedaris who left France for England sometime last year. (The title would eventually be changed to *When You Are Engulfed in Flames*.)

With pencil in hand, Sedaris read for 90 minutes with the grace and ease of a man tracing his finger around roses on wallpaper, marking his manuscript without pausing in accord with whatever groans, guffaws or empty silences his fans offered up as spontaneous reaction. During the Q&A session on this first night's performance, he admitted that sometimes simply writing the word "death" next to a passage too leaden to lift itself from the page was sufficient. Of course, inviting such a generous level of audience participation into the writing process is nothing new for monologists such as George Carlin and Bill Hicks and Rodney Dangerfield, or for any number of playwrights hoping to streamline the momentum of their scripted conversation. It is, however, unique to an author of literary nonfiction, which is what an increasing number of critics, university department heads responsible for drafting curriculum and subscribers to the New Yorker now consider Sedaris to be. Doubtful that one could ever expect others similarly classified — such notables as Tom Wolfe or Joan Didion or Hunter S. Thompson — to embark on this sort of tour specifically designed to elicit the opinion of the rabble as part of the editing process.

Indeed, if Wolfe was ever so open as to invite the opinions of the reading public into his creative process, he would've been forced decades ago to decide between his idiotic white suit and his typewriter. Likewise, Didion might've developed the right kind of paranoia that would've prevented her from naming her daughter Quintana Roo and Thompson might've found even more drug dealing, anti-authoritarian gun enthusiasts to hang out with.

That said, anyone at all familiar with Sedaris's work knows that the generosity with which he listens to the reactions of his audience during his workshopping tours is merely an extension of his desire to avoid the self-absorption and pomposity and isolation so pandemic through the profession. His books, after all, might best be described as the plain-spoken meditations of one man hoping to explore all the pain and beauty that comes from a writer's personal relationship with a universe that doesn't give a shit about him. Ironically, it is a universe that we typically read other authors to escape from. It is a universe that is indifferent to our pointless search for an existential narrative that requires the inclusion of archetypal heroes and villains to achieve its balance. It is a universe that, when we're honest with ourselves and feel as if no one is threatening us with judgment, makes a home for all our most despicable and mawkish and petty ideas. In other words, it is a universe that is willing to be a vast and exquisitely massive asshole into which we can scapegoat our failings.

Of greatest meaning to his readership, myself included, it is a universe that looks and feels the most authentic to our most private thoughts and our deepest insecurities and our most unifying imperfections as a species.

When asked by a member of the audience at the end of the first evening's reading if exposing such imperfections within his own family was a strain on his relationship with them — his family, of course, famously seen as being an inexhaustible fuel source, the Saudi Arabia if you will, for some of his brightest and most electrifying pieces — he didn't even crack a smile. It was almost as if to assume the treachery of such a betrayal on his part bordered on real unforgivable stupidity. "Everybody has secrets they don't want anybody to know about, my family included," he said. "I'd never expose anything private [they] didn't want me to talk about. They read every story I write before it's published."

As a credit to the mastery of his craft, everyone seemed genuinely shocked by this news, for to read Sedaris is to assume that such meticulous detail surrounding every unflattering blemish and character flaw introduced as part of his literary portraiture could only have come as a result of him picking over every last bit of debris left from demolished relationships and broken trusts and secrets pulled kicking and screaming into the light.

Put another way, David Sedaris was telling us that he'd never use the excuse of honesty to deliberately fart into the face of his audience and insist that it was art. Instead, he'd prefer to pass gas into a whoopee cushion and then place it under the collective sofa cushion of our more pompous and elitist and self-aggrandizing misconception of ourselves as noble creations with the understanding that the inappropriate sound of flatulence is only half of what's truly comical and absurd about the human condition. It is the stinkiness of life, after all, that forces us to celebrate our virtues as counterbalance. ✳

"But what if it's a First Class shit?"

It was Brock's disdain for spooning that led him to that
sweet piece of ass, Karen.

*"And for those of you who can't have my body as bread,
I invited my friend, Glutino."*

"Yeah, his last name is 'Dick.'"

"My heart says 'no,' but the tiny voices say 'yes.'"

"Sure it's sick, but think of the literary contribution."

DENNIS KUCINICH HAS
FIVE MINUTES FOR YOU

TO SAY THAT ALL POLITICIANS are nothing but puppets whose many strings are haphazardly attached to a diverse network of competing special interest groups is an oversimplification on par with saying that all cancers are bad. They aren't. At least not when they're compared to other cancers. So to say that Congressman Dennis Kucinich is less a puppet and more the living boy that Pinocchio became at the end of the fairytale with no strings attached is not much of a compliment, particularly when both have the same exact origins as tinder and, therefore, the same instinct to avoid exposure to too much heat.

I didn't know this. Now I do. Here's what happened.

❋ ❋ ❋

Dennis Kucinich carries around a miniaturized copy of the U.S. Constitution in his pocket like he's a 13-year-old virgin with a condom that he hopes to use one day. It has become his trademark prop, like Bob Dole's pen or Charlie Brown's bag of rocks.

Still, once you get past the initial embarrassment of pitying the metaphorical 13-year-old who believes that his orgasm is verging on the greater legitimacy of happening outside the self-aggrandized confines of masturbation — perhaps even clearing his skin and broadening his shoulders and deepening his voice into the confident baritone of whatever the political version of Barry White might be — you must admire him for unabashedly demonstrating his dweebishly patriotic enthusiasm for what many assume to be the blueprint for American democracy, really an assemblage of Pickwickian axioms insisting, in the grandest tradition of existential absurdity, that the best way to experience freedom is through strict adherence to the claustrophobia of rules; rules, in this case, that were written down more than 220 years ago with a feather and then immediately rendered almost completely meaningless by a myriad of ever-present prejudicial hang-ups, the usurping of the government by private corporate oligarchies organized on tyrannical and virulently anti-democratic business principles and, finally, the perpetuation of gargantuan economic and social disparities among the population.

You have to admire him because few politicians seem to be as genuinely moved by their own political peacockery as he is. It's charming. And then it's as depressing as hell, particularly when, from afar, you see him, with all his measured and brilliant oratory to end NAFTA and repeal the Patriot Act, go from being the Eugene Debs of East Capitol Street to, after you meet him, becoming Miss Cleveland of Hooterville, USA.

"I can only guarantee you five minutes," I was told by the Senior Advisor for all of Kucinich's West Coast stumpings, Sharon Jimenez, whose uncanny resemblance to band manager and lovable curmudgeon of the *Partridge Family*, Rubin Kincaid, allowed me the grace to forgive her persnickety manner as having less to do with me and more to do with the character that I imagined her to be playing. We were standing in the middle of a park in Sierra Madre on an autumn Sunday morning as crisp as cider and smoke, surrounded by volunteers, who were busy setting up chairs and sorting placards and stacking flyers for the congressman's speech. Twenty feet away, at a lopsided picnic table beneath a lopsided tree, sat Kucinich wearing a ginger-colored blazer that immediately made me wonder how many Winnie the Poohs had to die to make it. With his familiar squint and little boy haircut that always appeared as if it had been combed with a hot buttered roll, he nodded in response to the conclusions of a Pasadena Weekly reporter.

"I thought you were going to get me a ride-along with him to the airport," I said.

"Oh well," said Jimenez, smiling and shrugging her massive shoulder pads.

"But I don't have any five minute questions," I said, holding up my notebook. "All my questions are conversational — they're Bill Moyer questions."

"Like I said, I can only guarantee you five minutes," she said, looking at her watch. "The congressman goes on in about eight minutes and then he has to be in San Mateo for a straw poll at two."

"Which airport is he going to?" I said. "LAX?"

"No, Burbank," she said, shortening even the drive time that I was bargaining for to a ridiculously puny degree.

"Burbank?" I said. "I'm not sure any of it is worth my time," I said, looking at my notes.

"Here we go," she said, shooting past me in the direction of Kucinich and trailing perfume the same way that a tuna casserole might trail cats. "Congressman, this is Dwayne Booth from the LA Weekly," she said, just as the candidate was shaking hands goodbye with what he, no doubt, was hopping would be his last one-on-one of the morning. "I promised him five minutes," said Jimenez in a hushed tone, as if I were from the *Make a Wish Foundation* and was there to ask Kucinich to grow a third nut for me in the hopes that the magnanimity of the gesture might send my mucopolysaccharidosis into remission. The congressman sighed and looked at his watch.

"I know, I know," said Jimenez like a ventriloquist.

"All right," said Kucinich, weakly shaking my hand, "five minutes."

"Well, actually," I said, sitting down with him at the crooked picnic table, both of us moving slowly like two people lowering themselves onto either end of a seesaw, "I had been promised an interview with you on your way to the airport. All my questions are pretty longwinded, and five minutes isn't enough time."

"Oh, well then let's do that," he said, calling past me to Jimenez. "He's going to ride with me to the airport!" I turned to see Jimenez cup her ear. "He's going to ride with me to the airport for his interview!" he shouted. "Put him in my car." Jimenez nodded.

"Thanks," I said, "I really appreciate it."

"All right," he said, looking at his watch. "We got five minutes — do you have a short question?"

"Sure," I said, taking a second to turn on my tape recorder. "What non-political source material informs your idealism? In other words," I said, "a lot of your ideas seem to stress the importance of peace and humanitarianism and, certainly, you can talk about those things as political ideals, but politics don't really offer the best insight into those subjects. It's like Richard Nixon's peace sign, for example, meant something entirely different than John Lennon's. Most people don't look to politics to help them sustain their understanding of humanitarianism — they usually look to art and poetry and literature and philosophy. What are your cultural reference points?"

"Well, you know," began Kucinich hunching forward with the melancholy of somebody who had just been handed cotton candy and asked to knit a cake, "you can talk about the 20th Century and look at the writings of Erich Fromm, the work of Carl Rogers, [Abraham] Maslow, the humanistic psychologists. You can look at the English Romantic poets from centuries ago who had a sense of the perfectibility of humankind, of our deep connection to nature, of the importance of upholding a natural world. You can come back to Walden Pond, to Thoreau, to Emerson, to their understanding of intellectual integrity and of freedom. But you could go back thousands of years, too, to the basic structure of moral law that's reflected in the teachings of all the great religions." He stopped. I waited. He stayed stopped.

"What about more modern influences?" I said. "Are you in touch with any of the artistic or cultural movements that are contemporary; ideas and artistic trends that excite and motivate people, particularly young people, to view humanity as a whole rather than as incongruent pieces, which is more what politics tend to do? I don't guess that all the values that inform your political identity are as antiquated or esoteric as Thoreau or the Bible — you were a product of the '60s, right?"

"Look," he said, "my philosophical underpinnings relate to concepts that are really timeless, that go back to two thousand years of Christianity, thousands of years of the Hindu religion, that go to the tradition of Buddhism, to the moral teachings of Judaism, to the peaceful expressions of Islam. All of these are tributaries of a spiritual understanding that I have."

"Well, I guess what I'm wondering is what connection do you have with contemporary culture that isn't politically grounded? The reason that I ask is because it seems to me that most people don't trust politicians very much. People want to interact with ideas that are hipper and deeper than those narrowly defined by politicians and the political agendas of either party. I would figure that if you wanted to build a sizable movement that inspired people to get involved with politics and to participate in democracy — to vote for you! — you'd want to offer them something that has some artistic integrity to it. Isn't that what made the counterculture so powerful [in the middle of the last century], the fact that it was an *artistic* political movement?"

"Well, the social conscience of the Sixties percolated powerfully from what was called the counterculture, which actually was more than that, expressing mainstream articulations which had been suppressed." He stopped, confused by the broken crockery of his last sentence. He looked at me for some response, but I didn't know what the hell he was talking about, either. He looked at his watch. "Nixon's silent majority," he finally said, perhaps with a little too much authority, like he was trying to explain the virtues of internet pornography to an Amish family, "was actually a larger establishment unwilling to listen to what mainstream had to say and what mainstream had to say was powerfully at odds with what Nixon was doing. So my analysis would be a little bit different. What I want to do right now," he said, standing up and sending my side of the picnic table thudding into the ground, "is I want to get started over here, then you and I can talk more in the car."

"Oh, okay," I said, watching him walk away. I recapped my pen and closed my notebook and began packing up my gear when Jimenez appeared behind me.

"Make sure you're close when Dennis finishes because we're going to move fast and you'll miss getting into the car with him if we can't find you."

"Don't worry—I'll find you," I said, and walked off to practice my promise by finding a donut that I didn't really want.

❋ ❋ ❋

Sitting down in the grass with pastry glaze stuck to my fingers, I opened my notebook and uncapped my pen to streamline my list of questions for the congressman while the worst bow-wow oratory imaginable blasted from the stage behind me, beginning with the obligatory song sung by a child about the Earth being like a marble and humanity being like a rainbow and the future being like a bright and smiling sun, images whose crayon equivalents are studied in mental hospitals to determine the severity of a patient's inability to cope with the real world. Then there was the obligatory African American woman who was introduced to tell a horribly sad story about being fucked over by the healthcare industry, followed by Kucinich who, before pulling the miniaturized version of the Constitution out of his pocket and waving it around like a tiny recipe book capable of transforming the republic into something that the Forefathers promised would be both yummy and nutritious if followed precisely, recited the Star-Spangled Banner like it was Keats and did five minutes on courage, providing no more insight into the subject than Bert Lahr was able to as the Cowardly Lion by asking, *What makes the Hottentot so hot?* and *What puts the "ape" in ape-ricot?*

I wondered if that's what bothered me most about Kucinich's candidacy, his willingness to name all the most pressing problems facing the world without then demonstrating the ability to deepen the conversation beyond an understanding that was seldom expressed as anything but the most sophomoric pandering to the worst elements of patriotism and false hope and sentimentality. Listening to him speak after being so moved by

his reputation as a fearless David in disdainful pursuit of every despicable Goliath currently threatening our continued survival as a species was often times as heartbreaking as I imagined it must have been for an audience forced to listen, for the first time, to Bob Dylan, worse than going electric, going ecclesiastic.

As an example, I thought about the copy of the Constitution that I had on my shelf at home in hardback that was given to me by my grandfather, who had gotten it from his father, who had gotten it through the Immigration Office when he came over from Ireland in 1919 and who saw it as little more than a study guide designed to help him pass a test that, once passed, would qualify him to become something that he never would've become had he stayed in Ireland: a despised foreigner. I thought about how the book never meant beans to me, partly because I never knew my great-grandfather except through stories told to me by my mother who remembered him fondly as a foul-smelling lunatic, and partly because a book reputed to be about our rights as free citizens seemed as dull and undeserving of my attention as a book written about gravity. Gravity, I figured, like democracy, always seemed quite capable of existing without my having to contribute any thought to it whatsoever; it simply was, just as the color *blue* was, whether I existed or not. And just as I would never presume to have the kind of power to fine tune the properties of gravity to fit my own concept of how I'd prefer physics to operate, nothing in my experience had ever given me any reason to presume that I could, or even should, attempt to fine tune the Constitution to fit my own concept of what I believed freedom and democracy to be.

Maybe what bothered me was how I never saw any indication that Kucinich would ever want to align himself with any of the unflattering and lazy justifications that many Americans might have for not giving a rat's ass about the diseased substructure of our democracy. It seemed to me that he'd rather perpetuate the idea that we were being murdered as a society by dangerous men in high office as opposed to committing suicide with our own intellectual shortcomings as unimaginative people because the latter is not an electable platform from which to jump into public office; it was just one more example of a decent man wishing to quadruple his decency by publicly weeping over the plight of the lepers of which, if he ever hoped to achieve sainthood, he'd need a steady supply of.

In the end, his love of what the country could be made him something less than an expert on what the country was, which was perhaps the most compelling reason why nobody should ever call an idealist to fix a broken toilet; his solution might forget to consider the existence of the asshole. Like me.

Suddenly seeing the emphatic wave from Sharon Jimenez from across the park indicating that it was time for me to chase the congressman around his car with a dirty plunger, I gathered my things and hurried over to meet more members of the Kucinich posse huddled behind the stage. "This is Marcus and he'll be driving you and Dennis to the airport," said Jimenez, naming the last person in the group.

"That's the car over there," said Marcus, pointing past me to the parking lot, "the silver blue one, the SUV that's pulled in backwards."

"I see it," I said.

"The door should be open. Go get into that one because we're ready to leave," he said.

"*Quickly*-!" insisted Jimenez.

Walking as fast as I could, I got to the car and reached for the side door handle and stopped when I noticed a middle-aged Asian woman wearing a black pageboy haircut and a Kucinich *Strength through Peace* T-shirt sitting behind the wheel. I opened the passenger door, startling her some, and said who I was, and that Marcus told me to

get into the silver blue SUV so that I could interview the congressman on the way to the airport. "Oh, okay," she said, half her brain as tight as a fist and still focused on the mace in her purse, the other half, mellowed by the frayed wiring of an ex-pothead, as warm and inviting as pudding.

"Well, they said that they're just about ready to leave," I said. "Where should I sit? Is he getting in the back?"

"I don't know, I'm not sure," she said, furrowing her brow and looking over her shoulder, back towards the park where the crowd was just beginning to disperse.

"Well," I said, "should I get in the front or the back?"

"Umm," she said, meaning every *m*. I waited for a moment, long enough to watch her blink the concentration completely out of her eyes.

"Why don't I get in the front," I said. "We can always switch around when he gets here."

"Yeah, get in the front," she said, clearing papers off the seat and stuffing them into the center console amid schedules, itineraries and napkins. I climbed in and opened my messenger bag, took out my notebook and started to unpack my recorder. We spoke briefly about where each other was from and how long we've been toiling in our own separate professions and how boring the weather in Southern California could be. She gave her name as Mary, I think, and I gave her both my real name and my cartooning name, Mr. Fish. She swore that she knew my stuff and went on to describe what I think was a Tom Tomorrow cartoon as one of her favorites of mine. I didn't object, flattered by the praise, not the mistake in identity.

"What a great turnout," she said, "don't you think?"

"Yeah, I guess," I said.

"It's really important for people to hear what Dennis has to say," she said.

"I'd say," I said. "That's why I'm here," I said, wagging my notebook and pen in the air.

"What kind of stuff are you going to ask him?"

"Mostly stuff about peace," I said. "My feeling is that when a politician bases his candidacy on peace, he needs to be pretty precise about what that means. He can't be poetic — you can't legislate poetry."

"Uh! There they are," she said. "Here we go."

"There who is?" I said, looking around. She put the car in drive and edged out behind a dark blue Oldsmobile. "Wait a minute," I said, "where are we going?"

"To the airport," she said. "That's Dennis in front of us."

"What?" I said, glimpsing Kucinich and his wife in the backseat of the car in front of us. "But I'm supposed to be with him!" I said. "I'm supposed to be interviewing him!"

"Let me in, let me," she said, talking to her side view mirror. "Thank you, *bastard*," she waved politely. "Fucking California drivers."

"Can we stop?" I asked. "I need to interview him — this is my only chance."

"Maybe he wants you to interview him at the airport?" she said.

"I need more time than that!" I said.

"Well, I don't think we can stop. His plane leaves at 11:35," she said, rooting around for Kucinich's flight information, as if paper and ink were the ultimate authority on the content of whatever words they formed.

"Aw, Jesus," I said, closing my notebook and stuffing it back into my bag, "I give up."

"Sorry," said Mary, sweetly, her right foot nullifying the sentiment by slowly pushing down.

We rode in silence for awhile while I, never more than 30 feet away from the back of Kucinich's head, wondered which narrative of the day's events the Congressman wanted me to believe, 1.) that he was too much of an idiot to remember that he'd promised me an interview or 2.) that he was smart enough to figure that the press I was attempting to give to his candidacy was a meddling distraction to the vaguely progressive platform that he was running on in his bid for the White House — which one, I wondered, did he consider to be the most flattering for him?

Ten minutes into the drive Mary's cell phone rang and she answered it. It was Marcus calling from Kucinich's car in front of us. He wanted to make sure that his GPS navigation was not feeding him bogus directions.

"I don't know," said Mary, "I've never been to Burbank."

"We're fine," I said.

"What?" said Mary.

"Tell him that we're headed in the right direction," I said.

"Mr. Fish says that we're headed in the right direction," she said.

That's right, I wanted to say, *the fucking genius that makes you laugh so hard by drawing that fucking penguin with the goddamn visor will get you to the airport on time, just so you can drive him home again afterwards.*

"Huh?" said Mary into her phone. "Yeah, the journalist…he's with me…I know…he says that he's supposed to be with you…uh huh…"

"Ask him if I can do my interview with Dennis over the phone?" I asked, shooting in the dark not caring who I hit. She held up her finger, asking me to hang on for a second.

"Yeah…yeah," she said. "Can he interview Dennis over the phone?" She paused. "All right," she said, and then turned to me and asked, "Do you want to interview Dennis over the phone?"

"Yeah," I said, "if he'll talk to me."

"He said yeah…okay…okay…all right, here he is." She handed me the phone.

"Hello?" I said. There was the sound of some confusion, then the muffled sounds of chubby consonants being bled through a hand deliberately covering the mouthpiece on the receiver, then Kucinich.

"Yeah, hello," he said.

"Hi," I said.

"What's your question?" he said.

"Hang on for a minute," I said, "I have to uncap my pen since I can't record this…hang on…all right," I said. "Wow, I feel like a real reporter now, having to write everything down the old-fashioned way."

"What's your question?" he said.

"You refer to our presence in Iraq as an illegal occupation," I began.

"Right," he said.

"If our presence in Iraq is an illegal occupation, then doesn't that automatically mean that our mission as occupiers is criminal and that those

I first heard the name Kucinich — not to be confused with *koo-cinich!*, the onomatopoeic precursor to *gesundheit* that we've all heard all our lives — in February 2003, while attending a peace vigil at the town center in Sierra Madre with my then pregnant wife. It was around eight o'clock at night and there were perhaps fifty people in attendance, all standing around with drippy white candles, everybody genuinely terrified of what the next few years might bring as a result of the Bush Administration's über fascination with 21st Century beatific pyrotechnics and, specifically, what fire might look like when mixed with massive amounts of bullshit. There was very little talking, everybody concentrating on their own private version of doomsday, with the exception of six or seven GAP hippies, all teenagers, who were set off slightly from the rest of us, each of them drawing on a cigarette that he or she lit with his or her own candle. Occasionally, another teenager would ride by on a skateboard or lean out of a passing car's window to heckle somebody in the smoking circle and receive a "Fuck you, Wallaceton!" or a "Suck it, McGinley!" as a result, the good humor of the exchange being lost on me whose dissatisfaction with the powerlessness of nonviolent protest to prevent the war we were only days away from seeing launched on the world made my experience of every mockery of our pacifism, however benign, a potential excuse to start a fist fight. Part of me yearned for just such a release.

With the exhaustion of pregnancy beginning to widen the sway of my wife's shifting stance coupled with the fury tightening in my jaw, I leaned in to her and suggested that we try walking the few blocks back to our apartment with our candles lit where we could set them into holders next to our bed. She agreed and, passing closely enough to the GAP hippies to catch a scrap of their conversation, I remember distinctly hearing one of them say, "Chemtrails are real, man," referring to the conspiracy theory that suggested the government was dumping unknown substances on the population from high-flying aircraft for undisclosed purposes.

"Congressman Kucinich is the only guy in Washington who said he'd look into it," said somebody else.

"That guy's got balls," said another.

"We can't bring that on the plane, it's too much," said Kucinich four and a half years later at Burbank Airport while looking down at two

actively engaged in the occupying, specifically the troops, are essentially criminals?"

"Those aren't my words! Those aren't my words!" he shouted.

"I know," I said, "I know, I'm just asking a question. The question is: Is it possible to have an army of good guys when their combined efforts contribute to the perpetration of a massive crime against the population of another country? How can we support the troops when we abhor what their duty requires them to do? Isn't that like supporting the word *motherfucker* and being against obscenity?"

"Hello? Hello?" said the congressman as clear as a bell.

"Yes, hello," I said back.

"Hello?" he said again.

"I'm here," I said, watching him through the rear window of his car, furious at what I knew was about to happen.

"*Hello?!*" he hammed.

"Hello — I'm here!" I said.

Then came the sound of the line going dead. "You've got to be fucking kidding me," I said as I watched Kucinich close his phone, lean up and hand it to Marcus. Then he sat back and opened a newspaper as calmly as a man who'd just finished watching the evening news and had gotten up and locked the door to protect himself from his own imagination.

❋ ❋ ❋

grocery bags overflowing with vegan baked goods as heavy as dung bricks wrapped and perspiring in cellophane. Presented to Elizabeth Kucinich, the congressman's wife, in Sierra Madre by campaign groupies wishing to acknowledge her food politics with a birthday gift that she might actually be able to enjoy — which she might've had she been bovine and free for the next 72 hours to chew.

"Well, what can we do with them?" asked Mrs. Kucinich, her British accent as kind to the ear as a tinkling bell. "We can't just throw them away." She looked at me and sighed, smiling.

"People sure are, well," I began, not knowing how to react to such excessive and misguided affection as exemplified by the food.

"Nice," said Mrs. Kucinich. "They're very nice, aren't they?"

"Marcus," said Dennis abruptly, "can you put these back in the trunk? We've got to get moving."

"What do you want me to do with them after that?" Marcus wanted to know.

"I don't know," said Kucinich. "Can you ship them to us?" You could almost hear the dumpster two blocks away licking its chops.

"Can I walk along with you?" I asked the congressman, picking at the scab of our now obvious mutual disappointment in each other. Seeing the request as obligatory with my having made the trip all the way out there, Kucinich replied with an obligatory *yes*.

"Stay close," he said to me like a platoon leader just before entering the jungle in South Vietnam. *Stay close?* I thought, as we walked into the terminal, his luggage being wheeled behind us on a massive cart by a valet. *Is he shitting me? This is Burbank Airport, for Christ sake — it would be easier for me to get lost sitting in a car with him at a carwash than get displaced at the fucking Burbank Airport.* Walking too quickly for me to ever get beside him, I watched in amazement as he zig-zagged around in the strange pantomime of a confused tourist, sluffing off every attempt I made to ask him a question with a, "Hang on a second," his eyes bouncing back and forth between the airport signage like pinballs in a flashing machine.

As I ambled along behind him, I began to feel like the 13th Century Sufi philosopher, Nasreddin, who was found one day searching intensely for something in the street in front of his house. When asked by a neighbor what he was looking for, Nasreddin answered that it was a key that he needed to unlock all the secrets of the universe. The neighbor asked Nasreddin what he was doing, exactly, when he lost the key. "I was rummaging around in my basement," said Nasreddin. When asked why he was looking in the street for something that was probably lost in the basement, Nasreddin replied, "Because the light is better here."

It was then that I started to realize that an interview with Dennis Kucinich for the purpose of understanding his politics might've been as foolhardy as my attempting a deep understanding of a Shakespeare sonnet by interrogating each individual letter of the alphabet. Or asking a meteorologist to give meaning to a sunset. Sometimes the truth, I figured, is in the periphery of reality, reflected more in what it inspires in other things than what it states definitively with its simple actuality.

No longer interested in hearing what he had to deflect, I quickened my gait and trotted up to him to say that I was leaving just as he was cornered by walls and made to stop. "You stand in line to get the boarding passes," he told his wife, "and I'll wait here with the luggage." Turning to me, he said, "Okay, you've got a few minutes."

"All right," I said, snapping my notebook out of my bag, reflexively bowing to my duty as a journalist one last time. "Orwell said that the quickest way to end a war was to lose it," I said. "How difficult is it for you to talk about immediate withdrawal from Iraq without essentially asking

Americans to embrace the decidedly un-American concept of losing?"

"The longer we stay there, the heavier the loses. People understand that. It's time to recognize that it's a war based on lies. Orwell raised the question of the destruction of meaning…um…so, uh…hold on, I gotta…" Again, he was gone, off to stand with his wife at check-in, carrying some of the luggage with him. After waiting for a few minutes and realizing that he wasn't coming back, I walked over, packing my notebook away as I went.

"This isn't going to work out," I said, standing next to him.

"No," he said.

"Can I email you the questions?"

"No," he said, "I'm going to be flying…a lot."

"Can I call you?"

He thought for a second. "Do you have a cell?"

"Yes," I said.

"Gimmie your cell and I'll call you later." I wrote down my number and handed it to him. I thanked him and put out my hand. His hand remained down at his side. "I trust that you won't make any of the stuff that went on here at the airport part of your story," he said, making real eye contact with me for the first time that day. It was the equivalent of a guy saying, *I took a big steamy dump on your living room rug and I hope you won't tell anybody about the crappy car I drove home in afterwards.*

I didn't say anything.

Stepping back outside and feeling like a whore who had just been forced to deepthroat her own pride in front of a tiny king, I looked around for Marcus so he could drive me back to Sierra Madre and, if at all possible, to the other side of my vast and wasted morning.

❊ ❊ ❊

According to Mesoamerican myth, Quetzalcoatl was born after a four-day gestation to become, like every other deity, the God of (*Your-Opinion-Here*). For some he was a compassionate god of self-sacrifice and butterflies, for others an absolute bastard of water and wind. There are many who believe that he wasn't divine at all and in actuality was a wayward Viking, or, if not a wayward Viking, then a wayward Buddhist missionary or a wayward extraterrestrial. That said, nobody can know exactly who or what anybody else is com-

pletely, whether he or she is a rush job created in only four days or something allowed to evolve over eons, god or Adamite. Everybody and everything is a conundrum and must be, to some degree, in order to reflect the innumerable opinions, many of them conflicting, that exist in the world; the more confounding a personality or a thing can be *en masse* the more reality he or she or it will be able to reflect back into the world by being able to be read as truth by as many opinions as possible. Example: the registered Democrat who has Republican values, the freedom-loving president who authorizes the use of torture in secret prisons, the millionaire who imagines no possessions, the meek who will inherit the Earth.

That said, and by odd coincidence with regard to the Aztec God of Miscellany, it took the political conundrum that is Dennis Kucinich four days of gestation to present himself to me *re*-born as his own opposite, at least as compared to my impression of him following our first meeting. By contrast, this Dennis, speaking to me on his own reliable cell phone, not 30 feet away, but 3000 miles away, from the floor of Congress, had humor in his voice and the confident chumminess of a friend of a friend. More importantly, he seemed as unlikely to dodge any potentially controversial or complicated question put forth by me as Quetzalcoatl would've been to suddenly cast off his feathers and to whiten his green serpentine skin and to embrace the humiliation of becoming as vulnerable and gullible and worshipful as his inventors; a god will never look at himself in a mirror because, in a mirror, he is a *dog*.

And, by the sound of it, this Kucinich was no *boob*.

❊ ❊ ❊

Last time we spoke you mentioned Erich Fromm, who was one of my heroes when I was in college.

Absolutely, I mean you take the *Art of Loving, The Anatomy of Human Destructiveness* — here was somebody who had a very deep understanding of human potential and a deep understanding of love. I was reading him in high school. You had a number of people who were writing at the time, whose books were getting popular circulation. Carl Rogers was somebody else who I've long admired. Rollo May was another. Morris Berman's *Reenchantment of the World* was a great book. These were humanistic philosophers, important people to the health and wellbeing of a society.

The overall premise of Fromm's *The Sane Society* was how, in the broadest, non-clinical sense, sanity is subjective and that if you have a community where most of the people believe that the moon is made out of green cheese and you're in the minority who doesn't, then you're the lunatic.

Exactly.

Do you ever feel that because of your views on peace and labor unions and impeachment and so on that, when compared to other members of your own party, that you're marginalized for equally subjective reasons? I guess the question is, are you the lunatic in Washington? And the second question is would you be proud or offended by that characterization?

Well, I happen to know that the moon is made out of vegan cheese (*laughs*). I look at it this way — one must have the power of one's own convictions and you really have to have faith in that. It's much like what Emerson wrote about in his essay on self-reliance, when he said, "Above all, to thy own self be true, every heart vibrates to that iron string."

Some of that is Shakespeare.

(Speaking away from the phone.) Madam Secretary, how've you been?

Huh?

Condoleezza Rice just walked by. I'm sorry, go ahead.

Well, one thing that I wanted to get back to that we were talking about on your way to the airport the other day before the phones cut out was —

Hang on for a second.

Sure.

(*"Aw, crap!" I thought to myself. Hearing the phone muffled by his palm, I feared that, once again, I'd moved too quickly with my troops question and not spent enough time engaged in the rigmarole of intellectual foreplay. Had I flung myself at the congressman's*

cognition clitoris with all the cloddish enthusiasm that one typically reserved for the scratching off of a lottery ticket before making him feel like the most beautiful ass in the Democratic Party? I wondered if what I needed to do was to remember the respect that I'd had for him before I met him — when I thought he was a decent guy standing on a soapbox before deciding that he was really more a decent guy pictured on a soapbox, with a personality no more ingratiating than any other label on any other product advertised as being capable of replacing the doldrums of life with something lemon-scented and affordable — and work forward from the premise that I had something to gain from our conversation.)

All right, go ahead.

I wanted to talk about the concept of supporting the troops —

The *conflict?*

No, the concept. It seems like it's something that can't ever be talked about in any depth. Specifically, there seems to be a contradiction in our supporting the troops and our not supporting the war — the troops are the ones engaged in the actual violence, and, of course, that's their job; the violence is what defines their role as soldiers, as occupiers —

Well, you know, actually, it's extraordinary that you're talking about this, because you're the first person in the media who've I've talked to, in the 40 years that I've been in public life, you're the first person who —

(*I was literally squinting in anticipation of what I expected to hear him say next — something along the lines of, "you're the first person who, if I could just get my peace-loving, little girl hands around your lousy fucking throat for sniping so relentlessly at our beloved servicemen and women who suffer horribly everyday at having their humanity compromised by the inherit inhumanity of their duty! Do you think it's fun to have to be reminded everyday of the death and violence and mayhem that your presence is causing? Our soldiers have to look at the blood they spill and that's yucky!"*)

(*Continuing*) You're the first person who I've talked to who put his finger on really what is a deep philosophical question. In a way, we're in times where to take a stand for the truth seems to some anarchical, which shows you how meaning has been so powerfully inverted. It is really the fulfillment of George Orwell's prophecy about the debasement of language, the destruction of meaning and the destabilization of civilization.

(I only had a second to be shocked and then half a second to be flattered and then no time at all in which to realize that I hadn't said anything worth the compliment.)

It's about the perpetuation of confusion, so to say that you support the troops when —

This is what I saw when I was the mayor of Cleveland and I took a stand to save the city's municipal electric system. Everywhere I turned it was as though I was speaking heresy in saying that the people had a right to own their own electric system. You go back, the date would be December 15, 1978, when the biggest bank in town was trying to force me to accept their dictation that I would sell the city's municipal electric system, giving the private utility in Cleveland a monopoly on electric power in northern Ohio or the bank was determined that it would put the city of Cleveland into default on loans that I hadn't even taken out. What had happened was the entire social reality had been upended as these special interest groups worked their way through the media and people didn't know what was right. It took 15 years for the truth to be sorted out. And if I hadn't had that experience I would have found it very difficult to stand up to a war based on lies. Because in human experience there are very few things as powerful and compelling as a struggle for survival and war touches that instinct and people respond, not with their highest faculties but from the lower limbic system. And that puts us in the position where public policy is guided from levels that reflect earlier stages of human evolution.

That's why the idea of supporting the troops —

This is why we end up in war, because people don't stop to think, "Hey, what are we doing? Is this necessary? Do we need to be doing this? Is this based on truth?"

So, when people say that they support —

When I stood up and I wrote that analysis in October of 2002 that defiantly dismissed any call for war there were many people who asked me, "Hey, what's wrong with you? Of course, Iraq has weapons of mass destruction. Of course, Iraq had something to do with 9/11 — what's wrong with you?" And because I'd been through this before in Cleveland I understood the way that an entire social reality could be manipulated to make wrong right. Hang on for a second, I gotta vote.

(While waiting for Kucinich to return, I put a gigantic asterisk, the size of an impossibly large sphincter, next to my troops *question, figuring that the question was something to reintroduce later — the equivalent, to extend an earlier metaphor, of suggesting anal sex only after the joy of handholding had been fully explored and appreciated and accomplished without sweating. After all, I had some questions about peace that, if I ever planned on writing about the encounter, I felt I needed to ask, if only for the sake of allowing the congressman the opportunity to expound upon something without measuring his words.)*

All right, sorry about that.

Let's talk a little bit about your running for the Presidency on a peace platform. Typically, peace to a politician is a trade agreement, which seldom has anything to do with real peace. You can have the absence of overt physical violence in a trade agreement, but then isn't the commodification of people's lives a kind of violence, not to mention the violence to the environment that usually goes hand in hand with modern commerce? Then there's the question of what's being traded. We're at peace with Israel, for example, yet we sell them helicopters to perpetrate violence on Palestinians — what kind of peace is that?

You're exactly right. What happens is this: I'm in Washington and everywhere you turn there are myths being made which are all now dealing in fear and terror and, as a result, it's destroyed other myths which have to do with America's benign position in the world, freedom, democracy.

(The myth *of freedom and democracy? Was this a slip of the tongue that revealed some compatibility between us or merely a slip of the tongue that revealed the slipperiness of a logic that had been held in the*

mouth too long, mulled over by the cowardice of political propriety, and rendered as unstackable as rounded ice cubes?)

So, the dominant myths now are fear and terror and if you don't buy into them you're not a patriot.

Right, you're either with us or just like us.

And now I'm seeing a war gathering against Iran and it's happening under everyone's nose and people are either oblivious to it or they feel that that's just how it has to be.

Which goes to the heart of what I mean about our society's concept of what real peace is. Everybody will stand up and clap when they hear somebody talk about peace because it's widely understood to be the absence of war, of violence, which it is, but that can't be it's complete definition, just like the complete definition of love can't simply be the absence of hate — [peace] shouldn't be defined just in terms of what it's not. If peace is defined only as the opposite of war then doesn't that automatically make war a necessity because peace needs something to exist contrary to?

You're right about that, but let's go one step further — let me take your awareness of that to a Presidential election where candidates change their position every week so you don't know anybody's position on anything. It's all polled to the point where it's not the soul of the politician that becomes of interest; it's the poll of the politician. There again, truth doesn't matter. Stephen Colbert was absolutely right when he called it *truthiness*. That's why half the people in this country still think that Iraq had something to do with 9/11. So, look, I am absolutely amazed that there is someone out there asking these questions because I didn't know there was anybody — I didn't know there was anybody out there to talk to about this stuff.

Well, how frustrating is that for you, to be in a profession that doesn't typically invite the kind of conversation that matches your curiosity about the world? I notice, for example, how unpopular real anger is in Washington, like with Pete Stark [Congressman from California] saying, when the Democrats couldn't get the support they needed to overturn Bush's veto of SCHIP, that the Pres-

ident couldn't find the money for healthcare for kids but he could fund their deployment to Iraq where they could have "their heads blown off for his amusement."

Who said that?

Pete Stark, from California, on the floor of Congress. And after he said it there was this tremendous outcry for him to apologize and he wouldn't, for something like four days, but then he finally did and I thought his apology was a tragedy. How can you have an honest conversation about something when there are people demanding that you first qualify your emotion before they'll listen to the content? He was talking about the politics of war, for Godsakes, and outrage has to be a part of that, especially when we're talking about the illegality of [the war in] Iraq. Stark's frustration and anger resonated with a lot of people, it's part of the reality that we're all living in and we need to know about it if we're going to navigate [the world] with any expertise.

Well, you know, you're right about that and, again, you get new insights when you experience it first-hand and my job gives me a great opportunity to see how it all gets put together.

How slippery is that ground for you when you're talking to people in public, or when you're out in front of an audience? To maintain some level of popularity do you sometimes feel you need to be as inoffensive as possible? How impossible is that given the state of the world nowadays? Some things really do require deep and sloppy conversation.

I think it's important to approach things with an open heart and with clarity and courage, that's it. Lincoln said it well when he said, "With malice toward none; with charity for all; with firmness in the right, as God gives us to see the right." He was talking about binding up the wounds of a nation, but in a sense we have to continually work at binding up the wounds in our society and wounds to people's physical, emotional and spiritual selves and wounds to the truth that provide the social reality where we live or refuse to live. Do I get frustrated by that? No. The real test of power is whether you can countenance the approval, disapproval, ups and downs, acceptance, rejection with a sense of equanimity. That's how I proceed. I do my best to tell the truth the way I see it. The one advantage I've had through forty years of being involved in public life is I have a trained eye and it's clear. So, listen, I've got to run but I'm very interested in reading your article and I'd like you to send it to me.

(Well, like they say on Broadway, "You can't sell last night's ticket," I wanted to say, but thought better of it.)

I really appreciate your time and your patience.

You bet.

❀ ❀ ❀

He gave me his email address and disappeared into the legislative branch like a monkey into a tree, his request to show him the portrait that I'd be painting making him, given the level of intellectual fidgeting and ideo-*illogical* subterfuge he'd displayed, either a masochist for asking or a man completely unaware of his own inabilities to probe the lower depths of the more ethereal campaign points he was running on; specifically those regarding peace, love and misunderstanding.

Additionally, the request made me remember something that my grandmother once said while eating a popsicle made out of cheap orange juice, her eyes Buddha-like after decades of prescription drugs and crosswords puzzles. She said, while watching Larry King's very famous and excruciatingly respectful 1992 interview with Richard Nixon, that, given the choice between being a turd or a flower in life, I should consider being a turd. "Flowers are always getting trounced upon," she'd said. "At least a turd commands enough respect to be stepped around."

And perhaps that's what I found to be the real tragedy about Dennis Kucinich: he was not a turd. Nor, however, was he a flower. He was simply a man satisfied to stink in either direction, hoping that his do-gooder reputation — coupled with his being so open to interpretation, like any stench is — would deflect enemies sensitive to crap and attract those wishing to have a sweet-smelling political hero in Washington rather than just another complacent jackass to blame our collective and very real misery on. ✳

AMERICA'S PEACE CANDIDATE

THE ARTIST STARTING TO WORRY THAT HIS CONDEMNATION OF DOOMSDAY IS
BECOMING TOO ARTISTIC TO INSPIRE ANYBODY TO GIVE A SHIT ABOUT THE END
OF THE WORLD BECAUSE THEY'RE TOO BUSY DEBATING THE AESTHETICS OF HIS PANIC

MR.FISH

MASTURBATION: THE TYPING REQUIREMENT

WHEN IT COMES TO THE CREATIVE ARTS, the only profession that seems capable of purging its weaklings is sports. Why is this? Why is there always an audience for excruciatingly mediocre artists in this country, but not for clumsy, uncoordinated ballplayers? If Mookie Betts, for instance, suddenly started trying to catch line drives with his cap or if he continuously forgot to bring a bat with him to home plate, he'd disappear from public view. And, yet, there's E.L. James at a tiny signing table at the head of a bug-eyed chow line made up of people starved for the J. Peterman version of *Lady Chatterley's Lover*, as if chewing fifty shades of Tic Tacs is enough to change the meaning of the word *shit* without altering the pronunciation. And there's P.J. O'Rourke in an Alfa Romeo, speeding along the Gulf of Mexico and, miraculously, not sitting alone and unshaven in a dilapidated trailer in Toledo, Ohio, spreading marshmallow fluff on a Pop Tart and wishing that he knowed how to work a hammer or sumthin'.

Again, why is this? I have a theory.

There are two kinds of activism. There's the organized kind and the individual kind. The organized kind is typified by all the marching and leafleting and fundraising that come out of a group of people who wish to cure a perceived social ill that has either atrophied into the norm or, if unopposed, is threatening to atrophy into the norm. These are people who want to stop the natural gas industry from fracking up the environment, for instance, or on the other side people who think that creationism should be taught in public schools in place of Darwin's theory of evolution.

The individual kind is simply the act of not adhering mindlessly to either the demands or expectations of the dominant culture or what is verging on becoming uncontroversial public opinion. It may manifest itself merely in having a disagreement and then a conversation or a debate with somebody else, usually in an attempt to change his or her mind; specifically, it is not shutting up when faced with controversy in the name of politeness, cowardice or sheer stupidity.

Both kinds have benefits that, when unified, can affect the most positive change. Or, conversely, together they can have the most deleterious effects and inspire the most treacherous results. And that's the point: Typically, when one decides to save the world, he or she is deciding to save only the parts of the world that he or she finds most flattering to his or her ego and sense of right, wrong and beauty. After all, what good is a savior's concept of moral law without the implied lawlessness of contrarians who embody a contrary point of view?

When Buddha said, "There has to be evil so that good can prove its purity above it," he was speaking more as a keen observer of human nature than as a moralist who sits in judgment of some intrinsic good or evil. He recognized how, by observing the symmetric physics that determine the symbiotic truisms that constitute the material balance of the universe, a human being is prone to confusing his or her interpretation of reality with reality itself, thereby investing his or her own subjective understanding of things with the irrefutable concreteness of objective matter.

Such a person will imagine the light of his own

moral judgment to be precisely what determines the darkness intrinsic to all other competing moralistic visions.

Saviors, thusly, can never be trusted to be anything but mere amplifications of the dimmest wits among us, who are those who imagine that their concept of virtue is the version best suited for everyone. In fact, I always thought that the unfortunate deification of Jesus Christ and the subsequent scriptural moralizing that his biographers had him engage in for the sake of inflating their own importance were grotesquely unethical. Wasn't the notion that we should all help the sick and poor and love our neighbors radical and mind-blowing enough? Did we really need to have a savior who could also communicate with fish like Aquaman and get a dead guy to wipe the pus out of his eyes and start turning cartwheels around the room, yipping and yahooing like a goddamn hyena? I mean, why create a fictional Jesus who is immortal, *knows* he's immortal, yet still goes around pretending that his being crucified is a merit badge signifying some kind of sacrifice, as if trading in mortality for immortality wasn't the tactical equivalent of abandoning a sinking ship or escaping a burning building. Who among us wouldn't jump at the chance to exchange the slow, meaty disintegration of our own imperfect biology for, among other things, telepathy, the power to turn invisible, the ability to travel through time, to blow shit up with our mind, to be able to fly, to get to hang out with every celebrity who will ever live, all the while maintaining a perfect swimmer's physique and a blood/alcohol level that hovers somewhere around the typical monster truck rallier's 20 minutes prior to the fucking awesome arrival of Bigfoot? The only thing I felt that we should pity Jesus for was his fashion sense, which has never advanced much beyond what Roald Dahl's Uncle Joe wore for decades prior to Charlie yanking the golden ticket from his Wonka Bar. Like Charlie, I think it might be high time that we demand that Jesus put some goddamn underpants on and humble himself by walking among the living.

Now, before I pretend that

After years and years of not performing routine maintenance on his soul, Brad was sickened to discover that Amazon did not offer a replacement.

I was never ever guilty of thinking that I, myself, might make a halfway decent savior as a writer — having fooled myself into believing that I had been *saved* by the writings of S.J. Perelman, Albert Camus, Chuck Jones, Friedrich Nietzsche and Woody Allen — let me share with you the form letter that I used to send out to the publishers and editors of magazines and newspapers and publishing houses who rejected my work with their own form letters back when I first started out as an author:

Dear Publisher/Editor:

Thank you very much for your recent rejection note.

I would very much like to respond personally to every rejection I receive, but the volume of rejection is prohibitive. This is not an indication of the time and consideration devoted to your rejection note, but merely my desire to respond as quickly as possible. Please understand that this does not reflect on your profession but rather on my needs at present.

Fuck you and your shortsightedness. You wouldn't know a genius if one came up and bit you on the ass, even though the simple desire to bite you anywhere should be evidence enough.

Nevertheless, I encourage you to continue rejecting exceptionally good submissions as eventually someone will kill you.

Sincerely,
The Writer

This was back in the late '80s, when mail was still made out of paper and submitting one's work to an editor involved much more legwork and menial labor than it does now. (Try explaining to anybody born after 1985 the concept of licking a stamp and he'll look at you as if you just crapped your pants and started reminiscing about how cheap sodie pop and illegal abortions used to be.) In fact, the chore of writing, itself, was much more laborious in the past and required a greater commitment to all the many stages involved in the job of being an author.

Think about it. Before there was Microsoft Word and email and Wikipedia, there were dictionaries — I'll wait while you take a minute to Google the word — which one had to leaf through in order to confirm word definitions and proper spelling and usage, and there were libraries which one typically had to leave the house in order to find, and there were books which had to be opened and closely examined for the purpose of corroborating facts and theories and assumptions, and there was the collecting and the collating of research data and the handwriting of notes into notebooks, then there was the returning home and the pounding on the keys of a typewriter, which included the whiting out of mistakes with a tiny paintbrush and the blowing on the paint to make it dry, and then there was the leaving again and the xeroxing of all the pages of original type and the assemblage of copies for both storage and distribution, then there was the buying of the envelopes and the paying for the double postage, which included the self-addressed stamped envelope wherein the form rejection letter would be contained, and then, as I indicated earlier, there was the licking of the stamps and the mailing — followed, of course, by the waiting for weeks, sometimes months, for a response. It was easy then to make the sloppy deduction that all the hard work inherent in the preparation of a submission translated directly to the significance of the product.

Of course it only makes sense, given the preposterous verbosity of the human animal, that most published writing is exactly as useless and uninteresting as all the unpublished writing that comes out of nonwriters as longwinded uninterrupted speech, the only difference being that, by virtue of the printed page, a writer is less likely to shut up even when the reader puts his or her hands over his or her ears. And while such immunity to outside interference may sometimes inspire the kind of fearless intelligence necessary for the writing of such books as "Native Son" and "The Catcher in the Rye," most of the time it simply inspires the kind of fearless stupidity that imbeciles use to publish "Going Rogue: An American Life" and "The Bell Curve" and to make likeminded publications the kind of loud and wacky bullshit that enjoy the same kind of mass circulation as herpes, hula hoops and all the different mispronunciations of *Sartre* and *Goethe*.

Only when I first started reading what other people had written did I begin to realize that possessing the ability to write shouldn't automatically demand that a person become a writer, just like being able to swallow a live mousetrap shouldn't automatically demand that a person become an idiot. More often than not, being able to write about something has very little to do with having something worthwhile to say about it. My best friend all through college, for example, spent the first 15 years of his life learning how to draw with an attention to detail that made his pencil drawings appear as precise and realistic as photographs, only to piss away the 10 years after he graduated copying publicity stills out of music magazines of his favorite rock bands and implanting himself in the lineup. Not only should a person like that not be encouraged to believe that his art is anything more spectacular than a beautifully illustrated, albeit terrifically longwinded, suicide note that would guarantee no confusion among friends and family as to why, upon entering middle age, he decided to kill himself, but a person like that should probably have his air guitar confiscated and replaced with the Help Wanted section of the newspaper, which it was, thankfully. Now he's a top-notch alcoholic with a mortgage and a shitty office job and absolutely nothing to live for. Ironically, minus the office job, he's a more legitimate artist nowadays, being more like Jackson Pollack than he would've been had he continued doing what he was doing.

One thing to recognize about writing, too, is that the job of being a writer is populated by those who began as fans of the profession. In other words, wanting to be a writer is all that it takes for somebody to become a writer, especially when no one ever becomes a writer because he or she *has* to become one the same way that somebody *has* to become a dishwasher or a cashier or a house painter in order to pay the bills. As a result, the abilities of a writer are seldom what determine his or her talent, but rather it is his or her ability to simply wish to have talent that's enough to qualify him or her as a recognized artist — which, by the way, is why art has come to have no more value to the public at large than money would if everyone were allowed to print it. Most writers, in fact, are no more able to write spectacularly than baseball fans would be able to play baseball spectacularly if all of them were suddenly put into uniforms and organized into a league of teams made to define the sport. Not only would such a scenario dumb down the game to the point where the truly gifted players would be unable to demonstrate what previously made them great because the pitches they'd be getting would either be rolling across the plate or sailing over the backstop, but the yardstick necessary for measuring the talented against the untalented would be nonexistence because everybody would be crammed onto the same diamond, their feet rubbing out all the chalked boundaries, the mass misconstruing the consensuality of the chaos with a deeply meaningful camaraderie.

I hope that clears everything up. ✳

OBSCENITY

WHILE I WAS being dragged out of my bedroom, away from my open window, down the hallway and through the house by my mother, my fist still clutching the magic marker that I'd used to draw a mustache on myself when I first heard her slippers charging up the stairs like fuzzy mallets, I sort of knew that I wasn't going to save the world that day. Not only did she not fall for my panicked attempt to mute the severity of my crime by trying to make her laugh with the mustache, but she seemed more determined than ever to make an example of me to the rest of the neighborhood that political agitation through leafletting was not in our family's values. In fact, the overly flamboyant French accent that I used to confront her with when she burst into my room didn't fool her into thinking I was somebody else, partly because the phrase *Wee wee, mademoiselle déjà vu, déjà vu!* made absolutely no sense whatsoever and partly, I assumed, because the mustache that I'd drawn on myself, as confirmed by the dining room mirror that I passed on my way into the kitchen, looked much more Zapata than Chevalier. Senorita! Mi sancho pantza esta muy mal! Y donde, por favor! Qué guapo tamale? Arriba! *Arriba!*" *Slam!* went the backdoor and there I stood, no cap for my marker, surrounded by one hundred paper airplanes all bearing the words FUCK YOUR ASS written in a wounded and barking penmanship, the scattered notes a dule of dead doves inspiring to no one.

This was in 1973 and I was seven and had just figured out there was no such thing as obscenity. Listening through the kitchen wall to my mother slam cabinets and yell at the dog in the hell that I'd made of her morning, I decided, too, that there was no such thing as virtue either, neither qualifier able to exist in any true sense without having the other to be measured against, like there was no tall without short or light without dark or me without we.

There was only the cruel profanity of complete freedom.

❊ ❊ ❊

I drove out to the Beverly Hills Hotel, an hour and a half in traffic while the oily Tuesday afternoon sun melted into the toxic rainbow sherbet that is the Los Angeles sunset, for the singular purpose of snubbing Ken Starr. I'd been imagining the scene for weeks, the sophisticated crowd, the sound of Dave Brubeck's *Take Five* sashaying through the room like a sumptuous Pan Am stewardess, the tap on the shoulder, me turning with my glass of Romanée Conti to see Ken Starr standing there completely scentless and emitting no heat, his face split into the sort of well rehearsed smile that comes from decades of overachievement and never joy. He extends his hand. I look down at his chubby fingers, the manicured fingernails as shiny as wet cough drops, the soft puff pastry of a palm, the gleam of a watchband roughly approximating the value of Rhode Island. I do the classic gasp-chuckle of sitcom disbelief and turn back around, shaking my head. Starr's face begins to redden as if he'd just stepped into a freezing wind. I continue with my conversation, my voice elevated just slightly to be heard over the shrill whistle of steam coming out of his ears only moments before his head explodes like a hot coconut. I cover my glass with my hand to prevent bits of him from falling into my drink and lean in further to listen to the heiress finish her story about how she and Henry Kissinger and Mick Jagger bought a dazzle of illegal zebras and, following an all-night cocaine binge with Edie Sedgwick, freed them in Piccadilly Circus on Boxing Day in 1969. Applause. Curtain.

Why would Ken Starr ever want to shake my hand you ask?

Well, as a freelance artist I've always had to take in extra laundry to pay my bills and a couple years ago I took in a big stinky load from the Los Angeles Daily Journal, the preeminent law newspaper of Southern California, sometimes referred to as the Hillcrest Country Club of L.A. papers due to the exclusionary nature of its subscription-only availability, its content too hoity-toity to fraternize with other publications at newsstands, its Web content secured behind a pay wall like the sort of pornography that no decent person hoping to remain decent would want to see. My assignment from the Journal was to draw one hundred portraits for the paper's annual supplement dedicated to recognizing the top lawyers of California and Ken Starr was one of them. So was Gloria Allred, of O.J. Simpson and Amber Frey

fame, and so was Harvey Levin, of the *People's Court* and TMZ fame, and so was Jerry Brown, of Linda Ronstadt and Governor Moonbeam fame.

❋ ❋ ❋

The idea to save the world by writing *FUCK YOUR ASS* on one hundred pieces of paper, folding them into airplanes and floating them out my bedroom window like dandelion spores came to me over Memorial Day weekend about fifteen minutes after I started horsing around with my older brother, Jeff, in the backseat of my grandmother's station wagon while it was parked in the street in front of her house. He was trying to wrestle me into a headlock so that he could spit an ice cube down the back of my shirt and I was trying to pin him to the opposing wall of the interior cab with my feet when I accidentally kicked him so hard in the nuts that I swear he blacked out for a full five seconds. Ten minutes later I was handcuffed to the neighbor's fence with no pants on while my brother, refusing to hand over the key, explained to my grandfather how I, without provocation, had kicked him in the balls. "Here's an asshole!"

"A jerk," corrected my grandfather, narrowing his eyes like a marine biologist who had just pointed out someone's misclassification of a dolphin as a porpoise.

"Huh?" said my brother.

"He's a *jerk*, not as asshole."

"Well, aren't they the same thing?"

"Yeah," said my grandfather, "of course they are, but just say *jerk*. Saying *asshole* upsets your mother."

❋ ❋ ❋

"We also have a party at the Beverly Hills Hotel when the issue is published," I was told by the Journal's editor when the job of rendering one hundred portraits was pitched to me. "We're going to have all the original drawings put in frames and give them to the lawyers as little presents," he said, "and you can be at the party — I'm sure they'll all want to shake your hand!" The whole time he was talking I was trying to figure out how I was going to get the words *fucking* and *asshole* into the Starr portrait with the same deft hand that Hirschfeld used to get in his *Nina*.

Taking the ticket stub from the valet twink and throwing on my jacket, I straightened my tie

and walked through the hotel lobby in search of the concierge to help me find the room where I imagined Starr was eating enough cocktail weenies to verge on some infringement of Megan's Law. Moments later I walked into the Sunset Room and, having had the point of my HB Staedtler pencil up the nose and inside the pupils and along the lips and in between the teeth of every lawyer's face I saw, suddenly had the uneasy feeling that I was a voyeuristic pervert who had been watching these people through a two-way mirror for six weeks. After all, these were the facial features I'd caressed into being with all the slow and deliberate attention to detail that a cannibal might use to eviscerate his victims into a delectable recipe, only I had done it in reverse. Instead of obliterating life, I had created it, the goriness of the accomplishment no less fiendish than if I'd murdered somebody.

Averting my eyes from having to look at all the familiar faces, I scanned the room for the bar in the hopes of blurring my vision when I felt a tap on my shoulder. "The portraits look great!" said the editor of the Journal, having appeared out of nowhere to shake my hand. "Did you see them?"

"Yeah, on the way in," I said, referring to the table just outside the entrance where all one hundred framed drawings that I'd done sat near a large sign requesting that each lawyer wait until the end of the evening before retrieving his or her portrait to take home. "By the way," I said, "I never asked, how did you guys determine who belonged on the list of top 100? Given the fact that the average person finds lawyers, as a group, somewhat despicable — individually, they find them repulsive — I'm guessing that it wasn't a contest that had been put to a public vote."

"It was very unscientific," he said, appearing uncertain as to whether he should be offended by my characterization of his bread and butter as *repulsive*. "Me and the other editors got together every morning for a couple months and talked about who should be on the list and who shouldn't."

Then he excused himself, leaving me to realize for the first time that I'd been hired to glorify the equivalent of the football team for a high school newspaper and that the primary purpose of the Journal was to publish insular stories that celebrated the victories and chastised the failures and mourned the disappointments and trumpeted the dreams of all the prom kings, prom queens, star athletes, sluts, burnouts, unassuming nerds, chess club geeks and mediocre C-student toiling in the profession, fuck everybody else. And as it was with every school dance that I'd ever attended, I dropped my sense of moral superiority like a glass slipper, letting it shatter on the floor while I took my place against the wall, *Clark Kan't* in my glasses, and waited all alone with my hands in my pockets for the room to empty.

❀ ❀ ❀

To suddenly realize that *jerk* and *asshole* referred to the same thing was a real eye-opener for me. That meant that the obscenity of the word *asshole* was intrinsic to the word, itself, and not to the thing that it was naming, making it a concept rather than a fact, invented as opposed to revealed. I imagined that the idea that there could exist in language something like an offensive and corresponding inoffensive word was analogous to the idea that there could also exist something like an offen-

sive and inoffensive thought, even an offensive and inoffensive person, which was bullshit to me. Still, tasked with the chore of picking up the trash of my idealism, flightless bird by flightless bird, I started to realize that some things fly because they exist in a vacuum, not because they're propelled by some greater purpose.

❀ ❀ ❀

I left the hotel at around midnight, just as the clean up staff began to bunch up the soiled tablecloths and remove the chairs and scratch their heads and wonder what they were going to do with all the framed portraits sitting untouched at the entrance to the room, while thirty miles away Ken Starr, having never left his home all evening, continued posing in front of his mirror like a star quarterback preparing to lead assholes everywhere to victory against all the jerks who continued to insist against all reason that they were somehow above all that. ✳

Timmy had a penis. Timmy was white. Timmy had terrific potential to grow up to make the world a living Hell for girls and for boys who weren't white. Timmy might never realize what an absolute dickhead he is. Go, Timmy, go!

MR. FISH

AND THAT'S THE TRUTH

I always liked the idea that America is a big facade. We are all insects crawling across on the shiny hood of a Cadillac. We're all looking at the wrapping. But we won't tear the wrapping to see what lies beneath.

—Tom Waits

JOKES, ACCORDING TO KURT VONNEGUT, have to be simple and naked to be understood and, like all naked things, should obscure nothing while offering the unique benefit of commanding all the attention in the room, making hyper-focused truth voyeurs of us all. Want to know about *WAR*, for instance? Consider the quote so often attributed to Mark Twain, "God created war so that Americans would learn geography." Want to learn about *PEACE*? Here's Ambrose Bierce's definition of the word: *A period of cheating between two periods of fighting*. Want to build a viable democracy? Revel in the comradery that usually comes with sharing a profoundly unadorned insight that reiterates the eminently useful wisdom of perhaps the last true master of stand-up commentary, George Carlin: *Fighting for peace is like screwing for virginity.*

These are hard truths that, were it not for humor buffing them into shiny pearls of wisdom, would appear as rather dull and heavy stones. Indeed, whether we're talking about comedians, orchard spiders, slot machines or the Catholic church, shininess has always functioned as a lure for those most prone to distraction away from the dun-colored indifference of a lifetime made up of days largely devoid of surprise or variation, which, of course, is all of us. And while there are those who use shininess as a predatory technique and whose guts have literally been nourished by the gullibility of the least critically-minded among us, there are others — *artists!* — who prefer the shininess they advance be the luminosity of their prey reflected back to them as a virtue worthy of celebration and conservation. After all, what better technique is there for leaving a vulnerable population uncon-sumed and considerably less susceptible to the political, religious and cultural subterfuge forever prowling the Earth in search of innocent oglers of incandescence to devour?

Look at it this way.

When Aristotle said, "The gods too are fond of a joke," he was commenting on the inauspicious similarity between gods and mortals and the pen-chant for both to delight in manipulation of others. How else to explain the ridiculous and sometimes cruel zigzag of the human experience if not on divine folly? "Most people enjoy amusement and jesting more than they should … [A] jest is a kind of mockery, and lawgivers forbid some kinds of mockery—perhaps they ought to have forbidden some kinds of jesting," he added, suggesting surrep-titiously that lawgivers should also be trusted with the profane and ludicrous task of forbidding gods, which are merely the anthropomorphic stand-ins for nature, from expressing themselves in the only way they know how—in the only way they *must!*

While the 20th century Greek classicist and literary critic C. A. Trypanis wrote that "comedy is the last of the great species of poetry Greece gave to the world," many famous Greek philosophers considered humor morally corrosive and antitheti-cal to sound reasoning. Plato believed that comedy, because of the anarchistic mood it promoted and inspired, needed to be controlled by the state. He went so far as to characterize humor as a malicious vice debilitating to rational self-control. "We shall enjoin that such representations be left to slaves or hired aliens," he wrote, "and that they receive no serious consideration whatsoever."

Nearly 2,500 years later and with several hun-dred decades of evidence to support an opposing point of view, it is now undeniable that Plato and Aristotle were wrong. There is no greater exemplar of sound reasoning—and no greater filter of pol-itics, religion and mammonism—than humor. It is arguable that without humor we would not have such a precise tool with which to ridicule—nor the incentive to deviate from—the myopic main-stream narrative that would have us believe that the government, or at least the party with which we choose to identify, is consistently maintained by wise and benign stewards of justice. Humor also shows us that morality is measurable by how well we surrender our natural curiosity about how the world works to unimaginative bureaucrats tasked with telling us precisely how it *should* work.

Put bluntly, comedy has the power to reshape our comprehension of absolutely everything in pur-suit of a surprising punchline offered in contempt of conventional deduction and humor upgrades the dexterity of our thinking and convinces us of the subjectivity of truth and of our need to interact with one another using means beyond the political, religious and cultural contrivances on offer from the more traditional modes of perception, reflection and motivation.

Here is my conversation with Lily Tomlin, one of the most important comedians to come out of the 1960s, that unique period in American history when adventurous chefs and pioneering home cooks of artistic, political, intellectual and cultural cuisine experimented with startlingly new menus that explored the thrilling and unpre-dictable multiplicitousness of taste and appetite, celebrating the full range, depth and efficacy of both deep nutrition and mad confectionery as it applies to truth, beauty and being. Infused with the Cyrano genius of her writing partner, Jane Wagner, she more than any other person-ality contortionist in performance satire made having a social conscience play and empathy for those with whom we might otherwise ridicule beautiful.

And that's the truth.

❀ ❀ ❀

What was it about pretending to be other people that allowed you to find yourself?

Ha—I'm not sure I've ever found myself! [Performance stand-up] was really just a way to communicate and connect with people. I used to see all these guys doing mother-in-law jokes and *please-take-my*-wife jokes and I found myself wanting to [hear from] the mother-in-laws. I wanted to show the perspective of the wives.

Which is something I've always found unique about your work, particularly when it comes to *show business*. So much tv and nightclub humor relies on the perpetuation of clichéd [identity tropes], but your characters always pushed past stereotypes in search of something beyond laughter.

Yeah, I guess I always thought everybody deserved to have their depth depicted.

And where did this come from — this empathy for a person's true nature?

Well, I grew up in working class Detroit and my mother and father came from the South and we lived in the D'Elce Apartments, a predominantly white building in a predominantly black neighborhood. Of course, four or five blocks away, on Chicago Boulevard and Boston Boulevard, there were these large houses where the professionals and some very rich people lived, and everybody went to the same public school, even the rich kids, so there was this incredible mix of [class and color]. So, I got to experience all kinds of different people and [different] attitudes [from a household maintained] by a young Southern couple that most people would refer to as *hillbillies*, although they weren't — I don't use that word pejoratively, justly merely as a designation. I watched my mother needing to adapt to [Detroit], having come from a fairly sheltered existence [in Kentucky], and I used to go to the South every summer when I was young and I was horrified by how black people

were treated, even by my own family — how they were dismissed. It upset me to see how all the black help had to eat by themselves [from] their own special dishes.

So, you knew early on from your own personal experience, from living in a mixed community where black people were just neighbors, that there was something wrong with the concept of *the other*.

If anything, [the racism] reinforced the idea that white people were *the other* — that *I* was *the other*. [Remember] I was living in a building where the white people were going to hold onto their whiteness for as long as they could, [despite the fact that] all the Jews had fled to Sherwood Forrest and all the rich gentiles had fled to Palmer Park, which was still in close proximity to where I lived.

You got to see racism from both sides, from the South where black people were a repressed minority and from the North where white people

were a minority that felt repressed by a changing reality that challenged [the legitimacy of their] white privilege.

That's right, yeah. And you know how all kids feel like they live at the center of the universe? That's how I saw my apartment house, which, in a way, it really was with all these concentric circles of different socio-economic groups surrounding it. I remember in grammar school how some of the lazier teachers would make us stand up and tell what we got for Christmas — and it was gruesome because you knew some of the kids were lying and that they were ashamed by their poorness.

Were you ever ashamed?

I don't remember ever being shamed by my status, no. I saw my father as someone who drank too much and gambled and I went to the bars and bookie joints and track with him, then I'd go to church with my mother on Sundays. It was a big ol' Baptist church and by the time I was ten I was absolutely horrified by the prospect that there was supposed to be a Heaven and Hell and that some people were destined to burn forever. It was so humiliating to watch these grown adults beating their breasts and sobbing and confessing their sins in full view of the [community] and I just couldn't go for that.

So, again, you had this instinct early on to empathize with others by being curious about who they were and maybe feeling shame for them because they weren't feeling it for themselves.

I was always fascinated by people! I loved going to all the different apartments in my building and playing the rooms. There was an older woman, Mrs. Rupert, who was a botanist who was pretentious and Republican and always wore a hat and fox furs to empty the garbage. She took a big shine to me because she thought I had the most potential of any kid in the building.

To do what, specifically?

To marry well and to run a big house with a staff. (*Laughs*) She had two boys who were much older than me, who I thought were in the CIA because they were real brainy and [were] always taking radios apart and putting them back together

again. One wore a plaid hat with earflaps. Anyway, [Mrs. Rupert] was alone because her husband worked afternoons and when her sons left, she was *really* alone, so I would go over after supper every night to walk her chihuahuas and I'd get 15¢ and we'd listen to Gabriel Heatter and Drew Pearson on the radio and she'd proselytize to me about the Republicans and the Democrats. She told me that she helped indict Alger Hiss and that she had been the heiress to the Phillips [Petroleum Company] fortune and that her family disowned her because she'd married Mr. Rupert, who was from a lower class. She was about as tall as I was and she'd teach me how to buy linens and match the tone of my stockings to my outfits and how a lady sits and comports herself. She'd take me shopping downtown every Saturday to Hudson's and I had to wear a hat and gloves and carry a purse and I thought it was all great fun.

Great fun, but also a remarkable education for somebody who would eventually [use her art] to reflect private truths about common people beyond how they presented themselves in public. Were you conscious at all when you were younger that you were different from your peers, particularly in how curious you seemed to be about how other people lived and behaved?

I never thought about it.

Were you aware that you may have had an artist[ic] or *performance* mentality?

I don't think I ever articulated it to myself, although I pitched on a police athletic team and I was in Mrs. Fitzgerald's ballet shows, and then I started putting on shows of my own on [my] back porch. I'd try to get other kids to be in [them], but they wouldn't show up for rehearsal, so I just started doing everything by myself.

Which brings us to the question of how and why a theater artist [like yourself] choses to communicate using the singular voice as opposed to becoming part of an assemble cast. One of the most important contributions to both modern theater and stand-up performance comedy has to be *The Search for Signs of Intelligent Life in the Universe*, which I read while dropping out of college and which remains one of the small handful of books I still point to as

groundbreaking, even beyond its reputation. How aware were you when you started as a monologist that you were engaging with your audience in the same way that a painter or a novelist typically does — that is, using a method that is more personal and intimate than what we typically see with traditional theater?

Well, Jane Wagner wrote *Search*. There's this misconception that I'm the source of everything that I perform and I'm not.

Right, and I know that Jane writes a lot of your material, but it's also important to recognize that writing a piece of music is meaningless until it's played beautifully, and you play that music beautifully! One of the things that struck me about *Search*, specifically the book version, was how it was formatted. It was typeset to read like a long poem, with its dialogue broken up into stanzas rather than straight blocked text, which made it function as a piece of literature and not just a blueprint for a production. Reading it was like engaging with a serious philosophical [treatise] — one that was as funny as hell! When Trudy asks, "What is reality, anyway?" — that's Socrates! The idea that there are only assumptions and not facts to guide us through the dark[ness] is not what you usually get on The Great White Way.

It is my greatest sorrow that [Jane] doesn't get the credit she deserves.

Well, to your point about authorship, maybe that has something to do with the deep intimacy of what you do onstage — if Jane is engaging with the world as a writer and writers typically communicate [using] the singular, internal voice, then you are, too.

Jane and I mesh perfectly, and we understand what the other is doing, totally, even if we can't specifically identify it. I'd sought her out to help with the Edith Ann album in '71.

Let's talk about Edith Ann for a moment [*the precocious five-and-a-half-year-old known for philosophizing from a giant rocking chair*]. There's something overtly political about her, despite the fact that she doesn't directly talk about politics. Maybe it's her lack of a filter that allows her to

be completely honest about what she finds wrong with the world or odd about how society is structured. In a way, she demonstrates how communicating honestly is a political act in a society that is set up to reward decorum and self-censorship and punish curiosity and critical thinking. Here's the question: when you did Edith Ann, did you feel on any level that you had a political responsibility to use her as an icon of free speech?

Yes, I absolutely did! I'd say that everything I did had that inclination. It was natural for me. I didn't ever want to do something just because it was funny, for example. I always wanted the material to be expressive of something [more than jokes]. And, I agree, everything that people do involves politics on some level, whether they're aware of it or not. My characters are political because of the situations they get themselves into much more than who they are. [Communication] isn't always about what people talk about — it's more about what they exhibit.

So, again, I'd say that the political nature of what you do has mostly to do with your honest portrayal of the human experience. [In other words], because your work reflects the human heart, it degrades the false authority of politics.

Which is what drove Ernestine [*the switchboard operator*], who delivered all her snappy one-liners out of her sense of power. I wouldn't say that she really reflected the human experience, although she had very sharp politics.

But she reflected power in a way that made it seem arbitrary and not endemic, which, in a way, reinforced the notion that the whole concept of authority is foolish.

Maybe that's why she was so popular — you might be right.

Let's talk about your work on [*Rowan and Martin's*] *Laugh-In*. Tell me what it was like to work on a mainstream television show — this was pre-cable — that wasn't afraid to point fingers and to name names when criticizing, maybe not the politics of the day, but the culture.

I didn't want to go on *Laugh-In* initially because I was already on a show called *Music Scene*, which I thought was going to be much hipper because it was tied into Billboard and was like a contemporary *Hit Parade*. We had people like Jimi Hendrix and Janis Joplin and rockers like that and we were canceled mid-season because parents were up in arms because of the long-haired dopers, blah blah blah. So, after that I just wanted to go to New York and be an actor, *just* an actor, although I was still making up monologues. Then I met with George Schlatter [executive producer of *Laugh-In*), who was the first person with any power who got what I did and he really wanted [Ernestine] because Judy Carne [who also played a switchboard operator] was leaving the show. This was for the third season. So, I went on *Laugh-In* and Ernestine was such a huge monster of a character. It was the first time I *physically* dressed her, although I knew what she looked like in her 40s blouse with the puffy sleeves and the salmon skirt and the big patent leather belt and ankle strap shoes, which were never even shown on the television although they were there. And the jewelry was a big deal! She was very graphic.

Did any part of Ernestine come from the phone operators on *The Jack Benny Show*?

No — I don't even know that.

Oh, you should! They were really wonderful!

Were they 40s operators like Ernestine?

Yup.

Maybe I was bitten by them and wasn't even aware of it! Did he have a whole bunch of [them]?

No — just two.

God — on the old tv show?

I'm sure they were on a couple episodes, sure, but I mostly know them from the radio show.

How did they talk?!

I'll send you a clip!

Yes, please! I'm just dumbfounded! That's so great!

He was always taking one or the other out [on a date].

Oh my God! Well, Ernestine always thought that she was the sexpot of the phone company, which I think is what's good about all my characters, if there's *anything* good about them: They all have an ego and stand up for themselves — but they also have heart. None of them are pathetic, although they can have pathetic moments.

Which is a graceful and forgiving way to see each other — individually we are seldom who we are and almost always only what we pretend to be.

That's something that I learned moving through all those different apartments and through my neighborhood when I was growing up, that everybody is really the same. I remember going in the houses of some of the rich people — you know, these big glamorous houses with big cars and everything — and when you're a kid you think that rich people are rich because they're smarter than regular people and they know something that you don't. I found out very early that they were not smart and that they were no different than anybody else and that we are all so much the same. (*This is when Tomlin suddenly found herself choking up.*) Oh, I'm sorry — these tears…God. This is just like that penguin movie [*March of the Penguins, 2005*] — that movie just killed me, it was so horrible! Everybody just kept telling me that it was so inspiring and that [penguins] are so indominable and so human - it was so awful! [These penguins] just keep doing the same thing under terrible duress and hardship — marching for months, or whatever it is, and the one stays back and guards the egg and the other one comes back and then the other one has to go out and swim for months to bring back food. It was just…

Too much.

Yeah, too much.

I love how sensitive you are and how, not just in this conversation but in your performances as well, you're able to let your private self bleed into a public space. You don't quarantine or hide your vulnerability — you give yourself permission to portray what can only be described as our *emotional mutuality*.

I'm not here to judge people. Of course, I have some very harsh judgments and will occasionally scream at the television at people like Trump and certain politicians and people who are being so mean and ugly and abusive, but if I had to meet them one-on-one, I'd be more tolerant.

Well, it should be pointed out that there are no villains in your monologues. I think that reflects the real world — specifically how villains are really just people who have forgotten their humanity because they have jobs or exist in a certain social class that insists they play the part of a villain, which at the corporate and upper class level pays very well. What's that quote? *Rich people are just poor people with money.* This reminds me, in fact, of the sketch you did for your CBS special in 1973 — the one you did with Richard Pryor [called] *Juke and Opal*.

Jane [Wagner] wrote that one, too.

Yeah, it was groundbreaking theater for a comedy special, most notably because there was no live audience there to react to it while it was filmed.

Right.

Was that a deliberate decision on your part because you didn't want the drama and pathos that was so key to making the sketch work to

MR.FISH

be ruined by laughter? After all, here you have Richard Pryor and Lily Tomlin sharing the stage together, two of the biggest comedians in the country — that alone would cue an audience to laugh at things that [may not have even been] jokes — and the subjects that you're exploring have to do with addiction, poverty, race, bureaucracy, etc. Were you trying to avoid the distraction sure to come from people walking into a circus tent and finding [a staging of] *Waiting for Godot* and reacting to it as if it were *Monty Python* because of the setting?

CBS wanted us to sweeten the whole special and, yeah, they had a real problem with that sketch. They made us put it at the end of the show. Perry Lafferty [producer of *M*A*S*H*, *All in the Family*, *Maude* and *The Mary Tyler Moore Show*], who was head of programming or something, called me up to his office and said to me, "You sweeten up that special or we'll do it for you!" Now, I had a sketch that I did for my first special with Mrs. Beasley [*suburban housewife from Calumet City, Illinois*] called *War Games*. This was when the Vietnam

War was going on and in the sketch Mrs. Beasley goes out into the backyard and there's a war going on and her white picket fence is being strafed and kids' legs are being shot off and stuff like that. I re-filmed that [as the added *sweetness* that CBS was asking for] so I would have something to bargain with and I showed it to [the executives] and told them I'd get rid of *War Games* but I won't get rid of *Juke and Opal*.

How frustrating was that to create a meaningful piece of art and then have to fight with executives to get it on the air?

It was very frustrating! We had hired Rosalyn Drexler to write for that show and she was so excited to do it. We contacted other writers off-Broadway, people who we thought would make a real contribution to the quality of [what we were doing]. We really thought we were going to get a series out of it, but Freddy Silverman [CBS programming director] wasn't even going to air it — it'd been shelved! Then he was having breakfast with Alan Alda [who was in the *Jake and Opal*

sketch], who had just started shooting *M*A*S*H*, but it hadn't aired yet, and he said to Freddy, "I was just on the Lily Tomlin Special and it was *so* great!" So [Silverman] went back and reneged on his dismissal of us and he put it back in the lineup and it went on at 10 o'clock at night. We never did get a series. I did six specials — four at CBS and two at ABC — and never got a series. NBC never gave me a special, even though they did *Laugh-In*!

I'm guessing that a multi-million-dollar media company is unlikely to reward an artist who [produces work that] has, as its subtext, an appreciation of people over power. I deal with the same thing all the time with my cartooning. People keep telling me that I should be a millionaire and I tell them that corporations and private investors are the only ones capable of making anybody a millionaire and that most everything I do is some variation of the same message: *FUCK CORPORATIONS AND PRIVATE WEALTH.*

We won two Emmys for that second special!

Well, you didn't win a Clio, and television grows its bottom line with business decisions, not artistic ones — right?

Yeah, it's about selling advertising. Still, a lot of taboos have been broken down in the culture and television is starting to reflect that.

Still, I would prefer that television, [rather than merely reflect broken taboos,] break some taboos, itself. During the 1960s and '70s, for example, the arts community was more likely to break taboos well before the mainstream even had the guts to face them. Now we're living in Trump's America, which is all about silencing progressive and radical voices. What hope is there for the future [of our democracy] if artists are not allowed to express themselves and to encourage critical thinking and a dissenting point of view?

I've been around for a while and it's been my experience that these things move in cycles. I've come to expect that it's always going to be four steps forward and three steps back — or, looking around these days, more like two steps forward and five steps back, because Trump is such a pathetic, sorry-ass motherfucker. I fucking hate him.

And I'm not sure that politics can save us, because there are enough parallels to the 1960s to how sharp the divides are in this country and it wasn't politics that saved us then. Waiting for bureaucrats to save us from other bureaucrats is ridiculous. If the counterculture taught us anything it taught us that change only comes when we don't ask for permission from mom and dad to redecorate our own rooms or follow our own dreams. Politicians were never going to see feminism as anything other than bad behavior and they weren't ever going to consider gay rights as a civil rights issue — not without pressure from activists. I mean, wasn't that your experience?

I think the broader question is what will touch peoples' hearts now and turn them what will make [us all] more decent and less lascivious?

Feeling the pain personally will change us — and with global warming and the never-ending wars and the secret surveillance state and a President who acts like a Mafia don, the pain will be felt by more and more people, by and by.

I don't know why people need to feel the pain personally [to know that something's wrong] — that's what gets me! It should be more obvious than that.

They don't believe the information that they're getting is truthful, so they ignore it. With art, though, you can tell them the truth in a way that will make them respond emotionally, whether they laugh or cry, and because they're moved they'll want to share the insight or experience with somebody else and then all of a sudden you got a bunch of people engaging with the truth in these private, unguarded moments. I think you only learn whatever you teach yourself and art is one of those things that allows you to meditate on ideas in a way that allows wisdom to creep into your soul, pain-free. *You* crept into my soul that way!

That's very articulate.

Well, I think we figured it out.

Thank you. ✳

MAD IN AMERICA

IT IS A QUEER FACT, indeed, that none of the most outspoken and anti-authoritarian radicals in this country are under 65 years old.

Queer because radicalism and the job of saying *f-you!* to the bureaucratic versions of Mom and Dad have traditionally fallen to much younger men and women, who, as they approach early adulthood, are suddenly outraged to find how disinterested the dominant culture is in their ideals and their passions and their deep desire to live, perhaps even raise a family, in a saner society.

One thinks of Voltaire, Rimbaud, Phil Ochs, the young Picasso, the Beats, the yippies, the hippies, the Panthers, Warhol's Factory riffraff, the Gen X, Y and Z-ers, that sort of thing. One doesn't typically think of somebody who might smell faintly of mothballs and Metamucil or somebody who is likely to loose his teeth in a sneeze or who might proclaim loudly and repeatedly that Velcro, microwave ovens and cable television are newfangled and faddish and cockamamie.

However, when Howard Zinn died in 2010 at 87 there was something about the silencing of his voice that seemed unfair and tragic. How could a spirit that was so intellectually vibrant and forward-thinking and balls-to-the-wall energetic die, literally, of old age? It was like reading the impossible headline: *James Dean Dies in Porsche 550 Spyder at Age 91.*

In fact, losing Zinn only compounded the loss, over the last decade, of fellow radicals such as Vonnegut and Mailer and Terkel and Said, whose interpretations of the day's events and predictions of future woes were often so relentlessly honest and thought-provoking and dead-on that our society can only become markedly less provocative and decidedly less thoughtful and increasingly more ill-prepared for whatever comes without them being here. Am I wrong? You tell me: Who are the public intellectuals whose social commentary and wry observations and very public self-examinations can be relied upon to advance the species and to deepen our collective and happy misunderstanding of why we're all here? Who will be left once Chomsky and Sahl and ~~Vidal~~ and Steinem and Ali and Lapham and Didion and Sontag and Scheer and ~~Krassner~~ and ~~Hitchens~~ and Hedges disappear?

I can't think of anybody.

In fact, when one considers the *un*reaction from the so-called radical wing of the anti-establishmentarianism movement in this country to the current Egyptian civil unrest — not to mention to the Kyrgyzstan riots in April and the Freedom Flotilla massacre in May and the G-8 and G-20 protests in Ontario in June and the massive protests in Spain, Belgium, Greece, Portugal, Ireland, Slovenia and Lithuania against austerity measures in September and the huge demonstrations in France over pensions in October and the continuing Tunisian revolution that began in December — there appears to be no reason to believe that the world-famous, democracy-championing, radically confident and self-aggrandizing American Dream, like any other dream, can be substantiated outside of sleep. Awake, we snore. (And before you embarrass yourself by bringing up the vast number of people who attended both Glenn Beck's Rally to Restore Honor and Jon Stewart's Rally to Restore Sanity, you have to recognize that these were show business events designed to attract spectators, not participants, with both being exactly as significant to the preservation of our nation's honor and sanity as a NASCAR race.)

How else to explain how little impact the publication of this generation's Pentagon Papers seems to be having on the American public? At least with the 1971 Daniel Ellsberg version — which was 83,000 pages shorter than WikiLeaks' Afghan War Diary, released in July of 2010, and 393,000 pages shorter than the Iraq War Logs, also released by WikiLeaks, in October of 2010 — there existed an anti-war movement that was massive, mobilized and pissed off and understood the significance of such damning documentation.

What do we have now? An anti-war movement that is so gutless and so savagely unimaginative that, rather than gaining purpose and momentum in the face of our government's ever-increasing disdain for peace in the Middle East, it has proved itself to be too lazy, even too cowardly, to face down the very disease of oligarchy that it had concocted itself to cure. When did the American version of a bleeding-heart-radical-hell-raiser

BRIAN FIGURING OUT HOW TO GET AMERICA INTERESTED IN THE PEACE MOVEMENT AGAIN BEFORE IT'S TOO LATE.

MR. FISH

WHICH HAS THE GREATEST POTENTIAL TO STOP GOLIATH FROM ACTING LIKE A COMPLETE DICK?

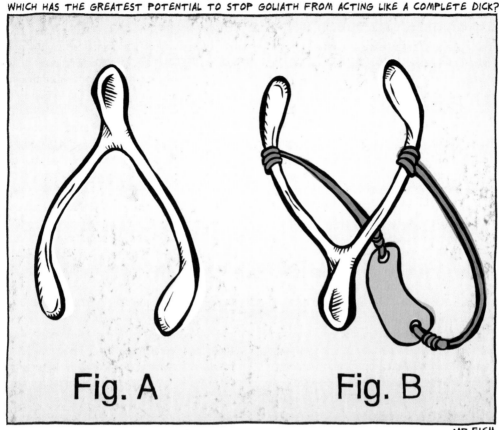

MR.FISH

become the equivalent of a vegetarian between meals of animal flesh, no more likely to dedicate his life to the teachings of Mahatma Gandhi and Martin Luther King Jr. than a devotee of the "Twilight" series would be to drinking actual blood and living forever?

By way of example, I once went to a MoveOn rally mounted in protest of George W. Bush's veto of a 2007 bill hoping to expand the State Children's Health Insurance Program (SCHIP) and experienced what came to represent the quintessential reason why I continue to worry about the future of the republic.

Here's what happened.

I arrived at the train station in L.A. at 5:25, five minutes before the demonstration was officially set to begin, a *candlelit vigil* I was told, and I found a seat on the wide lip of an enormous concrete planter on the landing where an underground train station emptied beneath a huge orange awning the size of a band shell at street level. Ten feet away from me stood two MoveOn organizers trying to recruit a pair of Awake! Jesus freaks into the protest, imploring

them to put down their magazines and to pick up one of the 50 stacked cardboard signs leaning against an adjacent planter and to spend the next few hours standing curbside with it.

Mimicking the uncomfortable *no thank you* shown to them several thousand times a day, the Jesus freaks *moved on*, leaving a total of four people to begin the event. Sighing audibly, the protesters grabbed their baffling signs — HONK FOR KIDS, BE A VETO BANDIDO, WE THE PEOPLE JUST SAY NO and an indecipherable one that was on a piece of dress shirt cardboard no bigger than a standard piece of typing paper with lettering that had been drawn with a ballpoint pen — and shuffled over to where the cars were whizzing by as impenetrable as 5,000-pound seeds in pursuit of soil.

In 20 minutes the mob of activists had swelled to seven people, two of whom were under 5 years old, one of them crying in her stroller because she'd been swatted for chewing on her sign. Thirty feet beyond the seven was a MoveOn photographer who was taking pictures of the demonstration, his shutter snapping just at the moment when somewhere around a hundred bone-tired commuters would exit the train station and crowd around the sign holders to wait for the walking green at the enormous crosswalk before continuing their commute on the other side of the road at the bus station. Then the light would change, the camera would be recapped and the hoard, composed of faces that looked as if the sign carriers were oozing something that might stain their clothes, would slide away from the minuscule number of protesters like sand being poured from a public ashtray around gum wads anchored where they stood.

"Get out of our way! Get out of our way!" hollered a man with widely spaced corn kernels for teeth and a limp severe enough to require airplane arms to help him keep his balance. He was headed toward the protesters, in the opposite direction of the commuters, and had noticed the MoveOn folks with their signs and assumed the hippies had taken over the world and he was speaking for all who hadn't yet been corrupted by empathy and optimism. "Anti-American sons-a-bitches!" he spat, on his way home, I guessed, to piss in the sink and to slurp dinner from the fistful of ketchup packets that he'd been warming over in his pocket since midafternoon, the notes that make up the refrain from "God Bless America" circling round and round inside his head like vultures.

Just before the demonstration broke up a little more than an hour after it started (it was never dark enough for candles or quite bright enough for camaraderie), I watched as one of the remaining three protesters left his curbside position for a daring final attempt to incite some support for the humanism that he and his comrades were hoping to stir in defiance of Bush's veto. Walking across the plaza with the deliberation of Jesus Christ moving toward the comfort of his cross, the man stopped at the top of the escalator leading up from the train platform below and hoisted his gigantic "HONK FOR HEALTHY KIDS" sign above his head, confident that he'd be impossible for the unwashed masses emerging from the underground to miss.

He stood there for 15 minutes unable to get a single honk out of anybody, his face souring and his eyes communicating a real disdain for humanity's inability to see what was right in front it. ✳

ABBIE HOFFMAN WAS HERE

ABBIE HOFFMAN, the wild-haired personification of both the noun and adjective form of the word "riot" in the 1960s, nostalgically revered by the current liberal Democratic wing of the Establishment Party as the Tourette's of the Anti-Establishmentarian Movement and the joy-buzzing co-confounder of the Yippies, his significance neutered by his infamy, his legacy no more useful to contemporary radical politics than the miniskirt or the lava lamp, famously said, "You measure democracy by the freedom it gives its dissidents, not the freedom it gives its assimilated conformists." This was in 1989, when Hoffman was just 52, the same year that he killed himself, making everyone wonder if freedom wasn't really just another word for *nothing left to lose*. His body was found in a converted turkey coop near New Hope, Pa., where I found myself a week ago, seated behind a small lopsided table on the sidewalk outside of Farley's Bookshop, trying to sell my new book of cartoons and essays about how we're all doomed to tourists and retirees in white linen shorts, crisp running shoes and "God Bless America!" T-shirts.

Roasting beneath the spectacular rage of the mid-July sun while the delicious scent of Abbie Hoffman's martyred ghost swirled around my starvation for attention like a home-cooked meal, I started to imagine that if only my book were loaded with chocolate chips and cut into bite-sized pieces and I were wearing an apron I might gain some acknowledgement from the public.

A week earlier I was at the Greenlight Bookstore in Brooklyn, drinking red wine from a plastic tumbler and standing before a microphone while the immense rain-soaked windows behind me fogged and perspired, the body heat and carbon dioxide from the overflow crowd overpowering the air conditioning like Bolshevism. The event had been organized by my publisher, Akashic Books, and featured short readings and presentations by a handful of the house's writers and felt not unlike what I imagined poetry readings at the Six Gallery in San Francisco must've been like in the 1950s, more like an Irish wake for the written word than a subdued Lutheran funeral. Following closely behind a short presentation by Adam Mansbach, author of "Go the F**k to Sleep," this year's "Chicken Soup for the Soul," I couldn't resist saying to the audience, in mock disgust, "Before I begin, let me just say that I've spent my entire artistic career saying 'fuck' to the most despicable politicians and the most ruthless warmongering men and women of industry and high finance, never realizing that if only I'd said it to sleepless children I'd be on the New York Times bestseller list and not counting nickels to buy my toilet paper." It was a party.

I remember back when I first saw Dick Lester's deeply significant 1964 film masterpiece, "A Hard Day's Night," and how the scene at the discothéque changed my life forever. It was the part of the movie where we find our lovable heroes, the Beatles, tired of being quarantined in their hotel room between public appearances and they decide to sneak out and go to a club to dance and meet girls. Most remarkable to me, and I was probably 12 at the time, was how cool John Lennon looked by *not* dancing as the other three were, choosing instead to sit and drink and talk — to *philosophize*, I guessed, judging by the attentiveness of his listeners and the *soigné* manner in which he held his cigarette! —with those around him. It seemed antithetical to all that I had been led to believe by the dominant culture about what grooviness and hipness were supposed to look like. What was hipness, particularly for a boy, supposed to look like? Well, the way I understood it was that hipness was largely determined by how well a fella could throw and catch a ball, how handy he was with tools and how gracefully he was able to communicate *nonverbally* with the opposite sex, whether through dancing, kissing or snubbing. Yet here was Lennon, in a black turtleneck and surrounded by beautiful women, appearing absolutely at home in his own skin, no ball or hammer or ChapStick anywhere in sight, just straight confabulation, pure and simple. The idea that one could appear gorgeous merely by having a conversation was somehow wonderful to me, and I decided to make it my life's ambition to define my own grooviness by engaging in a never-ending dialogue with as many people as I could. What would be the point, I suddenly realized, of wasting my time trying to emulate the wordless and episodic pantomime that I saw everybody else engaging in with one person at a time?

"Did you make this book yourself?" asked a sapid old lady in half glasses and a pair of powder blue Bermuda shorts approximating the size of the landmass they were named after. She was standing at my sidewalk table, having come from nowhere, caressing the cover of my book like she was hoping to provoke a purr, a needle-thin crucifix hanging from her neck on a chain the width of a thread.

"Yes," I said, smiling up at her in my black horn-rimmed glasses, fresh haircut and three-button blazer, the perfect picture of benign Christianity and cherry-cheeked Americanism. Then she opened the book and concentrated on a random page, mumbling silently to herself the gag line to one of my cartoons. In an instant the sweetness drained from her face and she closed the book and slowly returned it back to its stack, her eyes tearing as if she'd just uncapped a casket full of eels and bourbon. "Well?" I asked her.

"You should be ashamed of yourself," she spat, turning away and marching off in the direction of a live klezmer band playing the theme to "Rocky." What struck me as peculiar was how this woman, who no doubt had lived through the Great Depression, who had seen the bombing of Pearl Harbor and the My Lai Massacre and 9/11, who had witnessed the mind-numbing tragedy of the Holocaust and experienced the devastation of environmental decay and worldwide unrest and famine and public assassination, could react to something I'd drawn as if a new benchmark for unspeakable horror had been set.

"What is 'Go Fish: How to Win Contempt and Influence People' about?" I'd said at the Greenlight, referring to the book that I held in my hand, just as the light changed at a nearby intersection and a serpentine line of Brooklyn traffic slowly panned its headlights across my back and sent an elegant succession of shadows pirouetting around the bookstore like joyous slaves. "Let me answer that question by telling you about a young man who wanted nothing more in his life than to be a famous artist," I said. "He hated school, used to get in trouble for daydreaming all the time. He would lose entire afternoons meditating on the beauty of objects, on the aesthetics of light and shadow, his fingers forever smudged with oil paint, his clothes smelling of turpentine, his heart and mind awash in hope and optimism." I paused, afraid of choking up.

"For him," I continued, "there was no higher calling than to be a painter who created beautiful images for the public and who lived his life in service of his craft, his canvases designed for the singular purpose of inspiring people's souls to grow. That young artist's name ..." — I stopped, looked around the room, then back at the book in my hand — "... was Adolf Hitler. The moral of the story being that if only we lived in a world less inclined to discourage lousy artists from continuing to create shitty art and *more* inclined to discourage lousy politicians from becoming monsters hell-bent on conquering the planet we'd be a lot better off."

"True," I said, "if Hitler's artistic career had been allowed to continue and not been cut short there would be many more crappy oils of quaint churches at dusk and abandoned hay wagons at midday and misty covered bridges at dawn to clutter up the world, but at least there'd also be millions more Jewish doctors, dentists and psychiatrists to absorb all that mediocrity into gaudy frames in their waiting rooms."

❀ ❀ ❀

"What's your book about," asked a DNC canvasser with a clipboard and a blue T-shirt bearing the Obama logo just as the Pennsylvania sun was dipping behind the trees. He was watching me stack all my unsold books on my tiny table in preparation for returning them to the bookstore manager inside.

"Huh?" I said.

"Your book there," he said. "What's it about?"

"It's a coming-of-rage book," I said. He didn't answer me. "It's about how constructive nihilism can be when kept on the tip of a pencil and off the point of a fucking bayonet." It had been a long day.

"You registered to vote?" he asked.

"Yeah," I said.

"You supporting Obama?" he said.

"Why?" I said.

"I just want to know."

"No," I said, "I mean *why* should I support him?"

"Forget it," he said.

I did. ✳

BLAH BLAH BLAH

MR.FISH

IT WAS MY HABIT during school dances to never stop walking. For hours I would circle the dance floor and act as if I were scanning the crowd in search of somebody. "Booth!" a classmate might yell, hoping to head me off, oftentimes with a clotheslined-arm-offering punch, and I'd hold up my index finger and push past him, craning my neck this way and that, my brow furrowed, my eyes looking everywhere in an insane pantomime of deep concentration and reconnaissance. Inevitably, the news of my solitary bug-eyed schlep around the gymnasium would be reported back to my mother, usually by my twin sister, and the assumption would be made that I was afraid of girls. I'd shrug off the simplicity of the deduction and return to my room and practice not giving a shit about what people thought, feeling like Ichabod Crane charging toward the covered bridge of my high school graduation, beyond which the Headless Horseman of Manahawkin, N.J., had no dominion over my soul.

Manahawkin, N.J.?

Inside my third-grade social studies book was a map of pre-Civil War America that showed the Mason-Dixon Line in red. I used to stare at that line and imagine it as a great bloody gash set in the body of the country by sober and learned Northerners hoping to amputate the vicious and cross-eyed hillbillies in the South from our national identity. What worried me was the irregularity of the line once it hit Delaware. Moving east with the surgical precision of a straight line along the southern border of Pennsylvania, the incision seemed to suddenly hit a bone and be redirected downward, erratically tracing around the Union's First State and dead-ending into the sea. Anyone could see, looking at the map, that had the line been allowed to move uninterrupted it would've sliced through New Jersey just north of where I lived, thereby implicating me as a heehawing redneck.

Of course, had my third-grade social studies book suddenly decided to reclassify my hometown as part of the South, little evidence would be available for me to prove otherwise. For example, the one and only black kid at my school had absolutely no friends to speak of. And while this might've had less to do with the color of his skin and more to do with his penchant for having seizures and wearing velour, the effect of isolation was the same. And then there were the Jackson, Miss.-like summers, which had a way of attracting prophetic significance beginning in mid-May and ending in late October, as if God were using the whole of South Jersey to rehearse an End of Days scenario for more densely populated, potentially more repentant, parts of the country.

The signs would appear overnight when one day it would be springtime, with the scent of mud and dandelions and freshly mowed grass stirring something like swarming bees inside everybody's guts. There would be the almost audible explosion of yellow azaleas in everybody's yard and the storybook appearance of new rabbits and butterflies and birds. Then, the next day, you'd step outside and feel as if you'd just walked down into somebody's flooded basement. The air, heavy with pinesap, would be filled with dragonflies, grasshoppers and wasps. Green flies, as loud as incensed vibrators and as durable as seeds, would bite you through your shirt and on your face and the sun would no longer rise; instead, it would suddenly materialize at the center of the sky, swollen to the size of Jupiter, and radiate an impossible heat that seemed as unnatural as an electrical fire. At dusk, flatbed

trucks would chug through the neighborhood at 5 miles per hour, lugging what appeared to be a jet engine that had been stripped of its alloy skin, revealing a deep-fried skeleton of black metal harnessed to a giant fan which belched out a great wet cloud of pesticides aimed at controlling the mosquito population by making everyone's blood taste less like tomato juice and more like paint thinner. Midnight would bring the temperature down to 91 degrees, and moths, driven mad by the sound of a trillion chirping crickets, would trampoline their furry bodies repeatedly against your screens until daybreak, when the cycle would repeat itself.

Certainly, it is under such extreme and relentless conditions that a lifetime can be stripped of nuance and reduced to a preposterous simplicity. Often it is precisely because of those daily bombardments of discomfort and disquiet that a person will typically develop a strong reliance on the crude shorthand of prejudice and paranoia and deep rage to help explain the pain inherent is his or her victimization. Specifically, when self-preservation is made the top priority in any given situation, there is seldom room for the sort of charitable selflessness that allows a person to enjoy any peace of mind whatsoever, and without any peace of mind whatsoever a person will tend toward an active retaliation against existence itself. Consider, as a parallel, those made to endure inside prolonged cycles of poverty and war, or even

those made to persevere through long prison sentences or through monotonous jobs or marriages for decades at a time.

When badgered relentlessly by exterior forces contemptuous of either personal contemplation or any opportunity for blissful complacency, a human being will seek a certain numbing comfort by shunning optimism. He will eliminate the expectation that the situation will ever improve by excising the want for it to improve if only to minimize the torture that comes with the crushing belief that his desires are inconsequential. He will then deflect blame for his situation away from himself and scapegoat others, for only a comic book character would ever assume that he alone had the power to conjure such vast and debilitating hardship. He will then do his best to champion the mediocrity of his life, typically inflating every act of non-acquiescence to complete self-annihilation into a self-delusion capable of sustaining his pride and re-imagining his existential suffocation as the hard breathing that accompanies the difficult, though heroic, job of slaying dragons.

All of this came flooding back to me, rather circuitously, during a recent trip to New York, where I had taken an assignment to interview famed altruistic hippie-clown, self-titled psychedelic relic and professional self-parody Wavy Gravy during his 75th birthday celebration at the Beacon Theatre on Broadway. Promoted as a fundraiser for the Seva Foundation, an international nonprofit health organization started in 1978 by Gravy's best friend and former executive director of Google.org, Larry Brilliant, the concert featured David Crosby, Graham Nash, Jackson Browne, Buffy Sainte-Marie, Dr. John and Jorma Kaukonen, among others. Having been promised access to the artists backstage, many of whom were as famous for their social consciousness and commitment to compassionate hell-raising as they were for their music, I took the gig and spent the week leading up to the show trying to devise a line of questioning that might garner new insights and prompt fresh answers from these 1960s and '70s superstars whose combined 400 years of experience in talking to reporters made me feel as if I were facing down the impossible task of looking for a suite of new notes on a grand piano without touching the keys.

"Should I introduce you as Dwayne Booth or Mr. Fish?" whispered the publicist once we were about 10 feet away from Wavy Gravy's dressing room, which would've been a storage closet had it contained a mop, a bucket and a 40-gallon drum of bleach instead of a Wavy Gravy in grubby Crocs and a clown nose. "Maybe I should introduce you as Mr. Fish," she said, mentally high-fiving herself like a cheerleader suddenly overcome with the golly-gee neatness of her own cheer. "Because he has that fish on a leash, right? You know, the one he always walks around with?!"

"All right," I said, "I'll be Mr. Fish."

"You don't have a lot of time," she said, her face quickly becoming as serious as a heart attack. "He's trying to gather his wa before the show starts in about 15 minutes." His wa? "Sorry about that," she said. "I wish you had more time." Leaning into his dressing room and spotting Gravy sitting all alone and plucking at an ektar before a large cellophaned tray of cloudy cheese and deflated fruit, his white hair exploding from beneath a filthy white bowler sporting a black propeller, I wondered if gathering one's wa might be Japanese for coming to a quiet and dignified acceptance of one's questionable headwear.

Of course, having been hurled like a halved mackerel into the soft purple brain bath of Wavy's preshow meditation, it became immediately obvious to me as I closed the door and stood, struggling with my backpack to retrieve my notebook and tape recorder, my elbows pressed in close to my body as if I were undressing inside a sleeping bag, that I was an unwelcome guest. "I'm gathering my wa," he said, his eyes closed like he was Charlie Parker listening to the bebop rhythms of the universe, his mind awash in Gravy.

"Yes," I said, "I heard." Eight minutes later I was back in my theater seat, having gathered my wa-the-fuck-was-that? in less time than it took me to gather, just a week earlier, all my false hopes about the political and cultural viability of a man and a movement 40 years past their prime. Rather than prompting any new conversation out of my subject, my questions merely acted as non sequiturs signaling when he should begin his rote recitation of previously published quips and poorly reasoned declarations of victory against the status quo, the singular exception being when he interrupted my last question by sighing the words "blah blah blah," the exhaustion in his voice making me recognize him as a 300-pound Jack wanting to be returned to his box.

Then, packing up my crap and transplanting myself back into the audience and beginning what, over the next three hours, would be a series of fruitless texts with the backstage publicist for me to interview anybody else, I began focusing on the concertgoers now filing in through the gaudy and ornate archways at the back of the room. White beards and slow, shuffling steps and large wide bottoms. I watched them lowering themselves as gingerly as Easter eggs into their seats, tie-dyed and bifocaled, and I wondered, perhaps for the first time in my life, why I so constantly tried to convince myself that the Woodstock Generation was not only still an active and viable force for social and political change in America, but that it was also forever young and constantly regenerating its membership and expanding exponentially through bloodlines, like alcoholism or diabetes. Scanning the crowd and trying to find anybody under 50, I suddenly started to worry that the only threat hippies might pose to the dominant culture nowadays was the personal-injury lawsuits they were likely to file from accidental falls due to uneven pavement.

After all, here were people dressed in the universally accepted uniform of the beloved peacenik, nearly all of them, yet none of them seemed so much peaceful as sleepy. It seemed as if their uniforms, after decades of insular overuse, had become mere costumes designed to reflect the quaint nostalgia of an earlier era that was no more relevant to the present day than winklepickers, culottes or powdered wigs. Had not the peace sign itself finally become as trite and ineffective as the Live long and prosper hand sign popular at Star Trek conventions? With the same scant knowledge possessed by the average Trekker as to what it might mean to engineer and then pilot a vehicle capable of intergalactic travel, I imagined that there was nobody around me who might have the slightest idea as to what it meant to engineer a social movement and then to pilot it in the direction of Donovan's "Atlantis."

Sure, I thought, tonight's performance was guaranteed to provide the Seva Foundation, particularly the organization's Sight Programs, with a sizable chunk of change, thereby helping to bring the gift of sight to millions living in Tibet, Nepal, Cambodia and Bangladesh and throughout Africa, but — and here's the point — what else? It was as if I were surrounded by enthusiasts for alternative fuel who had convinced themselves that they were good guys because they knew that if everybody in the country went green starting tomorrow, in 20 years' time the United States would be a brutally fascistic plutocracy capable of sustaining itself exclusively on corn oil and windmills. In other words, by hijacking the music and the imagery of 1960s anti-establishmentarianism and forcing it to mellow along with its creators, the originators of flower power and free love had, I feared, unwittingly become the antithesis of the struggle itself, and by defanging the snake of radicalism so that everybody could safely hold it, the rats who used to constitute the predator's main diet were now running rampant. After all, here was Wavy Gravy — a man who at one time was such a threat to state power and straight society that he had to endure frequent beatings by riot police and who had been continuously praised by real revolutionaries — now voting for Barack Obama and rejoicing in the greater celebrity that he enjoyed as the namesake of a discontinued ice cream.

Leaving the Beacon Theatre that night and heading up Broadway with my "All access" press pass still strung around my neck, I figured that the news of my solitary bug-eyed schlep along the periphery of everybody else's communal optimism during the show would be reported back to my editor, most likely by the column that I planned to file, and that the assumption would be made that I was afraid of harmless do-gooders who believed that compassion and joy and togetherness was enough to save us all from self-annihilation.

Sadly, the assumption would be true. ✳

VOTE!

OTHERWISE YOU WON'T HAVE THE RIGHT
TO COMPLAIN ABOUT THE COLOR OF YOUR CELL

Riot police are not there to protect the peace

They're there to see that peace remains held for ransom by the profiteers of big business

JUNE GLOOM WITH LEWIS LAPHAM

THERE IS ALWAYS SMOKE around Lewis Lapham, as if he'd just been conjured by some sorcerer suddenly enraged by the placation of the status quo and alarmed by the myopia of contemporary culture and the rabid asininity of 21st century political discourse. The smoke, of course, is not supernatural, but rather comes from the Parliament Lights that Lapham has been smoking for decades. Like the man himself, who is never outside of the pressman's dark suit and tie, they hark back to a time when professionalism was decidedly masculine-chic and personal freedoms, even unhealthy ones, trumped the bullying demands, even the healthy ones, of the dominant culture.

I began reading him as a teenager in 1984, while working at a drugstore after school in southern New Jersey. Harper's Magazine, with Lapham as the newly reinstated editor, had just undergone

a redesign and his monthly "Notebook" column, always constructed with the care and meticulous attention to detail usually associated with those working with either scalpels or explosives, was one of the things that made me want to grow up to become an insufferable and excessively well-read know-it-all. Contrary to his academic lineage, Lapham impressed me, and still does, as the most plainspoken public intellectual ever produced by the blue-blooded coupling of Yale and Cambridge, a feat deserving of real praise if only because similar Ivy League inbreeding has been known to produce great litters of erudite ninnies and putrid snobs.

Anyway, I recently came across an interview that I'd conducted with Lapham in 2008, just as the economic crisis was beginning to unfold its magnificent class-conscious talons and just before Barack Obama was swept triumphantly into the

Oval Orifice. It was only months after the launch of his post-Harper's publication, Lapham's Quarterly, a themed literary journal that relies on the rigorous mining of world history, both ancient and present-day and everything in between, for its content. The conversation was supposed to be about the death of the mid-20th century counterculture and whether it had been homicide or suicide that'd killed it, and it was, or at least it started out that way, but the cacophony of current events eventually had the better of us and our talk quickly became early 21st century prophesying. We spoke for an hour and a half at Lapham's then-new offices in lower Manhattan, the two of us sequestered inside a tiny glass room in the corner of a much larger office populated by editors and their editorial assistants. As if he were representative of a rare and nearly extinct bird, his office felt like an aquarium that had been designed to allow the *Lewis-icus laphamogatus* to live out its final years in an environment best suited to its comfort and joy, meaning that the great tar and nicotine aroma that hung in the air like silt was being churned continuously by a refrigerator-sized air conditioner that roared like a riding mower and cooled the room with all the efficiency of a half-eaten popsicle that is waved through the air.

That said, what follows is a sampling of what we talked about that June afternoon, his voice as clear as a bell on the recording, mine compromised somewhat by General Electric and the helicopter gunship that the good general rode through my entire transcription. Luckily, the notes that I took during my discussion with Lapham, plus the questions that I prepared before our meeting, were able to fill in where necessary.

❋ ❋ ❋

Assuming that you recognize the same shift in the American culture that I do, namely that members of the artistic community — specifically those writers and philosophers and painters and poets most committed to exploring the perplexing and fascinating vagaries of our human identity — are no longer encouraged to participate in the national debate about who we are as a nation and what our responsibilities might be to our own moral and humanitarian ideals, all political avocations be damned. In other words, where are the modern day Picassos and Voltaires and Mailers and Twains?

I think that what's happened is that we have a new language. My answer comes out of Marshall McLuhan — McLuhan publishes *Understanding Media* in 1964 and makes the point that we shape our tools and our tools shape us and he sees the shift from print to the electronic media as a revolution in the settled political aesthetic order. Now his observations from 1964 have simply become more and more apparent and seemingly more prescient as time has gone by. He recognized that television is not a medium that lends itself to philosophy, literature or even straightforward narrative.

Nor does it provide a stopping point for contemplation, which is the only way [that people have] of deepening their understanding of things.

Right — with the electronic media there is no memory, it's always the eternal present, which is constantly dissolving and contributing to a great social anxiety.

The electronic media has also forced people to become much more private and much less engaged in the community and, therefore, much less politically active. For example, consider the difference between Jon Stewart and somebody like Mort Sahl. Back in the early '60s, if you wanted to see Mort Sahl you had to congregate with other people in a public space and that takes a certain amount of bravery because you're visibly aligning yourself with a specific point of view. Not only that, whenever you congregate in a public space you're making a statement — a political statement, even, given the stuff that Sahl was talking about — with your body and because there are other bodies the statement is substantial because it is amassed. Conversely, when you watch Jon Stewart you are not in public, you're in your house — you don't even need to be wearing pants! — and your dissent is not amassed. You pose no threat to the dominant culture because all you're doing is watching television. It's the same thing as wearing a T-shirt from the Gap that has a peace sign on it and thinking that you're part of the peace movement, even though you've done absolutely nothing of any real significance for the cause. In fact, you've just gone shopping and given money to a corporation that your peace sign speaks contrary to.

And you lose democracy that way because democracy is face to face and it's argument with people unlike yourself. Television keeps you inside your own set of circumstances where there's no risk, and dissent is a habit of mind that withers unless you use it.

[Norman] Mailer once said that television perpetuates the idea that one can learn the secrets of the world in some easy way. He [also] said [TV] was *frictionless*, which I always loved, and that it teaches us that boredom is better than dread.

That's very good.

I often wonder, though, getting back to the *friction* of face-to-face communication, if the problem of how we deal with democracy and human interaction isn't so much about *what* we think, but *how* we think. Ultimately, it becomes a question of how viable a tool human consciousness itself is when it comes to both perceiving and comprehending reality. If human consciousness is only able to use objective reality as corroboration for its subjective notions *about* reality — which I believe is the function of consciousness — then we are doomed as a species because it means that there is no perception of reality, there is only opinion and how do you get everybody to have the same opinion?

You can't.

Right — so what happens when opinion becomes our only concept of reality?

It's an epistemological question: How do we know what we think we know?

And that's how we wind up using something like capital as a unifying principle instead of some human element that cannot be manipulated.

You see a very clear demonstration of that in what's now happening in Wall Street. Here you have these guys who have been pretending that they know what they're doing, or that they're not stealing, or that there is somehow some substance in these entirely fictional debt instruments. They wish to preserve the facade. Our money is only worth anything as long as we believe it is. Money is the great abstraction. Schopenhauer said that,

"Money is human happiness in the abstract; he, then, who is no longer capable of enjoying human happiness in the concrete devotes himself utterly to money." Again, it's nothing.

And yet we're convinced that we can't *afford* to engage in self-preservation as a species, as if self-preservation had anything to do with capitalism. I mean, why is it necessary for us to fundraise before we can even attempt saving those most in need of humanitarian assistance, for instance, or to prevent some environmental catastrophe from happening? How has it become logical for us to refrain from doing all that we can to prevent self-annihilation without first squaring our attempt with an economic philosophy? When did peace, love and understanding become incorporated? Again, it may be a problem of human evolution and the fact that consciousness, itself, is flawed, particularly if our consciousness is blinding us from suicide.

Right.

And, getting back to what you were saying about McLuhan and the electronic media: As long as technology remains sexy to people it will justify the mechanism of industry that seeks to present itself as an addiction to a society that can never be satiated. So then the question becomes how can we make agrarian society sexier to people? How do we make wooden carts and dirt roads and no air conditioning preferable? Wasn't that part of the '60s mentality, figuring out how to get back to the garden?

And that concept is now what they mean when they talk about sustainable growth. The world's population is now 6 billion people and the estimates show 9 billion people by 2050. Now the thing that saves Europe in the 14th century is the Black Death. It kills one-third of the population and what you find, if you measure the curve, is that Europe can't feed itself before the plague arrives. It's starving. Take away a third of the people and suddenly there's more work, wages go up, land gets cleared, things improve. It's like democracy — democracy only really works in a relatively small circumference.

Which is mirrored by the anarchist ideal — the idea that given a small enough society where

WHEN THE CITIZENS OF A DEMOCRATIC SOCIETY NO LONGER RECOGNIZE THAT THEY ARE THE SOURCE OF POWER FOR THEIR ELECTED LEADERS AND THEY START TO BELIEVE THAT THEIR ELECTED LEADERS ARE THE SOURCE OF POWER, INSTEAD, THAT SOCIETY HAS BECOME FASCISTIC AND CAN NO LONGER CALL ITSELF FREE

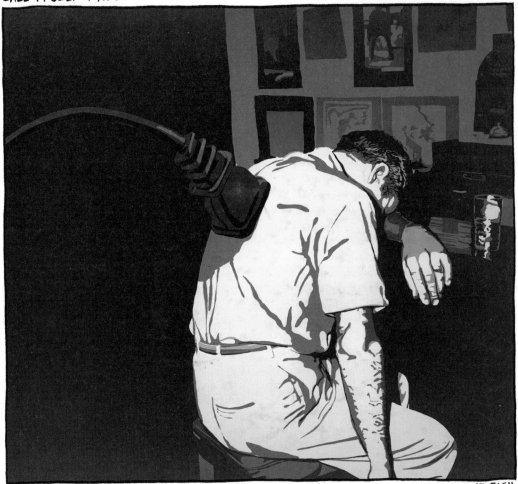

MR. FISH

people's natural desires are allowed to flourish and nobody is forced into doing anything that they don't want to do, the tribe will be able to sustain itself. It's really just an extension of the family model, where your natural tendencies are not to take food out of your own child's hand, or your mother's hand, or your wife's hand. It's when the community is allowed to bloat to a ridiculous degree, where the tribe is suddenly populated more by strangers than by those who you actually have some intimate knowledge of, that you run into problems.

We need some new big idea. The Enlightenment ideas are played out. Think of all the ideas that are dead and gone. What has to come along in the 21st century is a new uber myth/assumption/idea. There's a parallel, although no parallels are exact, as you know, between the death of Alexander, roughly 300 B.C., and the birth of Christ. And the birth of Christ rises at the same time as the Roman Empire — the old Roman Republic, after 100 years of civil war, gives way to the empyreal idea, in more or less the same few years that Christ is alive and well and walking the roads of Palestine. But in the 300 years between the end of the death of Alexander and the birth of Christ, there's no guiding idea and the only thing that counts is money. There's no other value. You don't get that much civilization coming out of that setup. I expect some idea to come out into the consciousness of the 21st century that will allow for some notion of sustained balance as opposed to unlimited growth.

Do you think it will take a catastrophe to wake people up to the necessity of that?

Yeah, I think so — but again, the language that that will be expressed in has to be congenial to the electronic media. Maybe we'll end up with a language that is more like a rebus or the Egyptian hieroglyph.

I would tend to think that the language would have to be detrimental to the electronic media — you know, that it should be the antithesis of the burgeoning shorthand that our increasing reliance on our technological advancements demand — if there's to be any hope for our survival. It's about learning how to deepen our comprehension of existence, to pause for contemplation rather than to merely ping-pong from one reaction to the next. Modern technology is much more prone to distracting people away from self-examination and self-discovery than encouraging [it], and we're getting to the point where we're able to create more and more abstract ideas that are more valuable than — and therefore more detrimental to — our own physical well-being. Again, I tend to think that the solution is often overlooked because of its simplicity and

that sometimes obviousness is a camouflage. Getting back to Jesus Christ and what made his teachings revolutionary — it wasn't the idea that if you structured your life a certain way that you'd be able to fly around in a nightgown with all your friends after you died, but rather it was about how the meek are worthy human beings. That idea was extremely radical at the time because it had nothing to do with any of the magic and fairy tale found elsewhere in the Bible, but instead it had the strength of being grounded in reality, the reality being that all human beings have value.

Well, yeah, [Jesus] is coming into the world when all of the societies at the time are based on slave labor. He was a radical and was perceived as such, which is why he was crucified. Garry Wills had a column once where he said that, if you're thinking about Christ, you're closer to the mark if you're thinking about Lenny Bruce than you are if you're thinking of Archbishop Russell. People don't like to hear the truth. You can go back to Plato who said that, "[People] see only their own shadows or the shadows of one another, which the fire throws on the opposite wall of the cave." The truth is like Plato's notion of the sun: You can't look at it, and the people who do either go blind or get killed.

That's a great metaphor as to how *trip-able* the trigger for doomsday is: we've been misspelling the subject noun of [the term] *Son of God* since its inception. It's spelled with a "u," not an "o."

He said putting on his /ˈsəŋˌlasəz/.

Exactly! If there is a universal reality it's most definitely being broadcast to us phonetically and we're transcribing it, removing the sound, which is *muting* it, and then pretending that the truth resides in our spelling.

"To the uneducated an *A* is just three sticks." [A.A. Milne]

And it is! ✳

BLURRED VISION

MY FIRST REACTION TO THE VIDEO released in 2012 of four U.S. Marines urinating on the bodies of dead Afghans was that it was too ham-fisted and bombastic a metaphor to add anything of real value to the ongoing critique and analysis of this country's über-mortiferous foreign policy. Similarly, if I were to see a video of a 500-pound CEO wearing a top hat, spats, a monocle and a watch chain walking through an Indonesian sweatshop while lighting a cigar with a $1,000 bill, I doubt that my disgust and outrage would have anything more substantial than an apparitional cliché into which to anchor its cleats. Watching these soldiers, deeply tanned from hours of volleyball back at the base no doubt, cheerfully peeing all over the bodies of indigenes, I felt as if I were looking at a Sue Coe painting that had been brought to life and then handed over to the Capitol Steps to assiduously overact, the stereotype of the Ugly American being turned up to 11 for those in the back of the Mark Russell Bawditorium who might be hard of sneering. Exaggeration, it turns out,

is no longer a tool with which a satirist can rely for enlightenment, not since the hyperbolics have been hijacked by ruthless plutocrats who discovered, through trial and error, that the best way to discredit the useful and telling symbolism of cartoon violence is to murder a *real* coyote with a *real* anvil in *real* life, or a *real* duck with a *real* shotgun, or a *real* rascally rabbit with a *real* stick of dynamite.

Rather than being presented with an inspirational image that rivals the famous Joe Rosenthal photograph of the five Marines and one Navy corpsman raising the U.S. flag at the top of Mount Suribachi during the Battle of Iwo Jima, the iGeneration is stuck with the image of four ebullient Marines outfitted with the most sophisticated weaponry available anywhere in the world, including body armor and what might be Versace sunglasses, pissing on three corpses of Taliban fighters who are all gaunt and barefoot and wearing clothes better suited for Frisbee or beach barbecue or Andrew Lloyd Webber.

What could turn out to be the most telling detail about the entire incident is how a number of online news agencies decided to censor the stills that had been extracted from the original video by blurring out the soldiers' penises while allowing a direct and uncompromising view of the dead bodies. Such a deliberate and widespread editorial decision provides clear insight into what the media, and therefore the dominant culture that they endeavor to reflect, consider to be obscene and what they deem to be innocuous and uncorrupting of our moral fortitude. Of course, as the proud owner of a penis myself — one that has undergone thousands of hours of excruciatingly thorough visual and tactile inspection, frank and glorious usability and withstood more rigorous endurance testing than a NASA chimp — I couldn't help but feel a little bit perplexed by the breakdown. To me it was like trying to preserve the innocence of a child who stumbles into his parents' bedroom while they're having intercourse and who continue to bump and grind against each other but decide, just before climax, to throw on hats and dark glasses and fake English accents. What is the fucking point? Likewise with the micturating Marines: Are not the cadaverous human beings pictured dead on the ground sufficiently off-putting to make the whizzing — the one and only detail depicted in the news item that is so mundanely commonplace and as familiar to all of us as breathing — the least offensive element, when isolated, of the crime? After all, we're talking about a 39-second clip that never would've been produced — never *could've* been produced — had we not decided as a nation to conflate invasion, occupation and mass slaughter with liberation, or foreign sovereignty with anti-Americanism, or war and murder with democracy building and peace-making, and yet what we decide to classify as being too disturbing to look at is the blatant demonstration of a bodily function that everybody and his grandmother partakes in 204,440 times over the course of a normal lifetime.

It seemed absolutely ludicrous!

Then, instead of choosing to scapegoat the blotting out of the male groins in the video on what everybody always scapegoats full frontal exposure of our human anatomy on, namely our oh-so preciously Victorian mores, I decided to consider an alternative explanation that was much less condescending of our character and much more deferential toward our intellectual moxie.

I began to wonder if I wasn't, in fact, witnessing the censorship of an enlightening fact rather than the shutting down of mere prurience. What if we were being encouraged to be afraid not of what these peckers might reduce us to but rather to what heights they might elevate our comprehension of ourselves as sentient beings?

Deciding to seek the grounding counsel of personal experience to further stoke my growing suspicions, I suddenly recalled some writing that I'd done on the subject of penile erudition back in 1986 and I reached for a journal that I had to blow the dust off of before handling.

When I was 19 years old, I posed naked for a life drawing class at Rutgers University and had this to say to what I imagined would be eager and receptive future generations afterward:

How did this happen? How did my pecker end up at the tip of 30 slow-moving pencils? More to the point, what business does my pecker have in defining for a bunch of teenagers what art is? That's like bringing Adolf Hitler into the room and asking him to teach the Foxtrot, or handing somebody a fistful of hundred dollar bills and asking him to appreciate the fine art of portraiture engraving. You'd think that a pecker in a classroom, set like a tiny basket of fruit before a sleepy mob of freshman boys and girls, is a little bit like a gnu forced to rest its great horned head on a filthy drain behind bars and before a wall painted to look like the African savanna. Rather than gaining some useful knowledge about the wonders of nature or the breathtaking majesty of the animal kingdom, one can only come away from gawking at such a spectacle a little bit dumber about the interconnectedness of man and beast.

Let me start at the beginning.

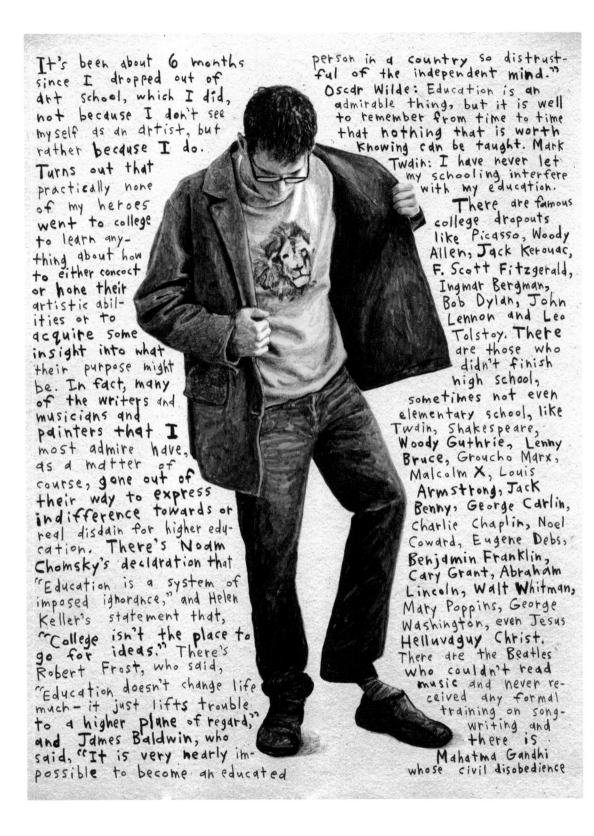

It's been about 6 months since I dropped out of art school, which I did, not because I don't see myself as an artist, but rather because I do. Turns out that practically none of my heroes went to college to learn anything about how to either concoct or hone their artistic abilities or to acquire some insight into what their purpose might be. In fact, many of the writers and musicians and painters that I most admire have, as a matter of course, gone out of their way to express indifference towards or real disdain for higher education. There's Noam Chomsky's declaration that "Education is a system of imposed ignorance," and Helen Keller's statement that, "College isn't the place to go for ideas." There's Robert Frost, who said, "Education doesn't change life much — it just lifts trouble to a higher plane of regard," and James Baldwin, who said, "It is very nearly impossible to become an educated person in a country so distrustful of the independent mind." Oscar Wilde: Education is an admirable thing, but it is well to remember from time to time that nothing that is worth knowing can be taught. Mark Twain: I have never let my schooling interfere with my education.

There are famous college dropouts like Picasso, Woody Allen, Jack Kerouac, F. Scott Fitzgerald, Ingmar Bergman, Bob Dylan, John Lennon and Leo Tolstoy. There are those who didn't finish high school, sometimes not even elementary school, like Twain, Shakespeare, Woody Guthrie, Lenny Bruce, Groucho Marx, Malcolm X, Louis Armstrong, Jack Benny, George Carlin, Charlie Chaplin, Noel Coward, Eugene Debs, Benjamin Franklin, Cary Grant, Abraham Lincoln, Walt Whitman, Mary Poppins, George Washington, even Jesus Helluvaguy Christ. There are the Beatles who couldn't read music and never received any formal training on songwriting and there is Mahatma Gandhi whose civil disobedience

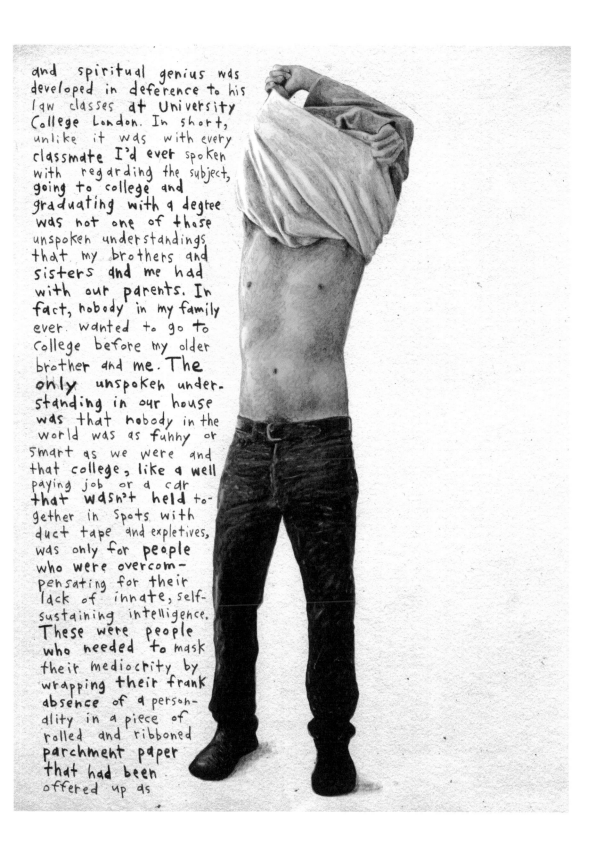

and spiritual genius was developed in deference to his law classes at University College London. In short, unlike it was with every classmate I'd ever spoken with regarding the subject, going to college and graduating with a degree was not one of those unspoken understandings that my brothers and sisters and me had with our parents. In fact, nobody in my family ever wanted to go to college before my older brother and me. The only unspoken understanding in our house was that nobody in the world was as funny or smart as we were and that college, like a well paying job or a car that wasn't held together in spots with duct tape and expletives, was only for people who were overcompensating for their lack of innate, self-sustaining intelligence. These were people who needed to mask their mediocrity by wrapping their frank absence of a personality in a piece of rolled and ribboned parchment paper that had been offered up as some sort of triumphant proof that they could memorize shit and repeat it back, their hollowness made somehow whole by the addition of an academic echo. In fact, the only reason why I went to college was to get out of South Jersey, which, after 17 years, was beginning to make me wonder if perhaps the only reason why my family was able to see itself as being so superior to everybody else was because we'd actually emigrated from Pennsylvania and weren't really from there, which appeared to give us an unfair advantage over people who seemed to have set the bar so low for themselves, not so much because they were stupid or lazy, but rather because — after ZZ Top, CB radio, fishin', crabbin', huntin', prayin', smokin', pokin', tokin', cokin', teen pregnancy and tournament level alcohol- ism — they where absolutely apeshit about limbo. "How low can you go? How low can you go...?"

So what am I doing here?

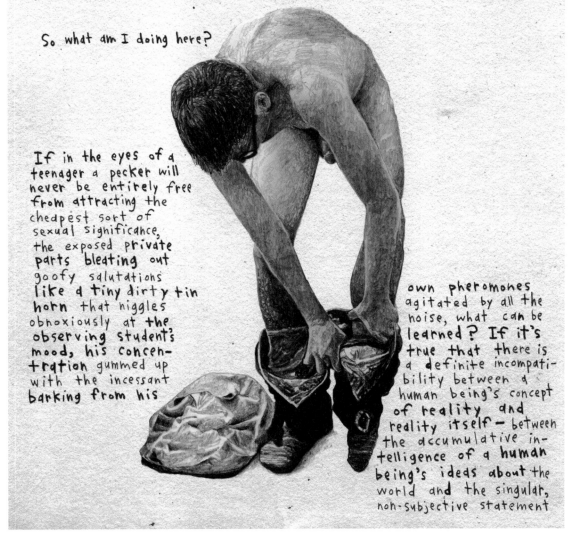

If in the eyes of a teenager a pecker will never be entirely free from attracting the cheapest sort of sexual significance, the exposed private parts bleating out goofy salutations like a tiny dirty tin horn that niggles obnoxiously at the observing student's mood, his concen- tration gummed up with the incessant barking from his own pheromones agitated by all the noise, what can be learned? If it's true that there is a definite incompati- bility between a human being's concept of reality and reality itself — between the accumulative in- telligence of a human being's ideas about the world and the singular, non-subjective statement of fact that is the world, itself, which is a world that remains unchanged and indifferent to what human beings wish or think about it — then an artist might best be described as a person who tries to fill the glorious and terrifying swimming space between those two points with objects and concepts that either celebrate the boundless freedom of weightlessness or embrace the spookiness of the unmoored anarchy so expertly revealed by the Existentialists and Dadaists.

So the question remains: How, precisely, is my pecker integral to the shaping of an art student into an artist? Should I assume, if I'm to trust completely all that is promised by the course description, that all peckers point, like compass needles, to the same creative nirvana wherein an artist can develop his expertise and ultimately find employment, power and influence? Or, I wonder, is it the purpose of my pecker to be an insignificant part of a life drawing class, the mere purpose of which is to teach a high school graduate whose SAT scores were too shitty to qualify him for an English program the cheap parlor trick, a mechanical skill really, of rendering a human body accurately, first naked and then clothed?

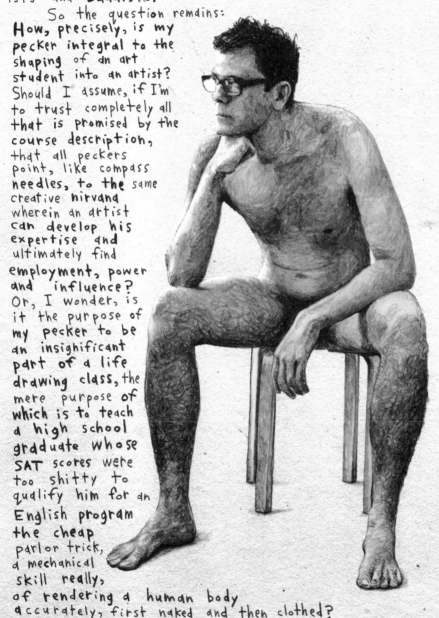

What then? Does he then matte and frame his crap and become just another asshole who can make money selling shit to people? I wish there were fewer of those sonuvabitches around, not more. But, then, maybe it isn't about the commodity that's produced by the act of art making that defines the artistry of the artist, nor is it about satiating the intellectual or emotional hunger of the observer first and foremost. Maybe being able to draw like a motherfucker brings an artist closer to some kind of insight about the human condition that other skills, like cross stitching and pillow embroidery, don't and then maybe the ability to render other people in the world with pencil and paper helps him dispel, for himself, the bogus notion that he is alone in the universe. Maybe it's that personal. Maybe all that nakedness machine gunned into an artist's brain, nude model after nude model, eventually teaches him to demystify the singular obscenity of the individual cock or the individual pussy, the balls, the tits and the ass, and integrates them into the rest of the human anatomy, like pouring notes into an allegretto or alliteration into a poem. Maybe it teaches him, then, to recognize the sameness that all people, naked beneath their clothes, share as a virtue, a grace: proof,

Somehow, that humanity is comprised of 7 billion specialized cells that conspire to create an immensely complicated planetary organism that requires cooperation and equal respect from all its parts to remain cohesive and alive and purposeful.

Is it then the responsibility of the art student to draw my pecker and to become an artist whose job it is to unify all of humanity around the same holistic worldview, his ability to grab the public's attention with his gifts merely the thing that he piggybacks his goal of rescuing the species from self-annihilation upon? Could my pecker really do all that? Have I been blessed by the great good fortune to be partnered with the wizened sage, the bald Mahatma, the bearded orator and Savior predicted to arrive one day by countless prophecies from practically every culture that has ever existed since the beginning of time for the purpose of setting the world ablaze with truth and beauty and spiritual glee?

(Pause to allow the sound, from offstage right, of Roman soldiers busying themselves with the gathering of the boards, the hammers and the nails.)

My mom is always telling me that I can be whatever I want to be when I grow up, usually capping the list with "even President of the United States." I only wish she had more faith in my ability to become a contributing member of society. Why doesn't she ever say I can be an "empathetic anarchist anti-authoritarian philosopher spiritually-grounded skeptic avant-garde dissident agitator organizing artist activist who is unwilling to compromise his humanity for a buck?"

Because that sounds an awful lot like "completely unemployable."

MR·FISH

CALVIN TRILLIN:
WHO'S YOUR DADA?

"Every good idea sooner or later degenerates into hard work."

— Calvin Trillin

IN 1913 ELSA VON FREYTAG-LORINGHOVEN found a three-and-a-half-inch corroding iron ring in the street on her way to get married at City Hall in New York City and called it art, naming it *Enduring Ornament*. Around the same time in Paris Marcel Duchamp attached an upside-down bicycle wheel to the seat of a small white stool, just to enjoy its movement on occasion the same way that one might enjoy a fireplace log, a windchime or the nearly inaudible twittering of a beloved child's hand set alone in a corner coloring. Designated as a new form of sculpture made from complete or partial objects found in everyday life — a concept further expounded upon in subsequent years by Elsa's *God* and Marcel's

Fountain, copied by Pablo Picasso with *Bull's Head* and eventually echoed with the wriest of smiles by Warhol's *Brillo Box* — these *readymades* presented themselves as the purest form of non-fiction in three-dimensional visual art.

Consider the revelatory thrill one must've felt upon witnessing the wholly unmiraculous birth of something mundane *NOT* being manipulated by either artist or audience into representing something grandiose, existential or metaphorical. Here suddenly was an artform made special by its not being special at all. For the first time in art history the very act of interpretation was being discouraged, where the peacockery of symbolism was being shooed away with haste so that the invisibly banal could be pulled into a spotlight and given a tin cymbal salute as a way to acknowledge with relief and glee that we are not gods capable of granting meaning to some subordinate reality rendered with us in mind. Instead, the message was this: *we are a family of winsome fools who have engineered an elaborate theatrical production full of distracting props and backdrops that are part of a grand illusion concocted to keep us from recognizing how we are little more than loathsome and lovable children who continuously mistake our goofy and prideful commitment to surrounding ourselves with impressive towers of balanced blocks for the expert execution of order, stability and security.*

In other words, the Dadaists were literalists who taught us that our dignity and intellectual and spiritual acuity have all the intrinsic worth of a rusty bit of metal scavenged from a roadway and all the extrinsic significance of eternal wonder — and isn't that endearingly absurd? Does not the sublime indifference resulting from a full-blown conflict between frank usability and conceptual obsolescence offer a recuperative break in the cognitive shitststorm that we all endure every day when attempting to square the many differences there are between what we experience with our five senses and how we interpret those experiences using a fickle and gloriously subjective imagination?

Surely there must be a certain amount of genius to the revelatory power of being caught in the stupefying crossfire of such silliness — right?

❀ ❀ ❀

Calvin Trillin began his writing career as a journalist for *TIME* magazine in the late 1950s, reporting primarily on the burgeoning civil rights movement in the South. Before long he had moved his reporting to the pages of *The New Yorker*, where he also began contributing casuals and humorous travel pieces chronicling the experiences he had on the road moving between assignments, later to become part of a reoccurring series called U.S. Journal. These are the essays that would eventually morph into columns about eating in small towns and cities all over the country. While working on staff for *The New Yorker*, he also wrote regularly for such publications as Hugh Hefner's *Playboy*, Victor Navasky's *Monocle* and had a regular column in *The Nation* called

Uncivil Liberties. He even contributed to a television pilot on New York's independent Channel 5 for a satirical comedy program called *What's Going On Here?: A Shrewd and Somewhat Rude Look at the News*, later to be picked up by CBS and boiled down to a short-lived segment on the *Ed Sullivan Show*.

All of this begs a question that one might imagine sounding an awful lot like one likely proposed by an art critic perplexed in 1914 by the sight of a drying rack for wine bottles displayed in an art gallery and called *Bottle Rack:* How does one move from excavating the facts about the desegregation of the University of Georgia in the Jim Crow South or investigating the tragic suicide of a Yale classmate named Denny to delivering, with the same measured tone and attention to detail, an exposé on potential bathroom scale tampering by a wife named Alice or the rage of a full-grown man losing a game of tic-tac-toe to a Chinatown chicken and then blaming his defeat on the flimsy rationale that the chicken had accrued more playing time than he had?

The answer, of course, is this: the only difference between hardcore journalism and joke-making is that joke-making tends to be more succinct, memorable and respectful of your time.

❀ ❀ ❀

I met Trillin on the morning of June 29 in 2008 at his home in Greenwich Village. He was in the midst of packing for his yearly sojourn into the Nova Scotia summertime and upon entering I was instructed to remove a pair of blue and white to-go Greek coffee cups from a paper bag. "I grabbed those for us a couple hours ago," he said. "I figured we could warm them up in the microwave." This from the most popular food writer in lower Manhattan, though, having never read any books or columns about food from other writers and not being able to cook, himself, he would insist that he didn't write about food as much as he wrote about consuming what different cultures and ethnicities expressed through various menus.

What follows is a portion of a conversation that lasted for two hours, which I would say was about the past, present and future of political satire and he would say was about the good, bad and ugly of apolitical humor that may on occasion singe bureaucratic folly just enough to make us all feel slightly more hopeful.

128

✱ ✱ ✱

When you were growing up in Kansas City, what forms of comedy were you most excited by?

Radio — Jack Benny. He was my favorite and I loved all the characters on the show. Jack with his stinginess, Phil Harris with his drinking —

Mary Livingstone with her wisecracks.

Dennis Day with his ditziness. Just amazing! Really great timing. I [also] used to listen to Fred Allen and *Fibber McGee and Molly,* but Jack Benny was by far the best. And that was really about it.

Was there any particular moment when you first saw the potential of applying humor politically? I'm referring, of course, to what inspired you to become a contributor to *Monocle* [satirical magazine] and *That Was the Week That Was* [NBC satirical tv show that aired in 1963 and '64, derived from the British version that aired on the BBC in 1962 and '63]. There was also a show called *What's Going On Here?* that you wrote for.

Is that what it was called? I can't remember the name of it. You're talking about the one that ended up on [*The Ed Sullivan Show*]?

Yeah.

I'm not sure I remember the details, but this is how I think it happened. I met Victor [Navasky] when I was in the Army on Governor's Island.

Was he there, too?

No, he was in the Army in Alaska, I think. He was out of law school and working for "Soapy" [G. Mennen] Williams [41st Governor of Michigan]. I met him through a friend who had also gone to Swarthmore — I don't remember the details, but that's how that came about, sort of accidentally. The thing about *Monocle* is that they didn't really pay anything for their articles, and, in fact, they once sent me a bill for a piece that they said was going to cost them more to process than they had. Richard Lingeman would be a good source for you if you want to find out about the early days because he's the only person whose life Victor managed to ruin twice. He was at Yale Law School, about to graduate and make millions of dollars as a Wall

Street lawyer, and Victor said, "No, what you want to do is become the managing editor of a doomed magazine of political satire." And then when [Lingeman] finally picked himself up from that disaster and got on the *New York Times Book Review* and was about to be vested in his pension plan, Victor said, "No, no — you don't want that. You want to be managing editor of a failing left wing political magazine." So, he's been there from the very beginning.

I once got a rejection letter from Lingeman that I have framed next to my writing desk. It has so many typos in it that's it's almost indecipherable.

Now you know why. Anyway, it was through Victor and *Monocle* that I met the remnants of the *Beyond the Fringe* people. As you probably know, *Beyond the Fringe* [the British comedy group made up of Peter Cook, Dudley Moore, Alan Bennett and Jonathan Miller] was a huge landmark in the satire boom in the 1960s and it wasn't just because of the subjects [they lampooned], but also who they were. They were college guys, and not just *college guys*, but college guys from Oxford and Cambridge.

Right — I guess the idea was that elite institutions weren't supposed to produce satirists. They were supposed to churn out the targets that satirists took aim at.

Yeah, they were very smart. And [at the end of their tour] they ended up in New York and a couple of them were still hanging around. So I found myself in a meeting with Peter Cook and John Bird, who wasn't one of the *Fringe* guys, but was on a Canadian show called *Quest* [an anthology series that featured dramas, musical performances and short documentaries] — this was around the beginning of 1963, around the time when I was leaving *TIME* and headed over to *The New Yorker* — and the idea was that we would try to do a show of political satire for [American] television. We made the pilot and Peter Cook was in it, and so was John Bird and a wonderful black comedian named Godfrey Cambridge, who died quite young. A really funny guy who was also know for carrying ball bearings around in his pocket so that if a cab passed him by because he was black he would throw them through the back window. He originally worked as a professional laugher — he

TheNation.

33 IRVING PLACE, NEW YORK, NY 10003-2332 TEL: (212) 209-5400 FAX: (212) 982-9000 E-MAIL: INFO@THENATION.COM

Dear Mr. Booth:

We can't qite see the cartoon but try us again. And I'm afraid the essay doens't work for us either. Sorry, but thants for letting us see he material.

Sincerely,

Richard Lingeman, Senior Editor

○ Printed on recycled paper.

was a great laugher. Anyway, I think Jonathan Miller was the director [of *What's Going on Here?*] and there were a bunch of writers, four or five, and it was on Channel 5 in New York and after it aired there was an attempt to get it on [national network] television, which of course was going to be hard because programming was a very narrow field in those days, [especially for political satire]. It was finally decided that it would be on *The Ed Sullivan Show* in ten or twelve-minute segments. It seemed like one of those ideas you see in a Mickey Rooney movie or something — *"This is so crazy that it just might work!"* I remember going with Clay Felker [tv producer, magazine editor, journalist and co-founder of *New York Magazine*] to talk to Bob and Ray [American radio, television and theater comedy duo whose careers together spanned fifty years] about whether they would be the anchormen on the show.

Was this the first time you had met them?

Oh, yeah. Anyway, they were very skeptical about coming onboard, with good reason. Sullivan had a son-in-law who was a producer and his name was Bob Precht. He looked like the guy who sits quietly in the office while the Nazi field officer says to the downed American pilot, "I hope you'll cooperate — if not, Herr Müller here has his methods." He was blond and may have had a scar. Maybe I'm imagining that. Anyway, Bob said, "I can see what'll happen. We'll rehearse on Monday and Tuesday and around Thursday Ed will come by to look at the run-through for the first time. He'll watch for a while then he'll call me over and say, 'Bob, is the Berosini Family around anywhere? I like those monkey acts. We can put them in instead of this.'" But we did do it, two or three times, and it was completely unlikely and, I assume, a terrible failure. We may as well have done it on the Lawrence Welk Show. Needless to say, we had content problems.

Why? Because it was truly dangerous satire or because any criticism of public servants or the culture back then was just considered rude and inappropriate behavior?

Yes, absolutely, it was the culture. I remember having this argument with Ed [Sullivan]. We went to see him in his suite at the Regency just above Grand Central. I had written a sketch with my friend, Gerry Jones, about two guys waiting for an elevator, a black guy and a white guy. They don't say anything while they're waiting and then finally when the elevator door opens the white guy says [to the black guy], "Oh, you must go first. You've endured 300-years of slavery." And they exchange these race relations clichés and the doors eventually close and the elevator goes down — that's all! And Sullivan said, "Oh, no, we couldn't possibly put that on network television!" Just the recognition that one of the guys was black and the other one was white and that they were actually *talking* to each other, *that* was enough to get us kicked off the show!

Maybe if you'd said *300-years of alleged slavery* or *300-years of living rent-free* it would've been less controversial. And what about your work on *That Was the Week That Was?*

That Was the Week That Was was a direct import from England, sort of the equivalent of the American *Office*, which was imported from Ricky Gervais. David Frost came over from the British show, which had been canceled, to do the American version. He always made me shudder whenever he read one of my lines. You know, one of the greatest things ever said at a memorial was said by Alan Bennett [English playwright, screenwriter and actor] at Peter Cook's [service]. Peter Cook was just hilarious! He was also a really destructive guy and drank a lot. Anyway, at the memorial Bennett said he'd been reading in the press that Peter had had a lot of remorse in recent years about how he'd behaved in his life. "Absolute nonsense," said Bennett. "I think I knew him as well as anybody and the only thing I ever heard him express regret for was that in 1963, in a house he'd rented in Connecticut, he once saved David Frost from drowning." (*Laughing*) That's just brilliant! At any rate, I was too involved with reporting to get enmeshed [with more tv] so I made a deal that I would walk over once a week from *The New Yorker* and hand them a packet of two-liners and fake news items and that was really my only connection with that operation. I don't think it was very successful.

Well, I'd guess that writing satire for television in the early days must've been close to impossible, particularly when, as a writer, you're trying to get your criticism of the government and conventional society past advertisers and network executives

who don't want to offend a mainstream audience that might not want to imagine the world is anything less than benign and serviceable.

That's right.

And speaking of humor as a vocation, I remember you saying something in your *Paris Review* interview from 1995 about being funny. You said that you're either funny or you're not and that wanting to be funny doesn't mean you're going to be.

No, I don't think it's a learnable skill. I usually compare it to the person in the family who can bend his thumb back and touch his wrist. It's a minor facility. It's not like being able to correct club feet or something like that and I don't think it's correlated with intelligence. There was this guy, a distinguished social scientist at Columbia, who used to send these things to *Monocle* all the time that were just awful. You could just see the cranes straining and dropping these giant concrete blocks that he thought were hilarious.

I've always thought that the arts were mostly made up of people who wanted to be artists rather than those who have no other choice other than to be artists.

Or they're artists because they see it as a birthright, like with academics. Sometimes it's a lineage thing that a person just adopts and they become part of an ingroup and they have no real contact with the outside world. Supposedly, and I don't know if this is an apocryphal story or not, but there was this study done where [pollsters] went to a supermarket in West Los Angeles and asked everybody who came out how far along they were on their screenplay and everybody had an answer. So, as long as you have an independent income from somewhere, or don't mind how you live, you can be a writer because, as a writer, there's no requirement that you're attached to anything external that might define you as one.

Which brings us to an interesting phenomenon that I think might have to do with the consolidation of media outlets and the concentration of ownership over the last decades. Art and information are meaningless without a distribution mechanism and it seems to me that the availability of certain kinds of artistic, journalistic and

politically radical points of view have been altered by a seismic shift in how material is shared with an audience. Specifically, it seems that mediocre writers and artists are the ones getting the jobs over the [truly talented] ones because the distribution mechanism is largely controlled by big business; big business that sees an audience as customers to be exploited for their income stream rather than as participants in a social democracy that need to be informed for the greater good. I guess what I want to ask you, since you were working in the industry and living in the world when art and information seemed better able to criticize power and enlighten a wider range of people and to break down barriers of prejudice and distrust between subsects of [the rank and file] — what happened? How did the counterculture become the consumer class without anybody knowing they should panic over the transition? Why do I now live my life every day feeling like a victim of your missed opportunity — or was it my generation's responsibility to revolt against your revolution? I keep looking for somebody to blame.

Said the forest through the trees. (*Laughing*) Listen, [pandemic enlightenment] didn't happen, but a lot of things did happen. For instance, the difference between what Jon Stewart is able to do on *The Daily Show* and what we were able to do on *The Ed Sullivan Show* is enormous. I actually thought once that I might have to leave *The New Yorker* because [William] Shawn (editor of magazine) wasn't going to let me say that Lester Maddox (Governor of Georgia) said the federal government could take its education money and ram it. He finally did let me say that, but it was a struggle. There's been a tremendous liberation in what can be published. I just wrote a piece where supposedly non-racist kids were rushing to a hospital with a friend who had just been shot and the 911 call they were one hadn't been [disconnected] and they thought it had and so you can hear them on the tape saying, "Turn right here, and turn left...!" and then the kid in the backseat says, "Don't worry, Dano. We're going to get those fucking niggers!" It never occurred to me that I would have a hard time getting that published in *The New Yorker* today. When I worked at *TIME* in 1963 all the writers were men and all the researchers were women by policy! I grew up in legally segregated schools. So, yeah, it really has changed a lot.

I'll grant you that women and minorities have greater access to rights, respect and opportunities, no doubt about it. My worry, however, is that the power of the dominant culture has increased so much and become so pervasive that nobody feels encouraged to exercise these freedoms beyond how they conduct themselves within the system. We're probably going to be electing our first black President, which will be positive on some level, but I can guarantee you that he's not going to be Martin Luther King. Same with Hillary Clinton. If she had won the primary and become President it would've been the same thing — she's not Gloria Steinem or Angela Davis, she's Margaret Thatcher with better teeth. You can see a parallel with the 1st Amendment. Everybody is so proud to point out that we have freedom of speech and that we can challenge [doctrinal power structures], but how often do you see that happen? Humor is only ever allowed to criticize [the government and big business] because it's largely assumed that jokes are harmless and, by and large, they are.

Harmless in the sense that they're incapable of doing anything on their own?

Right — but something had to be different about political satire in the late '50s, '60s and early '70s. What was it? Was it because there was a more radical element functioning inside the society that wasn't harmless and posed a threat to the dominant culture and knew how to use humor to tell the truth? My understanding is that these were [radical] elements that were attempting to exercise their freedoms *outside* the system — *contrary* to it, in fact! While I love Jon Stewart, at the end of the day he is Viacom and none of his jokes are ever [going to be] pointed enough to be used to question the legitimacy of [the prevailing hierarchy]. In other words, I'm never angry when I finish watching *The Daily Show*, the same way I might be after listening to Bill Hicks or George Carlin. I'm entertained, and then a little sick because I feel like a prisoner who just got finished coloring in a coloring book.

I'm not sure I agree with that. [Television] satire was barely satire [back then]. I mean, we were on *The Ed Sullivan Show*, which was the most mainstream show in America.

But that's my point — whenever you see political satire presented in the mainstream, aren't you looking at something that's signaling the death of [the artform], whether it was 50 years ago or now?

In the sense that the mainstream swallows up satire?

Yeah.

Oh, yeah! But that's the point I was making earlier — I think the mainstream has changed and [now it at least] understands satire better.

Well then maybe the conversation should be about where political satire exists away from the mainstream. In the 1960s, if you wanted to see somebody demonstrating the most fearless sort of satire, stuff that was never going to be on *The Ed Sullivan Show*, you had to go to a nightclub. Now consider that in contrast to watching Jon Stewart on television. To see Lenny Bruce, for example, you had to go to a public place so that when you saw him you were making a sort of declaration that you were interested in anarchism — or at least some sort of demonstration of antiauthoritarianism. And, because it was Bruce, you were also saying that you were willing to be an outlaw by association because the police might arrest Lenny and, by paying for a ticket, that you were willing to be an accessory to his crime of criticizing power. Compare that with Stewart. When you watch [*The Daily Show*] it's a private act and you're not risking anything. When you watch *The Daily Show* you're demonstrating your commitment to free expression by staying inside your house, which is the opposite of political engagement.

I think that maybe you're reading too much into it. I think that has more to do with declining nightclubs than anything else.

Regardless, the psychology component can't be ignored. It's like somebody going to Old Navy and getting a t-shirt with a peace sign on it and then thinking they're part of the peace movement. By the same token, it would be a mistake for me to get in my car and put on my seat belt and then pat myself on the back because I think I'm preventing traffic accidents in New Delhi.

Again, I think those people [who mimic social awareness and have none] have always been around. Also, I'd say there are people in nightclubs now who are just as far out as [Mort] Sahl and [Lenny] Bruce were. It's just that they're accepted now.

By whom? That's my point. If these people exist, they are so marginalized that nobody knows their names. I certainly don't.

Maybe they're on HBO. Remember, [there are] more places for stand-up comedians to perform than there used to be. When I was younger, there were no comedy clubs. There was the Borsht Belt and a couple small private clubs and some lounges in Vegas, but that was it. I'm going to sound like an old guy, but there was a time in America when there were no gyms, either. There were a couple for weightlifting, but other than that there were no gyms. There were no fitness centers in hotels or anything like that and nobody ran around the streets in shorts — *nobody!* Gyms and comedy clubs are both fairly recent phenomena.

I take your point, but I'm still suspicious of what happened to the caliber of [commentative] art being produced today as compared to previous generations. I'd suggest that there may be a [telling corollary] between art [as contrarianism] and cultural criticism. If I had to name the leading dissidents among public intellectuals nowadays, I'd say Noam Chomsky, Howard Zinn, Gore Vidal, Edward Said, Susan Sontag, people like that, and they're all in their seventies and eighties! In fact, they're the same people who were the leading dissidents in the '60s! If there are more venues for comedians then I'd still say that the best comedians are being drowned out by [a cacophony of] commercially acceptable artists, which, in the end, still qualifies as a kind of censorship.

I know what you mean. I read an article in *The New Yorker* all about how writers had changed and how Norman Mailer came to New York and represented a whole generation of writers who involved themselves more in politics and culture and all that. My take on that was the guy who wrote the article was upset because he wasn't Norman Mailer, as simple as that. Mailer was Mailer and he always intended to be a public intellectual.

He wanted to be part of things — he ran for mayor [in New York]! You're right that there aren't many people like that now, but I wonder if [people like Mailer] aren't just historical accidents.

The difference is that Mailer was asked to participate in our national discourse. So was [Kurt] Vonnegut, [Joan] Didion, Hunter S. Thompson — their opinions were sought after. Nowadays, artists are ridiculed if they offer an opinion about politics. During the invasion of Iraq, Tim Robbins and Sean Penn were always being told to shut up and sit down because they were actors who didn't know anything.

That was always the case, even during the Vietnam War — unless they were for the war; unless you were John Wayne.

Maybe actors aren't the best example — or maybe they are in this particular case because I can't think of any who spoke out against the war! So, I'll make my point that way! Sean Penn had to speak up because there was no Norman Mailer to speak up.

And forty years ago, no actor would speak up because the studios wouldn't let them, so that's progress. I didn't know what Robert Taylor's political opinions were because he wasn't allowed to talk about them.

There was the Hollywood Ten.

They were all writers — they weren't actors.

I do remember hearing tape of Humphrey Bogart and Lauren Bacall speaking out against the McCarthy Hearings. Maybe that's because Bogart was an independent actor without a studio contract. I'll have to look that up. At any rate, when it comes to communicating the human experience [during times of] both war and peace, I think we can agree that artists need to be involved in the conversation because artists are the ones best equipped to express those experiences in a way that others can't.

But, again, artists aren't the only ones who express those experiences, although they might be the best ones to do it. Where are the non-artists who [should also be] expressing those experiences? It's not as if [artists] are ordinarily vociferous and now they aren't vociferous and everybody else is — nobody else is, either.

And it's impossible to predict what will make people suddenly outspoken and what will suddenly make them silent again. It amazed me how huge the anti-war protests were before we invaded Iraq and how quickly they went away once the actual war started. There was something peculiar about having a movement against war going on when there wasn't one and then dissipating once there was.

That [reminds me of] one of Bush's great remarks. After watching the largest peace demonstration in the history of the world he said, "We don't govern by focus groups." (*Laughing*)

So, basically, you're saying that we shouldn't be asking how and why artists are failing us, but rather we should be asking how and why we are failing ourselves.

Sure — why should artists be any different than anybody else?

So, what makes everybody so disinterested in pushing back against the slow-motion doomsday that is [obviously] accelerating and seems [poised] to eradicate every living thing on the planet?

Cheap gas.

Not the internet? I'd say that modern technology has destroyed our ability to contemplate anything and that without contemplation we can only react to [things] and when we're only reacting to [things] we're not able to deliberate on all the complex narratives that confuse and distract us away from recognizing the real problems we face as human beings, forget about our politics and [the cosmetics of] our cultural differences.

Feel free to use *cheap gas* as a metaphor for [the internet]. I think we're saying the same thing — it's just that you're taking a lot longer to say it. ✳

DURING POPE FRANCIS' 2015 TOUR OF AMERICA THE PONTIFF MADE NUMEROUS OBSERVATIONS ABOUT THE WORLD THAT INSPIRED TREMENDOUS APPLAUSE AND PUBLIC RECOGNITION OF HIS VERY DEEP WISDOM.

I WONDERED HOW WISE MANY OF HIS PROCLAMATIONS WOULD BE IF PARAPHRASED AND OFFERED IN REGULAR SOCIAL SITUATIONS.

"PEOPLE SHOULD HAVE A JOB AND A PLACE TO LIVE. AND THEY SHOULD HAVE LAND."

"WHEN COUNTRIES WHO DON'T TALK TO EACH OTHER ACTUALLY TALK TO EACH OTHER, THINGS GET BETTER."

"BUSINESS IS REALLY COOL BECAUSE IT MAKES A SHITLOAD OF MONEY AND MAKES THE WORLD BETTER. IT ALSO MAKES JOBS."

PAY SOME ATTENTION TO THE MAN BEHIND THE CURTAIN

In those days, when we were all young and optimistic, I used to assure Navasky that the lack of a sense of humor was probably not an insurmountable handicap for the editor of a humor magazine."

—Calvin Trillin on Victor Navasky launching *Monocle* magazine

IN 1984 ILLUSTRATOR DAVID LEVINE CREATED a now infamous cartoon for *The New York Review of Books* depicting Henry Kissinger fucking the world. In the drawing, the former National Security Advisor and Secretary of State to President Nixon strains beady-eyed like a gargantuan rodent atop the naked and slight body of his conquest, the back of her enormous globe-head pressed forcefully into a pillow, her knees slightly bent, the Biblically-sanctioned missionary position perverted into a foul and nauseating display of crushing subjugation while the American flag covers them both like a distressed bedsheet.

First commissioned and then rejected by *The New York Review*, where Levine's work regularly

appeared, the cartoon was eventually published by *The Nation* following a week of internal protests waged by many on the staff to kill the artwork. According to Victor S. Navasky, who was the editor-in-chief of *The Nation* at the time, it was the only time during his 30-plus years heading the publication that the magazine personnel marched on his office and served him with a petition demanding that he refrain from running the drawing. Chief among the complaints was the criticism that "a progressive magazine has no business using rape jokes and sexist imagery to make the point that Kissinger revels in international dominance," as if commentary devised to condemn international dominance would or even could make sanguine use of pro-feminism imagery when excoriating the unfair domination of one entity over another.

Christopher Hitchens, who was a columnist for the magazine at the time, summed up the unfortunate episode this way: "How depressing that so many *Nation* colleagues should confuse the use of a stereotype, even as an artistic satire, with the reinforcement of a stereotype."

❀ ❀ ❀

I have interviewed Victor S. Navasky a number of times over the years and have never been able to use anything I transcribed from our long conversations. *Nothing*. As the founding editor of *Monocle*, considered by many to be the best magazine of New Left satire produced in *post*-postmodern America and the editor and publisher of *The Nation*, the oldest weekly of progressive journalism and cultural analysis in the country, not to mention a friend, mentor and enabler of practically every free press advocate, lefty writer, reporter and columnist alive, you'd think the man would have all the generous magnetism and gregarious charisma of whatever the I.F. Stone equivalent of a snow day might be. He doesn't. In fact, he is the most unassuming radical I've ever met, which, as it turns out, is his most inspiring strength and impressive asset. In other words, gravity too is unassuming, yet without it Molotov cocktails would never know to land on the polycarbonate shields of fascistic thugs nor would caricatured balloons designed to ridicule incompetent and reprobate world leaders be able to inspire us all by seeming to defy the very laws of physics in order to prove how impossible things like largescale levitation and a people's revolution are possible.

After considering everything Navasky had to say to me and my tape recorder and after finding only one quotation attributed to him in all the quote banks I could find on the internet (*"What's bad for the country is always good for The Nation"*) and after pouring over his many accomplishments in publishing and journalism and cultural analysis, I came to the conclusion that to look for egomania as proof of a person's legitimacy was ridiculous, not unlike attempting to measure the credibility of Rosa Park's legacy against her ability to do a handstand with a puppy on each foot or to snap a lit cigarette from the mouth of

a blindfolded audience member with a bullwhip while singing *Mule Train*. In fact, to equate one with the other would be to ignore every example from the past where ostentatious egomania was confused for legitimacy and suddenly there were warehouses full of shoes, hair and wedding rings and, silhouetted against a pewter skyline, greasy smokestacks full of swooping seagulls.

Here's an example of Navasky being pragmatic and unsentimental and me being, well, me.

❀ ❀ ❀

What made you want to launch a magazine of satire in the late '50s to begin with? Did you foresee the enormous cultural shift that was about to happen [with regards] to civil rights, the youth movement, the feminization of society, and free speech? Was it an instinct or an impulse to go into publishing instead of law after law school?

I was never in analysis, so I don't have the wisdom to tell you why, on some deep psychological level, I decide to do anything. Certainly, I thought there was something absurd about the assumptions of our political system and contradictions in society and I liked jokes just as much as the next guy.

Speaking of jokes, what happened to satire to make it less satirical and closer to being [mere] burlesque in the modern era? My guess is that whenever you have satire periodically interrupted by a commercial break, like with *Saturday Night Live*, *Robot Chicken*, *The Daily Show*, and shows like that, then it cannot possibly still be called satire because it is being used for the selling of products designed specifically to perpetuate a consumer class. And who does the consumer class benefit? [Pause] It benefits the very institutions of power that satire endeavors to undermine and disassemble in favor of a more equitable form of [egalitarian] living.

Yes. You're right.

Bill Hicks had a great bit about that. At some point during his career he was offered a sponsorship gig from a British cola company and the drink was called Orange Drink. He figured that the company had no idea who he was because he was famous in his act for telling people who worked in advertising that they should kill them-

selves. He imagined [doing the commercial and] saying, "You know, when I'm done ranting about elite power that rules the planet under a totalitarian government that uses the media to keep people stupid my throat gets parched. That's why I drink 'Orange Drink!'"

(*Laughing*) Okay.

So why do you think things are different now from when you got into the satire business?

When we started *Monocle* we had Lenny Bruce, Mort Sahl, *MAD* magazine, Harvey Kutzman, Terry Southern and those kinds of people. This was at the end of the McCarthy Era and it was generally understood that this was how you [broke] through after a period of repression. It's a sign that something good is happening in the culture after something bad.

How does that inform our understanding of what's happening right now, particularly when it comes to the apparent absence of a viable progressive art and alternative press scene? Are we really waiting for a period of repression to end before we react to it — should we be? I'm guessing that the repression we've been experiencing has been going on since 1980 and it doesn't show any signs that it'll be ending soon.

So do I think there's a satire shortage?

Not just satire, but all forms of open communication capable of forcing the dominant culture to engage with dissenting opinions and attitudes.

I don't think it's as bad as you say it is, although I might be wrong about that.

It seems that every time I see a panel discussion about politics or culture it's always the same people who say the same things. The debate is almost always [narrowly] defined as a disagreement between the Democrats and the Republicans and the only solutions [proposed by either side] are political ones. I always feel like I'm watching ESPN where everybody is talking about the strategies of how their team should be playing the game to win but there's nobody there to question the folly of the game. Imagine if you had an artist or even a social philosopher sitting in on one of

those panels! There's never anybody with an outside perspective to challenge the myopia.

Artists are unto themselves. Some can talk, some can't. Sure, they're geniuses, but what do they add to a panel except to sit there and to be incoherent?

But they're not even being allowed to communicate what their genius is using the language that they're expert in, that's the point, whether it's painting, music, poetry, satire, cartooning or even gonzo journalism.

I don't have a problem if satire doesn't work. What if there's a period [when] there are no good satirists? That doesn't bother me. Maybe it isn't a reflection of how repressive a society is. Maybe it has more to do with there being no good satirists at the moment. It can happen. That said, you're probably right that the only people talking about politics is a rotating repertoire company that should let other people into the discussion.

❊ ❊ ❊

There's an argument to be made that even Jackson Pollack would have lost coherency without being forced to communicate within the parameters of his canvas corners. Similarly, neither Henry Miller's *Tropic of Cancer* nor Kalkhosru Shapurji Sorabji's four-hour solo piano composition, *Opus clavicembalisticum*, would be legible at all without remaining within the confines a structured alphabet. Much of what Victor S. Navasky seems to communicate is that there are instinctual confines that exist within all people and that our mutual humanitarianism is structured and innate and nothing that should require strict regimentation from external bureaucratic mandates. He reminds us that we don't have to be livid to remain pissed off about injustice and that our panic over the possible eradication of independent thinking in the country isn't about facing the imminent death of free will, itself, as much as it's about misinterpreting sleep. After all, if anarchism is what the Oxford English Dictionary says it is, which is a "belief in the abolition of all government and the organization of society on a voluntary, cooperative basis without recourse to force or compulsion," then those who seem unable to recognize its purpose as anything other than to encourage unregulated mayhem may have simply never learned how to recalibrate their comprehension of themselves and the world to account for moments instead of millennia and persons instead of people.

Specifically, without people as exacting and practical as Navasky, the leading rabble-rousers in the trenches might not have the wherewithal to dot their i's and cross their t's, without which there might not be any demands from the most vocal champions of our social democracy for establishment toadies to *Eat shit and die!* — nor, of course, would there be the potential for the rest of us to warn those with the loudest megaphones not to mistake the volume with which they shout as anything other than the wailing infancy of a frustrated future authority. ✳

NOW THAT THE COCK
HAS WOKEN YOU UP

WHAT ARE YOU
GOING TO DO?

TUCHUSES AND NAY-NAYS

LENNY BRUCE, saintly believer in the First Amendment of the U.S. Constitution and eloquent teaser of all that had previously deemed itself to be unticklish, had a bit in his act where he talked about the greatest entertainment draw of modern civilization not being a Monet exhibit but rather being *tits and ass*. In his performance he described a pair of nightclub promoters on the Las Vegas Strip discussing what to put on their marquee to advertise tits and ass in such a way as to help their audience not appear so depraved at patronizing a show designed to perpetuate the not-so-fine art of ogling. *Tuchuses and nay-nays* was suggested as an option, which, to me, became a metaphor for what it meant to replace the literal meaning of something with the figurative meaning; that is, to replace the facts with a value judgment that had less to do with the truth and more to do with a particular interpretation of the truth,

which, contrary to the real truth, was much more user-friendly because it was exempt from needing to merely reflect reality and didn't need to be corroborated by anything or anybody. It became an opinion that could be carried around in the brain, where it could be edited and tweaked and reworked and perverted into something wholly self-serving, oftentimes gaining more detail and more prestige than the real world would ever be likely to lavish upon it. In fact, with the volume turned up on its appeal, an interpretation of reality will oftentimes seem more real than the reality that it's interpreting, even when the reality is standing in stark contrast and in blatant opposition to the outlandish claims of the interpretation. (Think of the divine celebrity of royal lineages or the groundless claims of the Aryans espousing genetic superiority over non-Aryans, where the proof is never in the putrid pudding.)

Tuchuses and nay-nays, thusly, became for me an explanation as to how only those willing to frame their understanding of the world in terms of how well their opinions interacted with the opinions of others could be counted upon to so consistently rebuke the First Amendment and to perceive the existence of a contrary point of view as being grotesque and inciting and completely unacceptable.

Rewind to mid-August in 1975. "Oh, for crap-sake," seethed my mother, rinsing the vodka from the small green plastic cup that she kept under the kitchen sink with all the other solvents. "Don't tell me that you're turning into that pot-smoking hippie freak who just lurched out the front door with her hair in her face?" She was talking about the babysitter who, with her patchwork bell-bottom pants, hand-sewn blouses fashioned from loud curtains and a fondness for the word *bullshit*, had become the secret love of my life.

"I'm not talking about Anna, no," I said, sitting at the dining room table painting blood on the hands of a Godzilla model. "I was just asking a question."

"If you think you're an incomplete person, somehow, just because I didn't eat your placenta like a goddamn hyena when you were born, you're way off, Buster Brown," she said, lighting a cigarette like a fuse for her mood. "*Way* off."

"I just wanted to know if, when I'm at school, I could give somebody my ring finger instead of my middle finger. I couldn't get in trouble for that, could I? I mean, technically?"

"What the hell kind of job does she think she's preparing for by joining the Peace Corps, anyway? What goes on the resume after that, I wonder? 'Has bad breath and wipes ass with hibiscus leaves and will refuse to stand for the "Star Spangled Banner" ' — wonderful! I'll tell you one thing, when that girl menstruates, everybody knows about it."

"She's a free spirit," I said, not knowing at age 9 what the word *menstruates* meant.

"Yeah, *free*," said my mother, chuckling and blowing smoke. "The only thing that makes that girl not a whore is the fact that she doesn't take money from boys who want to see what the top of her head looks like when its banging against the bottom of a steering wheel — I'll say that she's *free*. Birth control for that idiot is a stick of chewing gum."

"Mom," I said, impatiently drumming my fingers against the table, "can you just answer the question?"

"You'll figure it out for yourself when you're older, trust me," she said, shaking her head. "When a girl shows up at a quarter 'til nine on a Sunday morning raking at her crotch like a cocker spaniel and asking if she can take a quick shower before she starts work, well, you can put two and two together. All I'll say is that when she was done, her hair was still dry and the bathtub looked

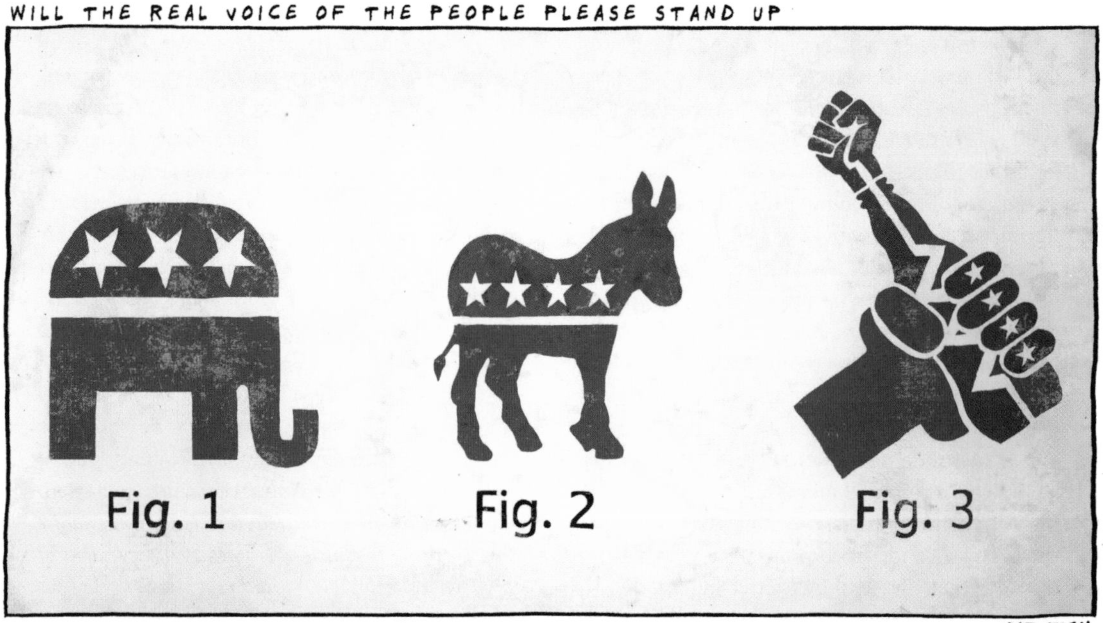

WILL THE REAL VOICE OF THE PEOPLE PLEASE STAND UP

Fig. 1   Fig. 2   Fig. 3

MR. FISH

like what's left over after you hose out the back of the air conditioner."

"So, you think I can hold up my ring finger at people and that's OK?"

"Huh?" she said.

"My ring finger," I said. Nothing. "Instead of my middle finger."

"Oh, right, yeah, don't hold up any fingers at anybody. Don't be stupid."

"And the only reason is because my ring finger looks like my middle finger?"

"Yeah, don't do it."

"So it isn't about my actual finger, right? It's what people think about a finger, one that they're not even seeing — right?"

"I guess."

"So my finger is really OK and people are getting upset because they think they're seeing something that they're really not?"

"I thought you had homework to do?"

"So if I do this," I said, holding up my ring finger, "and I get in trouble, I'm getting in trouble because people are beating themselves up with their own imaginations and that's somehow my fault?"

"Sure it's your fault!"

"How?"

"Listen, don't be a troublemaker just to make trouble," she said, essentially telling me not to be a bullshit detector just to detect bullshit.

Fast forward to early September 2007: I learned about the F-word incident like everybody else who I talked to the following day, by seeing it as the top story in the entertainment section of Google news, the headlines reading, *Gay rights group to Jerry Lewis: Apologize for f-word slur* and *In 18th hour of telethon, comedian may have let slip 'fag'* and *Jerry Lewis Calls Someone an Illiterate F-word on Telethon*. I followed the links to the clip of the flashpoint of the story and watched an 81-year-old Lewis, in a slack-tied tuxedo rumpled enough to give him the appearance of a half-opened Christmas present that had been abandoned by a sudden lack of interest, stumble around in front of his telethon cameras, loopy with exhaustion. "Oh, your family has come to see you," he says, improvising his trademark goofiness to the television audience. "You remember Bart, your older son," he says, gesturing in the direction of an off-screen cameraman, "and," he continues, moving to introduce another, "Jesse, the illiterate faggot, no. …"
He turns abruptly and skulks away, the stench of

the joke tethered to his wake like a flatulence that one could only wish to escape by swimming to the bottom of a pool. That was it.

Then, less than 10 hours following the show's final timpani, came GLAAD (The Gay & Lesbian Alliance Against Defamation) President Neil Giuliano's insistence that Jerry Lewis apologize. "[His] on-air use of this kind of anti-gay slur is simply unacceptable," his statement read. "It feeds a climate of hatred and intolerance that contributes to putting our community in harm's way."

Then, less than 10 hours following Giuliano's request, came Jerry Lewis' apology. "I obviously made a bad choice of words," the press release began. "Everyone who knows me understands that I hold no prejudices in this regard. … I am sorry." The whole episode from start to finish resembled a public spanking, the sort that you only half witness in the parking lot of a grocery store — the sort that might embarrass you into having an opinion about domestic abuse if only it lasted longer.

Dissatisfied with the assumed criminality of the slur and unconvinced that justice had been served by Giuliano demanding an apology — as if slaying a windmill has ever made it any less windy outside — I called GLAAD and said that I was a reporter and wanted to do a story on the whole F-word incident. I spoke with Marc McCarthy, senior director of communications, who requested that I submit my questions in writing before an interview would be granted, which I did. My questions, such as they were after a night of too much booze, went like this:

When Jerry Lewis, the oldest working clown in show business, says faggot in a teasing way towards an imaginary member of his production staff, and he does so in a way that bears no ill will towards the gay community — he could've been Harvey Fierstein for all the anti-gayness he exuded — whom does it hurt? After all, a word is not automatically a slur simply because it has the potential to be used by prejudicial people to convey hatred or stupidity. Specifically, doesn't hate speech require hatred behind it to qualify as defamatory; isn't the intention to be obscene necessary in order to transform a word or notion into something malicious, just as a bullet is not obscene or malicious if it has no deleterious trajectory? Are you battling prejudice when you demand an apology from Jerry Lewis or are you actually corroborating prejudice by suggesting that it is able to exist independent of subjective interpretation, like it's a fact reflecting the truth rather than a lie perpetuating a myth?

I waited four days for an e-mail response.

In the meantime, I decided to drive into West Hollywood, to a section of town barely 20 minutes away from where the very first gay organization in the country, the Mattachine Society, was started in 1950 by Harry Hay, to find out if GLAAD, like the Democratic Party or the U.S. Marine Corps, was nothing but a morality launderer for lazy idealists unwilling to aim towards the ultimate victory of complete and total obsolescence. I parked outside the Coffee Bean & Tea Leaf on Santa Monica Boulevard at 10 a.m. and, with notebook in hand, asked the first 15, mostly middle-aged, heavily perfumed dog owners I came across the following question: *Were you offended by what Jerry Lewis said during his telethon last Monday?* Six of the men I asked didn't know what I was talking about, seven knew what I was talking about and had not been offended, and two said that they had no spare change to give me, although I hadn't asked.

Not wanting to have my findings skewed by the opinions of a particular demographic, I returned to the same area 12 hours later to ask the same question of a much younger crowd. I leaned over outside tables at Rage and Trunks and loitered outside the Motherlode and A Different Light bookstore and gathered these stats: Four *nos*, one *nope*, seven *what-the-fuck-are-you-talkin'-abouts*, one *I thought Jerry Lewis died in the '80s*, one *Jerry Lewis Telethon? Don't ask me — ask my grandmother*, and one *that's a pimpin' jacket you're wearing*, which gave me all the information I needed to know in order to help me make sense of the short reply I received from GLAAD on the one-week anniversary, almost to the hour, of the outing of Jesse the Illiterate Faggot on national television. Here is what they said:

> *Hello Dwayne,*
> *At the end of the [d-word], this is a [s-word] that is too often accompanied by [h-word] and [v-word]. Our [c-word] has a [v-word] [r-word] to play in [c-wording] this kind of [a-word] [b-word]. GLAAD's responsibility is to ensure that [m-word] representations of our [c-word] are fair, accurate and inclusive. As long as [m-word] are sending a [m-word] that [u-wording] an ugly anti-[g-word] slur is either not a big [d-word] or, worse, something to be [e-worded], we have a [r-word] to [s-word] out, hold [p-word] [a-word], and ensure that these kinds of [i-words] don't go unchallenged.*

And then the world blew up. ✳

RE-BRANDED IDENTITY LOGO FOR AMERICAN RADICALS

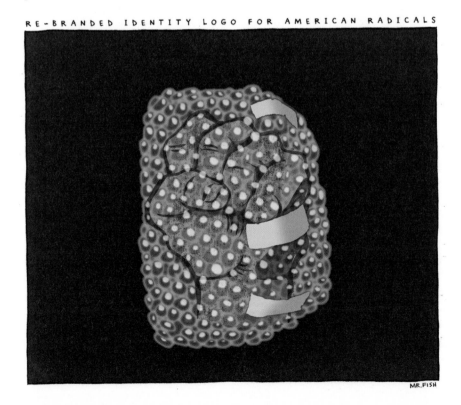

MR.FISH

BOB IS NOT A FOUR LETTER WORD

"Fortune," said Don Quixote to his squire, as soon as he had seen them, "is arranging matters for us better than we could have hoped. Look there, friend Sancho Panza, where thirty or more monstrous giants rise up, all of whom I mean to engage in battle and slay."

— from *Don Quixote*, by Miguel de Cervantes

THERE ARE BRICK AND MORTAR institutions all over the world whose identities derive from the unified opinions of those congregated within their walls. Some have charters known to the public, while others are defined by doctrinal allegiances upheld by the participants and rely very little on externalities. As operational factories of opinion, let's call them mills for wind; *windmills*. Because these windmills polka-dot the horizon all around us, they are often considered to be completely benign and as as likely to draw the point of an advancing lance from horseback as a tree, a cloud or a sunset. Of course, there is every liklihood that

these are the windmills owned and operated by many of the world's most insidious windbags from politics, churches and big business; powerbrokers who typically all know each other and who, like a circle of children in a backyard pool who decide to make a whirlpool, assume that through the unified motion of their perpetual follow-the-leader revolutions, will endeavor to get everything and everyone around them to abandon their free will and to move in only one direction; the boats, the plastic army men, the garbanzo-sized doot that nobody will admit having let float free from the mesh netting inside one of their swimsuits, the balls, everything, creating the grand illusion that their influence on the rest of us is invisible and imbedded somehow in nature, itself.

Despite being imperceptible to most, Robert Scheer has not only noticed these fuckers but has been slaying them for more than 60 years. Anybody can tilt at them, and many do from time to time, but he charges them, undeterred by the laughter or the accusations of dementia by spectators, a real serious rage in his heart, and he slays them. It is the best kind of carnage, too, as safe as granola, as unbarbaric as sitting alone with a purring laptop and an itty-bitty cup of cruddy black espresso: no people or animals or plants are ever really injured in the slaughter that he so enjoys; although *enjoys* is probably the wrong word. *Endures* is more like it, which is the case with most columnists and career journalists. I think of the overused Dorothy Parker quote: *I hate writing, but love having written.* Given the bullshit that he so often has to suffer through after publishing, say, a piece on the criminality of Israel or the not-so-lovable political ruthlessness of Barack Obama or Hillary Clinton, Scheer may sometimes hate having written much more than the act of writing, itself, but he does it because of those goddamn windmills.

And he's dying. Or at least his breed is dying. You can feel it in the wind.

❋ ❋ ❋

There's a job in the Catholic Church called the Papal Master of Ceremonies, the primary function of which is to make sure that all liturgical celebrations follow the proper ritualistic protocols and procedures. During the 16th century while Michelangelo was painting *The Last Judgement* onto the ceiling of the Sistine Chapel, Biagio de Cesena, the Papal Master at the time, deemed the Renaissance master's fresco obscene because of all the nudity, famously suggesting that it belonged in a bathhouse or a bar rather than a Papal chapel. In response to the official's imperious prudishness and very public condemnation, Michelangelo decided to cast Cesena into the Hell portion of his painting, putting his face onto Minos, the judge of the underworld, and outfitting him with donkey ears and a naked body bound by a coiled serpent that is also blowing him. It was an inspiring demonstration of real dissent that was allowed to remain, partly because it was assumed that the notoriety of the deliberate slander against a high-profile church official would eventually fade over time and partly because the painting would forever be 44-feet above the floor and such details would be rendered completely invisible by the limited optics offered by spatial physics. In other words, it exists because it is imperceptible.

That said, it is likely that other inspiring examples of real dissent must exist all around us all the time, yet they remain invisible due to the invented behavioral physics enforced by the social mores and cultural contrivances that frame our political traditions, myths and legends.

Again, you can feel it in the wind.

❋ ❋ ❋

With glasses that magnify his eyes to heroic proportions, meeting Scheer one might not have a hard time imagining that he is capable of seeing through all the complacency that has our participatory democracy stalled so much of the time, like he's Superman seeing through a mountain manicured to be arresting and unworthy of disruptive escavation. Reading him, particularly when you're pissed off about all the political bullshit that complicates our personal joy and demands the bipartisan labeling of our compassions, you might discover that his abilities are even more heroic than that; that he is perhaps even capable of seeing through Superman, himself, past Clark Kent, past Smallville, past Jor-El, through both Warner brothers, all the way into the most repulsive sectors of the plastics industry where tiny Chinese hands are toiling away through 16-hour work days to produce miniature *Happy Meal* figurines able to leap the FDA food pyramid in a single bound and to indoctrinate prepubescent American chubsters into the consumerism class where progressive politics and liberal concerns for fair labor laws are typically loathe to tread. Hell, even more impressive than that, he was the journalist who, in 1976, was able to see the lust in Jimmy Carter's heart when everybody else just saw peanuts. *Now* you know who he is.

My first exposure to the man was at the Los Angeles Times Book Festival in 2003 (when he was still employed by the host paper, more than two years before he would be axed in the fall of 2005 after thirty years of service for reasons murky at best and cowardly at least) when I watched him from the back of a very crowded auditorium use three words, *blow* and *job* and *bullshit*, to aptly describe the pistil and stamen and life-giving manure of modern politics, and also to lose his temper and to actually raise his voice to Christopher *hic* Hitchens, whose excruciatingly precise incoherence over his support of the freshly launched invasion of Iraq had the overwhelming majority of the bleeding heart eggheads in the room wishing, first, that rotten fruit had been permitted into the ballroom and, second, that the overwhelming majority of them didn't throw like girls. Like Nietzsche using exclamation points in his philosophical writings to shout down the most idiotic dictums of Christianity, there was something about Scheer's outrage that, besides attracting the loudest applause that I would hear the entire afternoon, spoke, by contrary example, to the lack of real passion in public debate over some of the more weighty issues facing the republic as, for many, it continued its inevitable slide into the ruins of a failed experiment begun by aristocratic hippies amused by charming and impractical inventions over two centuries ago.

"I think you're not a fully formed human being if you're indifferent to suffering of any kind," Scheer told me by phone in 2006 when I asked him if objectivity in journalism, particularly political journalism, was a myth; if, as it is for the wildlife documentarian, it was the job of the journalist to simply record the brutality of a political happening without interfering with its complete fruition. In fact, it was the only scripted question that I was able to peel off with any dexterity during our entire one-hour discussion on what I was hoping to frame as *inadvertent activism* in political reporting. Of course, I should have known that he'd overwhelm me with his response, having hung out with him a handful of times ever since becoming the staff cartoonist for his news and information website, Truthdig, a year prior to my phone call.

Let me just say here that Scheer in person is different than Scheer in print. In print he is the consummate ping pong player, never allowing the tiny plastic *ping* from his opponents to pass him unpaddled. He is quick and merciless and unbeat-

MR. FISH

able, largely because he is politically ambidextrous and his interviewees tend towards favoring, too heavily, either a right or left hand.

Conversely, Scheer in person has one of those fantastic brains that likes to answer a question with a zillion vaguely relevant responses that, in the end, overwhelm the room and block all the exits and amount to a precision that no single response from a more succinct thinker could've come close to matching. It's like asking John Coltrane to play *Mary Had a Little Lamb*: he'll play it, but by the time he's finished you might feel as if you'd also gotten to listen to a few bars of *Summertime*, read several dozen pages of *No Exit*, enjoyed a very satisfying glass of chocolate milk, gotten a reach around from the preacher's lunatic sister and laughed your ass off. Nothing in Scheer's conversation asks the world to prove or disprove the legitimacy of what he says. Instead, he leaves it to the world to aspire to his intellectual optimism; an optimism, of course, that is flown like a kite that's tethered to some real hardcore existential pessimism.

"Let's cut to the chase," he said, his Bronx accent made all the more musical by his early emersion into the beat pinko pre-hippie culture of 1960s San Francisco, where he was the editor in chief of arguably the flagship publication of the New Left, *Ramparts* Magazine (Castro, himself, thought Scheer was red enough to personally hand him the diaries of Che **Guevara** for publication in *Ramparts*), "if you pretend you're a dragnet cop, you know, *just give me the facts*, you show your stupidity, your mindlessness. I think the best thing that's ever been said on the subject of objectivity was said by the great Beat poet Lawrence Ferlinghetti who said, 'Keep an open mind but not so open that your brains fall out.' And what that means to me," he continued, "is that [when you're reporting] you don't lose who you are. You have your own ideas, your own background, and you just try to keep your listening ears open; you *listen* to what people are saying. You have to try to think logically and be guided by the facts – that doesn't mean that you're without values. I was on welfare as a kid, so when I came to write about it for the LA Times; I wasn't indifferent to the subject, I had feelings about it. But some guy who goes to prep school and then writes about it, he will also have feelings, maybe they're feelings of callousness, I don't know. But we all have to struggle with *why are we thinking what we're thinking?*"

"Doesn't that kind of self-reflection complicate your job?" I asked. "I'd assume that by asking yourself *why* you're thinking a certain way about something you're inviting your emotions into a deductive process best served by a colder calculation. Isn't a good journalist supposed to be a dective who's only interested in the facts?"

"No," he said. I didn't believe him, having recently argued with a couple of USC journalism professors at my wife's graduation party from the Annenberg School for Communication – professors who, upon hearing of my pending interview, find Scheer's emotional response to political outrage largely unprofessional and inappropriate and unbefitting of a serious journalist.

"But what if you were an AP writer and not a columnist, wouldn't your objectivity training demand that you not even consider your opinion when reporting a story?" I asked. "And isn't that the issue? Because your stuff usually appears on the op-ed page of the newspaper, do you feel that much of what you write can be shrugged off by people who might say, 'Well, that's not the truth, it's just Scheer's *opinion*. If what he's saying were *really* the truth then I'd be reading it on the front page or listening to CNN talk about it or, God forbid, I wouldn't be hearing the President saying the complete opposite over and over again?'"

"It isn't about objectivity," he said, "it's about accountability. If we'd gone into Iraq, for instance, and found weapons of mass destruction, if we'd found a connection to al Qaeda, if the people had greeted us as liberators, if democracy was now flourishing in the Mideast, I can assure you that I would have taken at least a sabbatical. I would've reevaluated what the hell I do, how I do my work, where I went wrong." He laughed, a gallows laugh, amused by the lack of anything funny. "If I got it wrong as often as Thomas Friedman of the *New York Times* – this is a guy who's gotten it wrong consistently, yet why is he valued? Because he has a certain style, a certain persona, a certain seriousness, he sits in the right cafes, he talks to the right people. What's the difference between him and Judy Miller for Godsakes? They both bought the same crap."

❊ ❊ ❊

Scheer has this deliciously discomforting way of saying stuff that is so nakedly honest (I'll leave it up to you to decide whether it's *truthful* or not) that

it feels crude to suddenly have it enthusiastically wriggling into your ear. It's almost as if half the time he's talking to you he's really trying to get you in trouble with him, like he's elbowing you and trying to hand you a suspiciously rolled cigarette in a public place. Why? I think it's because his sense of moral decency is totalitarian. He seems to lead his life as if morality were a form of physics that has somehow been corrupted by the biggest bastards in the ruling class and that, like gravity, morality only makes sense when it's applied equally and consistently to everybody. He truly seems to believe deeply that one group of people shouldn't be allowed to fly while another group is forced to live their lives pressed to the ground unable to move. The singularity of his contempt for privilege makes his most unrefined comments about injustice come off like he's farting in church – the farting, of course, being a metaphor for his refusal to believe that the presence of a church pew should automatically disallow any other *pew* access to the room.

"The same with Wen Ho Lee [the scientist accused of stealing secrets about U.S. nuclear arsenals for China]," Scheer continued with his criticism of corporate journalism unabated. "I wrote over 20 columns about it. How the hell did this guy end up being put into solitary confinement for 9 months, chained, videoed when he goes to take a crap, the government trying to break him, destroy him over totally phony information? And the New York Times leads the charge against him, totally distorting the evidence. Why didn't anybody in that building stand up and say 'this is wrong' while it was happening? You know, 'I object! What are you doing?!' There were people who knew it was wrong."

❊ ❊ ❊

And speaking of willful blindness, let's examine how willfully blinding a person may increase another's ability to exercise control and authority over a sightless subordinate. In consideration of all the biological systems and subsystems that make up a functioning human being, there is no reason to assume that the manipulation of a physiological attribute wouldn't exactly parallel the manipulation of a psychological attribute. Indeed, there have been experiments conducted where the eyelids of newborn kittens had been sewn shut for the purpose of seeing if the deliberate rendering of a

sensory organ as obsolete would ultimately make it obsolete. According to researchers, a kitten would attempt to see through its own eyelids for a period of approximately 3 months, reacting to the light used to stimulate the optic nerve and visual cortex, before its eyeballs would eventually lose the ability to perceive anything at all and stop developing. As the cats grew, their puny eyes would not, having become no more miraculous than table grapes. Similarly, it must be true that if privleged babies are born into a society that has rules and customs that deliberately bound their radically humane cognitive abilities and keep them from accessing their natural instincts to growl at injustice, laugh at piety and lash out against a state's demand for unquestioning loyalty to a perverse and brutal heirarchy, then they too will become nothing more than the demeaned and hollow host bodies for hearts and minds as dead and passionless as slag and scoria.

❊ ❊ ❊

Scheer went on. "You know, the Harris Poll recently published a poll that said 50% of America still believes that Iraq had weapons of mass destruction. You cannot look at that poll and feel optimistic about this country and celebrate its representative democracy. Where are the journalists who convinced these people? What about some-

body like Max Boot [author and military historian and apologist for U.S. international barbarism]? Does he not have a responsibility to tell the 50% that still buy that lie that, 'Hey, I was party to why you got this wrong and I'm now going to tell you that it is wrong.' Doesn't he have an obligation to do that? To reeducate the people who bought his lies?"

"Is it that journalists are like everybody else, figuring that it's easier to serve power than to debate it? Is it that simple?" I wondered.

"Let me tell you, buddy boy, it's not just power," he said. "The most depressing thing I've learned in this whole journalism business is that there really isn't much courage there. Journalism is a career and a journalist, particularly a mainstream journalist, will only report something if it doesn't jeopardize his job. These are people who are unwilling to risk a slight kink in their career curve – I'm not talking about having their fingernails pulled out or their testicles crushed like it is for journalists in other parts of the world. For instance, I assume that there must be one person at the Los Angeles Times who thinks that it was wrong to push my column out and I don't know of anybody [from the Times] who's publicly said that. Journalists are very brave when they sail out of the building and confront other people," Scheer continued, "but they're little church mice in their own building. They fail to let the reader in on the story that they know best: how does the mass media function, who's calling the shots, how does public information get formed? The Fourth Estate has been hobbled – they don't cover themselves. Take the Tribune Company (the Chicago based company that purchased the LA Times in 2000)," said Scheer. "They're basically operating in violation of the law because congress didn't pass the legislation letting them have the kind of consolidation that they wanted, so they got these waivers from the FCC and that's how they keep a television station and a newspaper in Hartford or in LA. They need the Bush Administration to get these waivers. Does anybody at the paper investigate that connection? Are they going soft on it? It's about courage!"

"Which means it could also be about fear," I said. "Both are equally motivating and, therefore, equally capable of moving humanity towards either ruthlessness or whatever the opposite of ruthless is. I guess what I'm saying is that fear might be the most effective form of courage there is. Take [for instance] the peace movement. Sure you can build a coalition of pacifists made up of middle-aged, white, college-educated, privleged ideologues. But what about a peace movement made up of underprivileged young people from every class, who are not particularly interested in pacifism, who are [unquarantined] by college or handicap or [disqualifying] transgenderism, but suddenly find out that the draft is being reinstituted? Then you have lightening in a bottle! I guess that one man's selfishness is another man's selflessness," I said.

He paused to smile; I could hear it through the phone. "More reason to avoid getting a job at The New York Times," he said.

"And every reason to be thankful that you were fired from the LA Times," I said, smiling imperceptibly back.

Then I heard him stand and walk across his living room to look out the window. I knew that the view was spectacular having been in his apartment before, not only because it took in the whole city and the mountains and the ever-expanding sky, but also because it faced away from the *L.A. Times* building, barely a block away, effectively putting it behind him.

"The quote at the top of Truthdig is a quote from A.J. Liebling: 'Freedom of the press is guaranteed only to those who own one,'" he said. "Well, I guess, now I own one."

"And I hope you never make a single penny from the proprietorship," I said. Fourteen-years later, in 2020, he hasn't. ✳

COMING OF RAGE IN NEVERLAND

G. GORDON LIDDY, noted Watergate thief and tournament-level egomaniac, once said that, "The press is like the peculiar uncle you keep in the attic—just one of those unfortunate things." Of course, such a quote, rather than maligning the press, ultimately serves only to label the quote's originator as a crackpot. Who else but a crackpot would want to shove another family member into the attic simply because he or she tends to ask a lot of questions about the world and expects a certain logic to be present in the answers?

It's a common phenomenon, this maligning of the press from the right wing, and it's what I love about blowhards like Liddy. Like the ancient geocentrists who believed that the Earth was the center of the universe and that all other heavenly bodies revolved around it, so much of the right wing's ideology seems to assume that its stubborn refusal to tolerate any point of view that doesn't recognize the values of the GOP as originating from some fixed center at the very core of the moral universe is some noble reflection of some permanent truth instead of clear proof that the

conservatism is too fearful and too unimaginative and too antiquated to be able to comprehend a reality that, simply by being chemically based, is anything but immovable. That's why Republican moralists perceive any criticism of their principles to be an attack on reality itself, and therefore believe that any disagreement with them is not only mad but also depraved and deliberately pernicious. It is also how they are able to so easily integrate the concept of absolute good and evil into their worldview.

Make no mistake, I find the liberal wing of the Democratic Party to be just as putrid and indefensibly contemptuous of democracy in its truly pluralistic form, although their pantomime of such a system permits at least a theatrical version upon which to model, upon the happy occasion of their demise, an eventual real-life staging. A conservative, on the other hand, would never have the sort of conversation that I remember having with my then-girlfriend, who is now my wife, right after I dropped out of college to become an insufferable know-it-all and condescending braggart.

Ardmore, Pa. 1992

All I'm saying is that one way to see if you really like somebody is to ask yourself, "Would I still go out with this person if he or she was the opposite sex?"

So, wait a minute, you'd still go out with me if I was a guy?

Yes.

A big hairy guy with a beard, testicles, hairy ass —the whole thing?

My mother has a hairy ass. It's not that big of a deal to me.

She doesn't have a guy's hairy ass.

Sure she does.

No she doesn't.

Next time I'm home I'll take a picture of the soap in her shower, it looks like a baby rabbit.

She doesn't have testicles!

Who knows what she's got down there? You know how when an Easter basket looks empty that a lot of times it's not — how there's always some loose jelly beans hidden at the bottom?

She wouldn't be your mom if she had testicles, you jackass! She'd be your dad.

No she wouldn't —that's like saying that if my dad had boobs that he'd be my mom.

Well, who would he be if he had boobs?

My grandfather.

Oh, Jesus . . .

It's true, I swear. The only way to tell my grandparents apart when they're swimming together in a pool is that when my grandmother goes underwater she comes up without eyebrows.

That's why I could never be a conservative, stomach-churning self-absorption and teeth-rattling paranoia aside, because my understanding of how the world works is based much more on truths that are circumstantial and completely subjective rather than universal and unalterable.

Imagine for a moment that you are a dog or a cat or a horse or a deer or a fox living in Germany in the 1930s. Because the Third Reich has passed the most comprehensive animal rights legislation ever known to man, and because Adolf Hitler and Rudolf Hess and Joseph Goebbels and Heinrich Himmler are all ethical vegetarians, these are the best possible times for you and your family. You might assume that you are living in Paradise and that your future will surely involve a myriad of personal freedoms that your ancestors would've never thought possible. And then the Allies show up and ruin everything and you're right back in the toilet.

The moral: Objectivity means different things to different people.

Which, I guess, brings us to the predawn killing of Osama bin Laden in 2011 by U.S. Navy SEALs in Pakistan. It has been said that the two things that people don't ever want to see being made are sausages and legislation. I'd amend that to say that doubly ugly to people is legislation that makes sausage. Wars are perhaps the most obvious example of that. Nobody wanted to look at the Iraq Liberation Act when it was passed by Congress and signed by Bill Clinton in '98, for example, nor did they want to look at the Iraq War Resolution or the Bush Doctrine or the Patriot Act that came later, for fear of being revolted by the grotesque notion that America might not be anything more than just a sloppy imperialistic plutocracy held together by a handful of Toby Keith songs and somewhere around 250 million late credit card payments.

In fact, I still find it reprehensible how purposely incurious the general public remained during Colin Powell's criminal behavior at the U.N. Security Council in 2002, really ground zero for the bloodbath in Iraq in which we ended up drowning. Criminal, because the sincerity of his plea for invasion, with his itty-bitty vial of white powder and hammy, faux-Gregory Peck pomposity, was about as convincing an expression of genuine statesmanship as Danny Partridge's bass playing was a convincing demonstration of … well, bass playing, yet it still led to the mur-

Craig had his MBA to thank for his amazing life and impeccable table manners.

der of, by some estimates, as many as a million people, and we're still counting. And we're still supporting the troops. Wherever we wind them up and turn them loose.

I did a cartoon in 2004 that made use of an iconic 1941 photograph taken by a German soldier of a fellow German soldier throwing a potato masher grenade during the Second World War somewhere in Russia. What struck me about the photograph when I stumbled upon it was how similar, minus the potato masher grenade, a 1941 German soldier and a 21st century U.S. soldier looked, particularly when it came to the shape of their helmets. Looking at the German soldier, who had been photographed on black and white film, his forest green camouflage indistinguishable from desert camouflage, I had to look twice to see that I wasn't looking at an American soldier crouching in the rubble of Tikrit or in a trash pile in Ghaziabad. The caption I chose for the image was: *I can't tell if this is a German soldier from 1944 or an American soldier from 2005 (and neither can his victims).* After posting it on MSNBC.com, I received upward of 300 emails mostly wishing to see my brains yanked out and stomped on by much more wholesome Americans than myself. I quickly followed it up with a cartoon depicting a squad of American Marines, an individual line drawn to each separate soldier labeling him as a *good guy.* Then I drew a bracket encompassing all of them and labeled the sum total as *bad guys.* "Dear Shithead," began the kindest email I received in response. "Since you are such a muslim lover, do the rest of us a favor and move to an arab country and STAY there. Scrawlings like yours have entertained defecators around the world ever since the invention of the rest room stall partition."

I immediately thought of the Antonin Artaud quote, *Where there is a stink of shit there is a smell of being,* and I sent a note in reply thanking him for the compliment.

Another email, by a woman named Lindsey, read, "I think your cartoon is a horrible affront to all the men and women serving in our armed forces. Good thing I'm not president — I'd have you tried for treason and hung at sun rise! Why don't you move to, say, Iran and settle down among those of your ilk?" I responded by saying that I didn't think the job she was describing was that of president. I guessed that it might instead be ayatollah, emperor, fuhrer, czar or perhaps Caesar.

Then I thought of the Bernard Shaw quote: *New opinions often appear first as jokes and fancies, then as blasphemies and treason, then as questions open to discussion, and finally as established truths,* and I shuddered at the thought of living long enough to one day be identified as a tireless champion of established truths.

Upon hearing the news that Osama bin Laden had been made to swim with the fishes after taking a bullet to the head, I couldn't help myself from thinking of the Mafia. The news came to me and a room full of journalists and activists and moneyed liberals during a fairly swank fundraiser at Disney Hall in L.A., probably just as I was being served a crème fraîche garnished by a sprig of mint and dusted with gold infused cocoa talc by servers who, as evidenced by their behavior, had no doubt been instructed not to speak and to remain as invisible as pixies servicing saints. Sickened by the elation on the faces of many of those seated around me at my table, as if the killing was somehow proof that Barack Obama had seen some sort of spooky justice served by targeted assassination and that his re-election would be both a cinch and well-deserved, I set down my fork and looked beyond the ostentation and noticed an airplane moving like a lit match across the black sky outside.

I thought back to the first week of October 2001 and remembered how peculiar I felt lying in bed with my wife in a Boston hotel room on the 26th floor with all the lights out, both of us feeling as vulnerable to targeted assassination by airbus as everybody else in America, the whole of Western civilization having been turned into an elaborate pretension of precarious and brittle dominoes by the 9/11 attacks. It was somewhere around 7 o'clock and our curtains were open to the great purple bruise of twilight, and we were listening to a radio program broadcasting original audio from a videotape that had just been released by Osama bin Laden. First, bin Laden would speak, his Arabic muffled as if spoken through a loaf of bread and then recorded by the crappiest Sanyo answering machine known to man, and then a translator would repeat the al-Qaida leader's words in a tone better suited to the wide-eyed, flashlight-under-the-chin, retelling of a ghost story.

Most disturbing about bin Laden's message, bat-shit crazy adherence to a voodoo-addled theocratic justification for mass murder aside, was how closely his disdain for U.S. foreign policy in the

Middle East mirrored my own, particularly when it came to Washington's megalomaniacal support of Israel's merciless occupation and savage mistreatment of Palestinians living in Gaza and the West Bank. Then there were the bombings by the Clinton administration of Sudan and Afghanistan and the harrowing sanctions, and occasional missile attacks, against the utterly defenseless Iraqi population. And then there was the construction of all the military bases in Saudi Arabia, Pakistan, Uzbekistan, Turkey, Yemen, Kuwait, Cyprus, Oman, the United Arab Emirates and Afghanistan. It pissed me off that the refusal of my own government to espouse humanitarian concerns for those it so unjustly threatened and brutalized had me reluctantly agreeing with a top-notch crackpot who would have no problem watching while his thugs sawed off my head with a sharp, prehistoric stone because his fucking Santa Claus found my atheism *naughty*. Worse than that, even, was what I imagined bin Laden's qualifying the United States as an imperial power would do to the West's likelihood that it would re-evaluate

its hegemonic tendencies and hubristic sense of global privilege. Knowing what Hitler had done to the complete eradication of the square mustache, I could only guess what bin Laden was doing to U.S. introspection.

With practically everybody behaving as if the world had suddenly been made lighter by the elimination of one man murdered at home in his nightgown, I left Disney Hall with the words, "There's no place like Rome, there's no place like Rome. ..." circling my mood like children dancing around a maypole, the pagan origins of their synchronized movement giving purpose to their muscles while simultaneously stirring nothing but optimism inside the absurdity of their pointless joy. ✴

PAUL KRASSNER GAVE A SHIT ABOUT EVERYTHING

"Irreverence is our only sacred cow."

— Paul Krassner

PAUL KRASSNER DIED ON JULY 21, 2019, at 87, and more than anybody else in his generation, he lived his life demonstrating over and over and*over*again how the best way to save our country from the relentless onslaught of polarizing politics that buries our enthusiasm for a kinder and gentler society is with friendship and humor, pure and simple. "Trying to save the world is a banker's mentality," he once told me while we were eating grapes at his kitchen table, "which is why I like to spend my time paying attention." He did that kind of thing all the time, to everybody he knew — that-*thing*being to camouflage his wisdom in an ad-lib phrase, improvised pun or invented idiom, which he'd then deliver as if it were nothing, a harmless ball of bubblegum, maybe. Only after you'd spend the next hour chewing on what he'd said would

you realize that what he'd given you wasn't glib or trivial or disposable at all. Instead, he'd given you something you found yourself replaying in your head and wanting to share with others, the-*wanting to share*part being precisely what brings meaningful cohesion to the multitude.

Of course, he always did claim that English was his second language, laughter being his first.

❀ ❀ ❀

On a chilly Friday night in 2007, when most of L.A. was still shoving Kleenex balls into its pants and mouthing the words "Please love me" into its bathroom mirror, a 75-year-old man wearing a dirty, red satin baseball jacket, a black T-shirt emblazoned with a pot leaf the size of a spinning boomerang and hair like steel wool said from the tiny stage of the M Bar, "I'd like to end on a note of hope, since I talked about a lot of negative stuff tonight." He went on to discuss the Doomsday Clock of the Bulletin of the Atomic Scientists and how it had recently been moved from seven minutes before midnight to five minutes before midnight, midnight being the end of the world. "The good news," he said, "is that scientists are people, just like the rest of us, and they're probably just as neurotic as we are, so they probably set the clock to be 10 minutes fast — so it's really only a quarter of."

The room went crazy with applause, and then everybody went outside to have their cars retrieved by the strip mall's valet service, while I stayed inside to watch person after person thank Paul Krassner for his performance — and for the work he'd done his whole life.

❀ ❀ ❀

Krassner, a founding member of theYouth International Party(known as the Yippies), a Merry Prankster, a contributor to Mad Magazine, the ninth member of the Chicago Seven and the father of the underground press, began publishing *The Realist* — which is now being called the "Charlie Hebdo of American satire," and which writer Terry Southern referred to as "the first American publication to really tell the truth" — in 1958 and stopped in 2001, finally upstaged by real-world events whose tragedy and absurdity trumped any and all satirical contrivances. After all, it was during that year, on Sept. 11, that the United States was attacked by 19 men with box cutters who ended up killing nearly 3,000 people. The date of the attack also happened to be the 126th anniversary of the initial publication of the very first newspaper comic strip in the U.S., "Professor Tigwissel's Burglar Alarm." It was published by the New York Daily Graphic newspaper, whose offices had been located some 5,000 feet away from the site of the World Trade Center.

Appropriately, the 1875 strip depicted a self-aggrandized egomaniac who attempts to protect himself from the threat of a home invasion by stockpiling excessive firearms and weaponry and installing a foolproof security system designed to prevent a surprise attack. In the comic strip, the firepower and security system don't work, and Professor Tigwissel is attacked, but he arrogantly

claims success afterward. He promises to patent his device to perpetuate the notion that we are best protected by the machinery of our paranoia and a weaponized mistrust of the world, rather than by a less hysterical adherence to truth, justice, humanitarianism and mutual cooperation. Such was the premonitory power of the cartoonist in the late 19th century, and such was the sickening plunge of real life into the realm of gruesome fantasy many years later, that rendered the satire of *The Realist* no longer allegorical, but literal — literalism being to allegory what a real fire is to a crowded theater.

Specifically, where there once existed a well-informed, anti-authoritarian audience for satire, 21st-century Americans became passive consumers of inconsequential burlesque masquerading as satire. People assumed corporate-sponsored jokes that merely used political personalities and circumstances as fodder the same way that slapstick used seltzer bottles and baggy pants were somehow the same thing as sharp and unforgiving criticism by uncompromising freelancers for the deeper purpose of revealing political and social injustices and commenting on them in a way that engenders more psychic pain than physiological pleasure. The idea became that humorists in search of laughter alone over frank and honest outrage are not satirists for one simple reason: Mirth cripples rage, and rage is necessary for the beating back of political, cultural and religious bullshit in service of change.

As the No. 1 progenitor of all the alternative and underground publications that followed it, *The Realist* taught us that the best way to rescue a panicked society from drowning is not to throw it a life preserver, but to teach it how to swim.

❀ ❀ ❀

I first met Krassner in 2007 at the M Bar in the crappy New Jersey section of Hollywood at the corner of Vine and Fountain. The bar was a very dark hole crammed into an enormous, two-story, L-shaped concrete monstrosity that has a Jewish deli, a Thai take-out place, an Italian take-out place, a Mexican take-out place, a Ramen/Japanese take-out place, a panini/tapas take-out place, a Cuban take-out place, a "European food" take-out place and a place with the words "A-1 Therapy" written on the door in a font only slightly more professional looking than masking tape. The foil covering the windows at A-1 Therapy suggests that it is a place that grows lizards or baked potatoes.

I had known his work from my college days in the 1980s, when I used to cut class and travel back home to pour over old copies of *The Realist* at an anarchist bookstore called The Wooden Shoe in Philadelphia. In many ways, Krassner gave me my career as a cartoonist by both proxy and demonstration. When it came to the politics of being a smartass, he was the one consistent practitioner of prankster journalism, social commentary and political satire that, because of his relentless presence on the scene, gave some measure of credibility to the First Amendment and, yes, democracy, itself.

When Jack Weinberg said, in 1965, not to trust anybody over 30, Krassner was 33, an old, *old* man, and certainly an exception to the adage. With the gargantuan reputation of his magazine, *The Realist* — the flagship publication of the radical left at the time, perhaps of all time, and indispensable rag to the hemorrhaging heart of the Vietnam War-addled counterculture — he had established himself as the Walter Cronkite of the underground press and was considered the most trusted investigative satirist working in A *mock* rica.

"The irony is that I've always tried to uphold the virtues of the Constitution and I never took an oath to do it, while [the politicians I target] did take an oath, and they're the ones trying to destroy the Constitution," he told me at lunch in Santa Monica six hours before he stepped onto the M Bar stage. Amazed at the clarity of his mind and the animated enthusiasm with which the septuagenarian still seemed to give a shit about everything, I asked him how he'd been able to survive while so many of his contemporaries, like Timothy Leary, Lenny Bruce, Ken Kesey, Terry Southern, Hunter S. Thompson, Allen Ginsberg and, most notably, his fellow co-founders of the Youth International Party and co-conspirators in the Chicago Seven Conspiracy trial — Abbie Hoffman and Jerry Rubin, who John Lennon called the Mork and Mindy of the '60s — had died. "Simple," he said. "I've never taken any legal drugs."

Having left Los Angeles in 2000 to live in Desert Hot Springs, a hundred miles away, he was only in town to do the one-nighter at the M Bar. "I've never played a strip mall before," he said. "I played the Brentwood bakery once, and anybody who came got a free pastry." I asked him if he missed Los Angeles. His wife, Nancy, who was sitting with us, said yes enthusiastically. He gave me this answer later, standing in the spotlight a mere 40 feet from A-1 Therapy:

"Desert Hot Springs is not like L.A.," he said. He explained how every clerk at every retail shop he patronized in his new hometown never failed to remind him at the conclusion of every business transaction to "have a nice day!" *Have a nice day! Have a nice day! Have a nice day!* — it followed him everywhere. *Have a nice day!* "Just on the way over here tonight," he said, capping a water bottle he'd just taken a swig from, "I bought this bottle of water from a girl who was sitting behind a cash register, looking really sullen. I figured that here was my chance to, you know, make her feel good with everything that I learned in [Desert Hot Springs]. So, after I paid for the water, I looked at her and I said (gleefully), 'Aren't you going to tell me to have a nice day?' 'It's on the fucking receipt!' she said." It gave him the biggest smile I'd seen on his face all day.

I left the club at 9:15 p.m., while there was still a line of people hoping to shake hands with Krassner. Stepping into the parking lot, I took a moment to notice that nobody was waiting to shake hands with me and, with Krassner's Groucho Marxism still ping-ponging around inside my mood, I decided to savor the freedom and to disappear into the darkness feeling grounded and blessed by the fact that it's never nighttime everywhere.

What follows is a portion of one of the last conversations I had with him.

❀ ❀ ❀

Besides attracting many of the most celebrated writers as contributors during its more than two decades in print — writers such as Norman Mailer, Ken Kesey, Kurt Vonnegut, Joseph Heller and Avery Corman — *The Realist* also attracted a number of famous cartoonists to its pages. In addition to running Ron Cobb, Wally Wood, S. Clay Wilson, Charles Rodrigues, Art Spiegelman and Dick Guindon, who were among the top counterculture cartoonists of the 1960s, you also published a handful of more mainstream cartoonists whose work typically appeared in The New Yorker, Esquire, Cosmopolitan, Good Housekeeping and the Harvard Business Review. These were cartoonists who wished to publish edgier work on racism, birth

control, the Vietnam War, censorship and women's rights, which were topics that conventional magazines would never run. These cartoonists included Jules Feiffer, Mort Gerberg, Sam Gross, Frank Interlandi, Lee Lorenz and B. Kliban.

Right — remember, this was a time when there were cartoonists who were basically gag writers and cartoonists who were more interested in satire. Gag cartoonists like [those] who drew for The New Yorker made a lot more money than cartoonists like Cobb or Guindon. But [publishing] *The Realist* was never about making money, and neither was creating [satirical cartoons] that attacked the establishment.

That's why Cobb eventually had to quit doing it and go into designing spaceships and aliens for fucking Hollywood. It's kind of heartbreaking.

That's what Lenny Bruce's *Lone Ranger* was about — saving people and not expecting any reward for doing it.

I was like that, too — I wanted to be Angela Davis when I grew up.

But Michelle Obama beat you to it!

Can a gag cartoon sometimes serve the same purpose as a satirical cartoon?

No.

Why not?

Because with satire, there will always be people who believe that it's real, that the government is capable of the most outrageous things, which, of course, it is. So, in a way, [satire] actually informs people of a danger that's real by attracting their attention to the truth with a lie. The New Yorker doesn't do that.

Because you have interviewed and/or published so many of the most important and influential thinkers and artists of the mid-20th century, I thought it might be smart to get your perspective on why, when it comes to contemporary culture, artists and writers and poets and painters

and social philosophers, either by accident or by deliberate design, have been removed from the national debate about who we are as a species and where we are going as a society.

I'm going to have to plead the 4th on that [*the Amendment which guards against unreasonable searches and seizures*].

Well, let me give you an example about what I mean. Besides the obvious superstars of the time, people like [Lenny] Bruce, [Marshall] McCluhan, [Norman] Mailer, [John] Lennon, [Mort] Sahl, you also had television personalities like Millicent Martin in 1963 on *That Was the Week that Was* singing a song, dressed as Uncle Sam, called, "I Want to Go Back to Mississippi," which contained the lyric:

> *Where the Mississippi mud*
> *Kinda mingles with the blood*
> *Of the niggers who are hanging*
> *From the branches of the trees*

Wow.

There's even a refrain that describes a, "…butter-colored moon" and, "cutting up a chocolate-colored koon." Now, what's remarkable about that is how brutally frank the social commentary was delivered and how bluntly the satire was played and how it was broadcast on mainstream television. Remember, this was not a nightclub or some underground cabaret somewhere — it was on the BBC.

Well, I did recently see a repeat of something from MAD TV — it was a sketch where there was a group of black actors who were all dressed as pimps waiting at an audition. It was a takeoff of the old Snickers Bar commercials, but instead of saying Snickers the announcer says, "Gonna be here for a while? Have a Snigger's Bar."

That's different, though. That's more like a parody that addresses the laziness of the culture and the inability of decent society to acknowledge the broader implications of racism in general, whereas the piece on *That Was the Week That Was* pointed a very direct finger at how ugly the prejudice is able to manifest itself in very specific acts of race-based violence within American society.

In fact, the song states clearly, "…If you ain't for segregating white folks from the black, then they won't hesitate to shoot you bravely in the back." In other words, [the TW3 segment] handles the issue with much more seriousness instead of merely playing it as farce.

I think Dave Chappelle does more of what you're talking about.

Maybe, but [he does it] in an atmosphere much less open to the free expression of ideas, that's my point. When you've got the management at the Laugh Factory [in Hollywood] fining performers for saying 'the N-word,' then the bar is lowered on what qualifies as dissent and what passes for social criticism. When there is nothing but debate surrounding how you should be allowed to say something, then there never comes a time when the content of what you actually say is assessed. That's when words become meaningless and language becomes a deterrent to knowledge.

You're right. I remember when George Carlin was asked why he didn't include the word *nigger* as one of the seven words that you can't say on TV and he said that there was nothing funny about it. He wanted to maintain what was humorous about the repression of certain words by religious fanatics who believed that bodily functions and sexual activity was taboo. That, he said, is funny as shit.

Then, I guess, the conversation becomes one about technique and different modes of teaching and sharing information versus just content. Making your ideas interesting enough to make somebody else want to repeat them to somebody else who will then want to repeat them to somebody else, over and over and over again, is how real education and real social change happens. [To] Carlin's point, jokes are probably repeated more often than dark satire because people prefer laughter over something ugly and depressing that leaves you staring at the wall and feeling hopeless.

Of course, to speak to your point about the state of satire today, which I think is where you were going with all this, is that so much of what passes for satire nowadays isn't real satire, at least not in the traditional sense. For one thing, it isn't even ironic — it's Sarcasm 101. Audiences will applaud for name-calling as a replacement for wit.

I agree — real satire begs a conversation to happen after the joke has been told. Not only that, [it] assumes that a conversation had been going on previous to the telling of the joke. [Satire] assumes that the audience is there to do at least half of the heavy lifting when it comes to getting the punch line and recognizing the irony or the hypocrisy of whatever is being lampooned.

And that's the subjective side of humor, all that [foreknowledge] that makes satire work. There are a lot of factors to consider when building strong satire. But there's also the objective side [of humor] that, if you can get it in with the subjective side, it really makes for [a good joke].

The difference between a clown eating a shit sandwich for no reason and the Pope eating a shit sandwich for some reason.

Yeah. In 1978, I went with my daughter, Holly, to Ecuador on a shamans and healers expedition, and we stayed with primitive Indians and took ayahuasca — I should say, indigenous Indians, because they looked at us as if we were the primitive ones. Anyway, we lived for a while with three generations of Chiapas Indians. There were about 15 people in our group, and one of them was an anthropologist, but after a while it became clear that we were the subjects and [the Chiapas] were the anthropologists. I remember watching a mother who was talking to us and how she was playing with her naked son's penis and how there was no internalization of inhibited social structures, at least none that I could relate to. [Similarly], they would watch us brushing our teeth or doing Tai Chi and wonder what the hell we were doing, you know. It was peculiar to them, like we were Martians who had dropped out of the sky. Regardless, I had these bright green sunglasses, and I let everybody try them on, and they all laughed at each other because [the visual] had elements of incongruity. They didn't know our language, but they knew what they felt in their gut, which was that it was silly. So, while so much of American humor has a lot to do with taste, and so much satire has an agenda that serves either the right or the left, there's a primal sense of humor that resonates with people because it transcends culture and is universal [to everybody].

Right, that's the appeal of slapstick, I guess. Maybe it's even the appeal of much of commedia dell'arte, stereotypes being much more closely related to our lower base functions [than our higher]. Still, what scares me is how society can sometimes misconstrue the ease of experiencing that primal sense of humor you mentioned as being the only genuine humor there is and, therefore, the only humor we should recognize. Way too often I hear pundits complaining that satire, like "The Daily Show" or The Onion or "South Park," is not real humor because it parodies political grandstanding and hate speech and religious buffoonery, that sort of thing. In other words, I'm uncomfortable when the definition of humor excludes irony and critical thinking and dissent because it is assumed that people are way too stupid to get the joke. I hate the notion that laughter cannot be used as a teaching tool and that censorship is somehow preferable as a mode of communication.

Exactly. With *The Realist*, I would never label an article as either journalism or satire because I didn't want to deprive the readers of the pleasure of discerning for themselves what was true and what was an extension of the truth.

I remember you saying that for years you received letters from people who thought that your famous piece about the Kennedy assassination was real investigative journalism.

I still get them!

And that speaks to how absolutely bizarre reality can be in comparison to satire. The fact that you were able to write something that was so fantastic and so ludicrous and still have people confused about whether it was fiction or nonfiction, even 50 years later, is really telling about how the world works. It reminds me of an argument that I have with 9/11 conspiracy theorists all the time. I'm forever telling them to expand their rage and distrust of the government beyond what happened on September the 11th, because if you're looking for examples of how distrustful Washington is and how the president is a complete asshole [who is] able to commit unforgivable crimes against humanity and [who can] kill thousands of innocent people for purely political reasons, just look at his domestic policies against poor and underprivileged people living in the country right now. Look at his foreign policy, which is not secret and is published in The New York Times and The Wall Street Journal every day. For fucksake, beginning with the sanctions against Iraq, implemented by the first Bush in '91, straight through until now, we're responsible for millions of deaths that could have been avoided. Then there's Clinton's bombing of the Sudanese pharmaceutical plant [in 1998] that destroyed the lives of millions of people. The point is, by sitting across the street from the White House in a windowless van with your night binoculars trained on shadows you see through the curtains, you risk missing what is already happening in broad daylight, which is stuff that is way worse than what you're trying to uncover.

Right, like looking for dirt on Eva Braun.

(*Laughs*) Exactly!

But, yeah, getting back to your point about satire, it is much harder to create satire when the world itself is naturally satirical.

So then we have to ask the question of what jokes do. Do jokes spotlight what is already funny about the world or do jokes reinterpret the world and create something funny about it? Is it funny, for example, that lawyers are cheats and politicians are liars, or is it unfunny that lawyers are cheats and politicians are liars, and jokes help us deal with the misery of that reality? Does satire defang the monsters that we feel most threatened by or does satire give us sanctuary from those monsters, the same way that being locked up in a prison cell protects us from the terror of having to keep up with a mortgage and maintain a lawn? Which came first, the chicken or the rubber chicken?

I don't know that there's an answer to that.

Well, I do feel that satire has opened my eyes to certain things, but I'm not sure if it is my inner eye or my outer eye that was opened.

I remember when I was a counselor at a summer camp and how they would show Charlie Chaplin movies and some counselor would inevitably get up and say, "Now the deep social message that

Chaplin was trying to convey in the scene when he had to eat his shoelaces …" You know? We were all talking about why we laugh, and the kids were saying, "I thought he had a funny walk." So, again, there's that innate sense of humor that we can all tap into and maybe that defangs the monster.

At least the monster that we project onto the world with our own pessimism. That was what John [Lennon] and Yoko [Ono] said when the press accused them of not taking the protests against the Vietnam War seriously enough. They said that they were willing to be the world's clowns [during their Bed-In event], the idea being that humor is anti-violent. They made the point that you're unlikely to attack somebody else, much less kill them, when you're having a laugh.

And yet satire is often called a weapon.

Which brings us back to the precariousness of jokes designed to do something more than just make people laugh. A satirist is either funny when you agree with him or downright mean when you don't. In fact, there are a lot of people who won't even call satire art, precisely because it involves [political subject matter]. They're the same people who insist that the surest way to fuck up a piece of art is to inject politics into it.

There again, it's all about the individual perception. Some people need politics injected for it to qualify as art.

I agree. There's also a pretty good argument for how injecting art into politics can fuck up politics — at least how one relates to politics on a personal level. The example that I always give is how watching "The Daily Show" and "The Colbert Report" can fool a person into thinking that he or she is being politically active when he or she isn't. It's because watching TV is a private act and engaging in political activity is a public [act], and when somebody is at home watching a television show, though he or she might be agreeing with jokes about, say, the criminality of the president or the injustice or a piece of domestic or foreign policy, he or she is not doing anything about it. In that way, laughter can deter political activity.

I know what you mean, sure. On the other hand, [my wife] Nancy memorized Mort Sahl's first album ["The Future Lies Ahead," 1958] when it came out, and when you memorize something like that, you really pick up on a lot of nuance about how the country works. You absorb a lot of critical thinking; it's a very subtle process. And that can be politicizing and make you politically minded at the very least and make you behave a certain way. I remember when I lived in San Francisco and attended the annual Comedy Day in the Park. This was in the '80s, in Golden Gate Park, and there was a long string of comedians, and the only thing I remember from the day was a guy standing up and saying, "Isn't Reagan an asshole?!" And the audience [went] crazy with applause and yells and the guy [said], "Oh, so you like the political stuff." So there are different standards of what being politically minded means. Sometimes you can be political without naming names. Guys like Mark Twain and H. L. Mencken and Will Rogers were all political.

And so was Bruce, though not overtly so.

Lenny Bruce died to make it safe for Jon Stewart to get laughs by saying words he knows will get bleeped out.

Further proof that Bruce didn't die for our sins, but because of them. God, I miss that guy.

Yeah, me too.

I guess what I worry about is the ability of a good political joke to diffuse the rage that a person might have for a politician who deserves all the vitriol that we can throw at him. Sometimes I think it's more important to embrace the discomfort that comes from being pissed off about something than to have your disdain obliterated by the relief you get from laughter.

Lenny and I used to talk about this stuff all the time, and his position was that people don't like to be lectured at. He believed that if you [could] make somebody laugh with a joke that [had] some truth about society embedded within it, the fact that they're laughing indicates that their defenses are down and that they're more likely to consider the information you're telling them. The joke makes it impossible for a person to guard against [the wisdom of the argument] you're presenting.

Plus, if it's a good joke, it will bear repeating to more and more people, and the information can become viral that way. It's like a catchy tune that you want to hear again and again.

Right — I'm relatively jaded, and if something really stirs me, either a contradiction or an absurdity or a horrible cruelty that has been euphemized, and that will set my EEG off, then I'll want to create a satire that crystalizes that contradiction or whatever it is, and I'll want to share it with people. Then, if it's funny, those people will want to share it, too. It's how *The Realist* grew. Steve Allen was the first subscriber, and he gave a bunch of subscriptions to a lot of other people, including Lenny Bruce, and then Lenny sent out a bunch, and the magazine really took off that way.

Of course, when it comes to the catchiness of tunes that people want to hear again and again, taste can sometimes trump nutritional value. There's the two-step, but there is also the goose step.

Right. Now that you mention it, I think "Malthusian" was the word they used to use before "viral."

Of course — yesterday's torture is today's enhanced interrogation.

And dead babies [have always been] collateral damage.

And, thanks to people like you and Lenny Bruce, "Fuck the government" will always mean "Fuck the government." Which's goes back to something you've said [many times before], which is that you shouldn't take yourself so seriously —

(*Interrupting*) That you shouldn't take yourself as seriously as your cause.

Right, as a strategy, I agree, you don't want to compete with a tragic situation [by insisting everybody notice the tears rolling down your cheeks] — but as a practicality you shouldn't take yourself seriously because humor forces you to maintain a parameter around your subject.

What do you mean by that?

Well, in order to make a joke about something

you need to have a complete understanding of whatever you're making fun of, particularly in the case of satire. You can't make a [satirical] joke about something that you don't comprehend, because with satire you're usually exploiting how the dominant culture sees something and your job is to either offer an alternative point of view or to force your audience to question their [blind allegiance] to a particular truth — right? In that way, humor [necessitates] comprehension [and] literally encourages a person to study something and to learn about it so the dissection is clean and accurate.

Oh — you know who made a great quote about that in a roundabout way?

Who?

Harlan Ellison — he said, "The real story of our times is seldom told in the horse-puckery-filled memoirs of dopey, self-serving presidents or generals, but in the outrageous, demented lives of guys like Lenny Bruce, Giordano Bruno [and] Scott Fitzgerald. The burrs under society's saddle. The pains in the ass." I always said that Bruce stopped people in their tracks to make them question what they stood for.

That's great.

But who are the pains in the ass now? I don't know. The society seems to be in a state of flux because we don't know how to make satire *work* anymore. In a way, politics has gotten so strange that [lunacy] is now public policy and people are [being forced to] actually *live* out satire as the butt of the joke. It's exhausting!

That's an important point to make — imagine how tired [we'd all] get of *knock-knock* jokes if every day [we] were forced to get up and down, over and over again, to ask, "Who's there? Who's there? Who's there?" to [an] endless [barrage of] pounding on a door.

There's so much anger in the world that the only jokes people are interested in are jokes that make us happy, which kills satire. It's not a satirist's job to make a person *laugh*.

What is a satirist's job?

To expose hypocrisy in a way that makes hypocrites look like fools.

So, again, it's about revealing a truth that, for one reason or another, has been camouflaged by either power or polite society and [doing so] in a creative way instead of a journalistic way, or a lawyerly way.

Sure — satire makes it possible to laugh and not feel guilty about laughing because it's usually coupled with a sobering truth, so there's insight there. I'm always wavering between hope and despair and satire can help strike a balance between those two things because it usually contains both.

You see satire as a form of art more than as a mere subgenre of humor.

That's right — it is its own unique thing.

And I guess that's because it's not always about *joke making* — sometimes it's about interpreting something that already exists or was created for some other purpose other than humor. A good example would be the videos that Osama bin Laden released after 9/11. I remember watching those and being horribly conflicted because, yes, he's a psychotic warlord speaking from a cave somewhere in the desert, but he's also talking about things that I really care about and that no U.S. politician would *ever* talk about — things like the plight of the Palestinians and how brutal [our] foreign policy is and how little we care about international law. I found myself thinking, "This guy should have a show on NPR, right after *Car Talk* — I'd up my pledge for that!" The whole experience had a real *Strangelove* vibe to it.

I know what you mean, and there's a real predictability to how [fanaticism from both sides] frames how we talk about things. I'm sure there were some people who walked away from the Sermon on the Mount saying, "Did you hear what that nut said about loving my brother — my brother's an asshole!" Anybody can rationalize themselves out of understanding [something] — everything is a euphemism for something else and the purpose of a euphemism is to hide reality.

So now we're talking about satire as a kind of activism, as agitation. Why are there fewer satirists working today than in the 1960s?

I think it's because things keep getting worse and there are more causes [nowadays] than there were in the '60s [to accommodate all the problems]. We've gone from *WE SHALL OVERCOME* to *WE SHALL OVERLAP*. Some groups want to agitate politically, and others don't. The New Agers started as [a] movement that was all about personal growth and healing and now it has UFOs in it. History is nothing but shifting sands that you can't draw a line in because there's always a new wind that comes along. We should also recognize that many of the seeds that were planted in the '60s are only just now blossoming — things like organic foods, sustainability, bioregionalism and how the health of the planet is in jeopardy because of the arbitrary borders [we draw] between nations. In that way, the history of the counterculture is still being written.

And to your point about more and more splintered groups overlapping with [one another], one can be fooled by the optics into thinking that the group they belong to is huge and effective when it's really not that big and [largely] inef-

fective. My brother called me in 2004 when I was marching in an anti-war protest in San Francisco and he was marching in Washington D.C. to tell me how excited he was by the size of the crowd he was in until he noticed that he was surrounded by pro-PLO supporters, environmentalists, one guy who wanted his foreskin back, some Pro Choice people and an anti-death penalty/Free Mumia [Abu-Jamal] group. Sure, you could argue that they're all linked by some common concern for justice and civil society, but when you have everybody leeching off the same psychic energy amassed in one space [it's possible to] lose perspective with regards to how best to sustain and properly weaponize your own [particular] cause.

Yes — fragmentation can be a big problem, but sometimes the links between the fragments are important. In the 1960s it was mostly middleclass white people who went to protests against the war, and then African Americans joined in and said, "No Vietnamese ever called me *nigger.*" And then the Hard Hats and the union guys who used to beat us up ended up saying, "No Vietnamese ever froze my wages." So, everybody has their own pain threshold and when the pain in society increases, more and more thresholds get breached and the more and more we're [able to unify our causes] and see how we're all in the same boat.

Still, I wouldn't say that black people were helped very much by joining the middleclass, white anti-war movement. In fact, I'd say the Civil Rights Movement was helped by middleclass white college students joining the Black movement.

Either way, breaching the color line was important because, in the end, both needed to become a people's movement to get anywhere at all. In other words, creativity is what propelled those movements forward. There's an Einstein quote that was given to me years ago by an 83-year-old massage therapist before he moved to Berkeley and the quote is: *Imagination is more important than knowledge. Forknowledgeis limited, whereasimaginationembraces the entire world, stimulating progress, giving birth to evolution. It is, strictly speaking, a real factor in scientific research.*

I get nervous when imagination meets scientific research.

Well, sure, with Oppenheimer and the atom bomb — but I was reading about how this 16-year-old kid created a bacteria that eats up plastic. I get inspired by things like that.

I heard about that, too, and I think it eats petroleum and then dies.

Yeah, yeah.

I also heard that companies like DuPont are doing research on a bunch of biotechnologies like that, not only for environmental cleanup but also for computer processing and nanotechnologies, and that lawyers are getting ready to argue the ethical ramifications of using lifeforms in this way. It's really a question of micro-slavery and how complicated an organism needs to be before we recognize that it has a right to be protected and not *enslaved* by a corporation. It's things like that that keep me up at night, mostly because I think a court is more likely to protect big business over the efficacy of life — look at fracking and strip mining, for fucksake.

That's true, you're right. It's an interesting time to be alive!

Interesting is one word for it.

There's an old Chinese curse that says, "May you live in interesting times." Of course, that saying was invented, evolved and manipulated by the ruling class who loved the status quo, so *interesting* meant trouble to them which is why it was a curse. But to the people who rebel against the status quo, an *interesting* time is a blessing! It's how they get their shackles off. So, when I say we live in interesting times, I'm not trying to be glib or [loquacious] — I'm really trying to be *interesting.*

So, let's end our conversation with what we started it with, and that's *satire*. Satire has always been the best tool to use for exploratory surgery on the body politic, particularly when one sees symptoms of disease in a society prone to shutting down debate and discouraging dialogue between two opposing points of view — which, really, is *every* society set up as a hierarchy that assumes that the opulent minority has a right to determine and control the destiny of the majority, which, of course, is *every* society because I can't think of

any contemporary society with a government that doesn't insist on a hierarchical structure where dissent against the ruling class is considered rude, criminal or a kind of madness. For example, one can broadly criticize the viability of religion by directly questioning its allegiance to the mystical over the scientific, thereby shutting down, or at least severely limiting, the potential for a conversation afterwards because a power dynamic has been established where one party is seen as the aggressor and the other is seen as a target, or one can ask a satirical question that invites a more measured response: *If Jesus knew all along that Heaven was Paradise and that He was going to exist there forever and get to hang out with all the celebrities who had ever lived and who will ever live and that his dad, who has the recipe for dinosaurs, rainbows, puppies and irony, is in charge of absolutely everything, how was dying on the cross a sacrifice?*

Ha! You're right, and that's how satire works — it finds contradictions in popular logic and exposes them. It takes a literal target, like [religious dogmatism in] your example, and makes it a figurative target that everybody can stand outside of and comment on. Remember that *New Yorker* cover that had the Obamas dressed as Muslim terrorists?

Yeah, yeah.

That was great because it had Democrats angry and not Republicans for once, because [the Left] didn't trust people from Kansas City or Nebraska to get the joke. It was the Party of the People essentially saying that *The People* were idiots! David Remnick [*editor of* The New Yorker] was right when he said that satire doesn't run with subtitles and that's the problem — people don't understand anymore that they're being invited [to participate in a conversation].

So, you're saying that satire isn't dead as much as the audience for satire is becoming tone-deaf to the artform?

Well there certainly is less of it nowadays, particularly on the printed page — satire I mean. When I was in college [*as a journalism major at Baruch College in New York City*] I discovered Bertrand Russell and one thing I remember [from] *Why I*

Am Not a Christian is [him] saying, "You don't see [Stanley Baldwin, *Prime Minister of Great Britain*] turning the other cheek!" which set me on this path of searching out hypocrisy. And that's what I love about the *New Yorker* cover; liberals reacting to a cover that lampoons them as fundamentalists from a Right-wing perspective by acting like fundamentalists!

Hence the hypocrisy piece that you mentioned! I remember the hard shift to the right that Obama took the day after he won the nomination, how he started to sound more and more like George W. Bush by saying if elected he might target Iran and how important it would be to maintain a military presence in the middle east, and on and on and on, and how those who [supported] him because they thought he was Gandhi became apologists for his rhetoric by saying, "Well, he has to say that stuff to get votes — after all, he is running for President." That's why we're fucked now because we're letting politicians frame our political conversations and we're becoming apologists for [campaign] strategies over critical thinking.

Right — *I'm going to sell helicopter gunships to Israel and maintain the embargo against Cuba!*

Which brings us back to how the counterculture dealt with those who toed the party line in the 1960s. It seemed to me that there used to exist an arts community that had a responsibility to call out bullshit, particularly the bureaucratic sort since [the bureaucratic sort] had the most potential to be lethal.

Still does!

I know! But what do we have now? I'd guess that the overwhelming majority of liberal [political and editorial] cartoonists working today would call themselves democrats whose job it is to argue in support of a party platform designed by special interest groups and public relations firms. Compare that to cartoonists working for the alternative and underground press in the 1960s and 70s who didn't have any party affiliations at all. It was their job to argue in contempt of [formalized] power [structures] that existed on both sides of the aisle.

I had a joke about that! I used to say that the New Left had to keep their orgasms to a minimum so they could save their strength to work the mimeograph machine.

So, in a way we've lost the ability to intellectually copulate freely in society with whomever we want, whenever we want, because we're being commanded to respect the sanctity of *mirage* — the corporate news media *mirage*, that is.

Ha!

I blame you for that! I never used to talk like that until I met you.

A meeting of the minefields!

I wonder if our [modern] technology confuses us into thinking we're something we're really not. For example, before the internet in order to be a dissident or a progressive you had to actually demonstrate that you were one in public, whether it was through marching or burning your draft card or staging a sit-in or [whatever]. Now all you have to do is share an Alan Watts quote typed across a shitty picture of a sunset or download a Michael Moore movie or get a Che Guevarra tattoo and suddenly you're fucking Eugene Debs or Mother Jones.

I know what you mean. I did [a live comedy] album a couple years ago when John Ashcroft [U.S. Attorney General under George W. Bush] was doing a lot of terrible things, like blocking the Oregon Death with Dignity Act and things like that, and I asked the audience to join me in saying, "Fuck you, John Ashcroft!" So I counted *one, two, three* and everybody did it — *FUCK YOU, JOHN ASHCROFT!* — and they laughed and clapped and then I said, "Doesn't it feel good to be a political activist?" Part of the problem is that people don't know what to do anymore.

I agree. I think that the protest population died when the middle class was eradicated [in this country]. Rich people aren't going to agitate for equality and poor people are too busy trying to stay alive to organize a sustainable protest movement [fraught with resistence]. Making art and trying to change the system is not a paying gig and it needs to be subsidized somehow. It was a middle class that permitted that to happen.

Well, the other thing that a middle class permitted was optimism in the community. Rich people don't have neighbors and poor people don't have optimism. In other words, people won't fight for a meaningful life if they don't see any evidence that one is possible.

Unless a meaningful life is revealed by the pursuit of meaning and not the attainment. Maybe meaning is arbitrary and only exists as a goal. Sometimes I wonder if it isn't our curse to perpetuate existential dread so that we can maintain our fury over its existence and that's all morality is.

Like feeding the bull flowers so he can shit out bullshit that will prove that the flowers are pretty by comparison to bullshit.

Yes.

Well, I received my journalistic apprenticeship with Lyle Stuart who published *The Independent*, which was a forerunner to the alternative press. It was part of a long tradition, because George Seldes' *In Fact* preceded that and *I.F. Stone's Weekly* and all the way back to the 1890s and [William Cowper] Brann's *Iconoclast*, all the way back to Thomas Paine. Anyway, [Stuart] ran a story on how the Anti-Defamation League was

subsidizing anti-Semitic publications and it was a huge scandal because people were surprised to find out that that kind of symbiosis could exist, where, to your point, it probably exists everywhere all the time.

That's why I think it's so important to have artists and satirists leading the conversation about what's right and wrong with our politics, our culture and [our] human behavior because artists and satirists are [best] equipped to tell the truth about who we really are as opposed who we wish we were or pretend to be. Naomi Klein can explain the disconnect between public and private institutions of power, but will she ever put herself into the equation and talk about her failings and inconsistencies? That's why people like Norman Mailer and Susan Sontag and even Gore Vidal were invaluable, because they let their vulnerability as human beings ground the stories they told in something murkier and more inviting than just the straight facts.

Hunter S. Thompson did that.

Yeah! And Carlin, Bruce and Hicks did it, too! Maybe I should just be talking about comedians here because that's really the job of most comedians. Jack Benny played a guy who was cheap and untalented and petty and self-important — plus, he had no luck with the ladies and made terrible movies and, still, he was the most beloved radio personality of all time because people saw themselves in his failings.

That's why I'm an atheist — because I see my superiority in His nonexistence.

Which is why you're such an inspiring fool. *

MR. FISH

GIVE US THIS DAY OUR DAILY SHOW

IN 1936, THE NAZIS organized a massive get-to-gether in Nuremberg for malleable nincompoops and called the gathering *Reichsparteitag der Ehre*, or "Rally of Honor." Watching clips from Glenn Beck's "Restoring Honor Rally" held in Washington, D.C., in August 2010, I was reminded of how, while growing up and flipping through channels, I would occasionally come across grainy footage of Adolf Hitler in Nuremberg and see the enthusiastic crowds applauding him and waving little flags, and I'd ponder what made these people so gullible to the nationalistic lunacy and bug-eyed, fascistic tribalism they were being inundated with. Is it really possible, I wondered, to imbibe fear and hatred with so much charisma that the end result of heeding its precepts will appear gleeful and positive and finally gratifying?

How, I asked myself, could such a whopping organizational feat as a Nuremberg rally even come off, with the weeks of preparation and all those opportunities for second-guessing by so many people? How, with all those workers setting up chairs and hanging banners and angling lights and arranging flowers and loading film cameras and proofreading speeches, did nobody suddenly stop doing what he or she was doing and say, "Hey, wait a minute — this is absolutely bat-shit crazy!?"

Of course, as a political cartoonist, such grand gestures of vaulting ignorance, particularly when marked by all the mindless rage and gaudy, ostentatious celebration of a sporting event, can often make my job way too easy to be at all effective. When Glenn Beck, the headliner at the most recent, though by no means the last, honor rally (the same Glenn Beck who regularly warns his radio and television audiences of the lethal concoction that is Islamic God and Islamic country) stands up in front of the Lincoln Memorial and says that the United States has been wandering around in the dark for too long and that it is time — a civic duty, in fact! — for every American to return to a position of complete subservience to a famously intolerant Christian god who has a long history of murdering and torturing his critics both in and *after* life, the joke has already been made. The cartoon has already been drawn. In other words, when somebody takes a crap on the floor it doesn't matter how good your thesaurus is, the actual stench of the shit will always trump any artistic description of it.

So, then, the question becomes obvious: How is it possible for people to so easily ignore, en masse, all the warning signs that typically come before manmade disasters, whether they're disasters engineered by ego or über-ego or fiat or hubris or whatever? The rallies at Nuremberg, as I've indicated, are a classic example. Joseph McCarthy's Wheeling Speech is another. George W. Bush's post-9/11 speeches are another. The post-crucifixion, transcribed paraphrases of Jesus

Christ are another. What is it, precisely, about the assemblage of a vast number of human heads that more often than not encourages a uniform stupidity rather than an accrued intelligence? Even the much-celebrated election of Barack Obama as president exemplifies a massive congruence of self-proclaimed liberal and progressive Americans suddenly blind by their own choice to the obvious fact that rather than electing a forward-thinking and radically compassionate and intelligent humanitarian — a living saint comparable in the press to Martin Luther King and Mahatma Gandhi and Jean-Luc Picard from "Star Trek: The Next Generation" — they were merely falling in line behind an establishment candidate no more likely to run afoul of the traditional values and deeply conservative principles of the Democratic Party than any ass hired to represent the brand.

(Look out your window and tell me that I'm wrong.)

And then there was "The Rally to Restore Sanity and/or Fear" on the Mall in Washington, D.C., which took place two months after Beck's rally and was hosted by everybody's favorite TV stars, Jon Stewart and Stephen Colbert. Did this humongous assemblage of, according to some esti-

IT WAS SO GODDAMN FRUSTRATING FOR TOM - EVERY ELECTION HE DID HIS BEST TO VOTE FOR THE CANDIDATE WHO STRUCK THE MOST EQUITABLE BALANCE BETWEEN THE MOST PLURALISTIC DEMOCRATIC IDEALS AND THE MOST AUTOCRATIC AND FASCISTIC MONISM AND THE WORLD JUST GOT INEXPLICABLY WORSE AND WORSE

MR.FISH

OF COURSE THE AGENCY HAS ENOUGH DIRT ON THE PRESIDENT TO SINK HIS ADMINISTRATION – THE TROUBLE IS WE ALSO HAVE ENOUGH DIRT ON EVERYBODY ELSE IN THE WASHINGTON ESTABLISHMENT TO MAKE IT SO IF WE PULL ON THAT THREAD THE ONLY PEOPLE LEFT TO GOVERN WILL BE THE ONES WHO CLEAN THE TOILETS AND TAKE OUT THE GARBAGE, AT WHICH POINT WE'LL BE STUCK WITH A REPRESENTATIVE DEMOCRACY AND THIS COUNTRY JUST ISN'T SET UP FOR THAT.

MR.FISH

mates, a quarter of a million people encourage a uniform stupidity rather than an accrued intelligence? Or, rather, did this rally's focus on joke-making exempt it from needing to adopt a hate-baiting, lynch mob mentality? If so, does such an exemption disqualify the gathering from just being Nuremberg-lite?

There's a story about Oscar Wilde walking through a birthing ward in a London hospital in the late 1800s and saying to an inconsolable mother who had just given birth to a pair of stillborn twins, "Buck up and be jolly, my dear lady! Stillbirth is a sign that God has a sense of humor!" It is a quote that can simultaneously give one hope for the future of humankind while also demonstrating why we are almost certainly doomed as a species. On the one hand, as a sheer spectacle it is an inspiring example of one man's ability to use humor in a real-life situation that the average onlooker would deem inhospitable to joke-making — the conceptual equivalent of striking a match underwater — and then, more important, it is somehow proof that reality itself, as it is defined by cold, hard fact, is never the sole determinant of truth in any given situation. That is to say that nothing, by mere virtue of its literal physicality, is wholly self-defining and nothing can happen in the world that cannot be skewed by interpretation and made into something else.

Jokes, like any other form of magic, can take a truth, usually a horrible one, and convert it into a satirical concept that, because it is an opinion

and no longer tethered to fact, is malleable and, therefore, capable of either rising above or nestling beneath, like a whoopee cushion, those truisms that the joke teller hopes to subvert. Humor, then, like any other form of mollification, can often dislodge the disease of hopelessness from any situation that appears hopeless and invigorate the joker's chosen audience with hopeful optimism. But, of course, on the other hand, when such a distraction is allowed to divert attention away from a situation that may in fact be *truly* hopeless and *really dangerous* then the diversion can prove disastrous.

In other words, readying a slide whistle and a pair of cymbals for the consequences of a safe that is being pushed from a 10-story window above a crowded sidewalk will not alter the physics of gravity sufficiently to temper the tragic consequences.

And that is precisely what I believe makes Stewart and Colbert, particularly in the context of a political rally staged at the nation's capital in obvious response to Beck's event, ultimately ineffective as either saviors of our collective cultural sanity or inspirational martyrs maligned unjustly by our savage indifference to our own fate. After all, when a clown is chosen by a society's pandemic fear of the dark to lead us all into the light, we can't be certain that the clown will think to move us all beyond the circle of his own spotlight. But why should he? A comedian's ultimate obligation is to a society's funny bone, all other bones be, perhaps not damned, but at least razzberried and machine-gunned by the fury of a seltzer bottle.

Thusly, when an average of 2 million viewers, myself included, were tuning in every weeknight to see "The Daily Show With Jon Stewart," they were there to jeer and hoot and ridicule the despicability and ineptness and sometimes criminality of both our elected officials and the media outlets that leech off their troubling antics and sell us our soap. They were there to see powerful men and women clobbered by their own exposed hypocrisies. Viewers of "The Daily Show," whether we're talking about the older version or the newer version with Trevor Noah, are there to have their anxiety alleviated, to have their mistrust of politicians justified and to have the pain and humiliation of their being continuously shat upon by oppressive forces from the upper echelons of government and industry and social pedigree lessened. Indeed, these are the noble tasks of the satirist: to help not only maintain but also to promote the concept that the power we invest in authority is power that we can also *divest*, to prove that laughter is much more likely than sorrow to inspire our desire to congregate as a democratic society and to shake the fear from our natural instinct to retreat from psychological hardship and to cower in isolation.

But, of course, enlightening people to the reality of bullshit is only half the task of the satirist and by no means an end unto itself. After all, it is not the diagnosis of a disease that cures the patient.

So, minus the existence of a well-organized, well-informed, deeply passionate and viable peace and anti-establishmentarian movement in this country, what will usually end up happening is that contemporary satire will often convert our rage at the dominant culture into whimsy and transform us from a threat to the social structures that berate us to complacent idiots. Political comedy, without practical application within a political strategy, will merely satiate our hunger for real change with a punch line and rob us of our sensitivity to any number of social and political injustices. Remember that levity provides a biochemical relief to our physiologies. It tells our insides that all is well and that there is happiness in our lives and that being buoyed by this temporary joy is justified by its own ends. Only when a wound is allowed to remain open and some measure of discomfort is permitted to pester our morality will we act to seek a solution to eliminating our pain and the pain that we empathetically feel in others. In other words, without agony, treachery and injustice can and will become dismissible.

"I'm sure a lot of you were just here to have a nice time, and I hope you did," intoned Stewart from the stage at the end of his rally, groping comedically for a reason why the event was organized and also why the overwhelming majority of his audience showed up to watch it. Such a banal and grandmotherly adieu left me to wonder if Americans shouldn't be looking for a more profound reason to stand shoulder to shoulder in a crowd of 250,000, in their nation's capital, carrying signs and wearing T-shirts demanding peace, love and understanding in every way possible, than just to have a *nice time*.

Contrary to the mood of those surrounding me, those who were continuously waving at themselves on the immense monitors set up all over the Mall, I refused to fool myself into thinking, even for a historical moment, that we were just too big to fail. ✳

"So after we make a shitload of money for the investors by turning the world into a toxic swamp of liquefied human refuse, let's take some time off for ourselves."

A BRIEF EXCHANGE WITH ROBBIE CONAL

WALKING INTO ROBBIE CONAL'S Westside studio on a recent Thursday afternoon, I found the guerrilla poster artist and political hell-raiser wearing green surgical gloves and standing before a brightly lit wall hung with several of his enormous triptychs, diptychs and paintings, all at varying stages of completion for a career retrospective at the Track 16 Gallery in Santa Monica. His clothes and skin were splattered, slashed and smudged with enough paint to make him appear as if he himself had been Jackson Pollocked into existence by some brilliantly joyful enthusiasm.

After he asked me to busy myself by looking around while he finished up with some things, I took my time to examine a pair of photomontages painted over with hilariously asinine images of electric-blue Smurfs, Simon Cowell praying beneath a skinny neon halo, the floating disembodied heads of many of the most despised American politicians of the past 30 years, Jack from *Jack in the Box*, the "Mission Accomplished" banner, the Death Star, ghetto-gold typography, J.R. from *Dallas*, innumerable skunks and just about every other stray image of American pop and political culture that anybody alive during the past half-century might be able to think of.

Invited to sit for what would turn out to be a four-hour conversation on everything from Conal's 10-month stint as a methed-out graveyard-shift cab driver in 1970 at the height of the Zodiac killings in San Francisco to his spiritual devotion to cat portraiture, I turned on my tape recorder and asked, "What is the longevity of glitter?" noticing that some of the pieces he was working on were completely covered with the stuff. All I could picture was the heartbreaking oxidization that had turned so many of the newsprint and paper collages from the 1920s and '30s into artless wads of dead leaves.

"It isn't about longevity, man," laughed Conal, slapping me hard on the back and looking, like L.A. itself, much younger than his age. "It's about living! It's about NOW!"

We were off.

❖❖❖

I figure that when you first began postering, few people really understood exactly what you were up to, but now, since you've created this huge body of work, people will actually invest time to contemplate your significance.

Yeah, the art happens when the viewer is looking at your stuff and trying to figure out what box it goes in — maybe a new box has to be built. And that only takes 10 or 15 seconds and then they can forget about you. But when you're postering for 25 or 30 years, you can link all that time together and reach some kind of critical mass that people can't shake.

An art gallery certainly provides a completely different viewing experience versus a street corner.

It's a completely different mindset. Those moments between receiving the image and figuring it out is where an artist does his job. In my case, this has always been both the curse and the blessing about living in L.A., where people are so receptive to superficial signage. They either don't mind it or they don't notice it.

Bob Dylan once said that the best place to hang art is above the urinal at a gas station.

He's not wrong.

You grew up in New York in the 1950s, and your parents, who were union organizers, dropped you off at museums while they worked instead of getting you a babysitter.

I didn't get dropped off — it was New York. I got a dollar bill and two subway tokens.

What did you get from that experience — a deep appreciation of art or a deeper appreciation of self-reliance and personal independence?

It was both, really. It all started with an Ensor painting, *Death and the Masks*, which I saw when I was 9 or 10. It was a painting that wasn't on my itinerary [of things to see], because I was mostly into knights and armor, the stuffed horses, the pyramids, the tribal costumes from New Guinea made out of woven reeds and mud — scary shit, powerful because it was to scale and not two-dimensional illusion, like painting. Anyway, that Ensor was so freaky, like one of those things that's so grotesque you want to see how long you can stand there before turning away.

Intellectual heroism — maybe that's where your dissent came from, practicing the ability to look at something head-on without turning away.

Yeah, it's fun. After that, the Abstract Expressionists became my guys. Still are.

I always thought the smartest thing your work did was to force the public against its will to consider ideas about dissent and to look at images of protest.

The kindest thing you can say about me is that I'm a conspiracy.

By embedding your work into the landscape, literally, you help prevent radical notions of free speech and liberal politics from becoming antiquated.

Creating signage that is out of place and doesn't belong because it isn't selling anything, particularly in a consumer culture, is important. The nature of reduction and what it doesn't include is ample justification for why it's there.

Did you ever worry that your vilification of certain politicians and religious leaders read as reactionary?

Was it character assassination, you mean?

Yeah, like responding to the vitriol of Bush and Reagan with your own vitriol, which pretty much amounts to a "Fuck you!" "No, fuck YOU!" type of conversation, and how that kind of back and forth really does nothing to deepen anybody's understanding of anything. I mean, isn't the problem with political discourse in this country that it's too simplistic and ridiculously shallow, anyway?

That's a really good point — that [what I do] might add to the problem, in the sense that it's polarizing.

Do you see yourself as a bomb thrower or a bomb diffuser? Are you providing an emotional release for people who feel too disenfranchised to say "Fuck you!" to the ruling class? By putting a face on what pisses people off, are you helping to keep us all sane by letting us know that we're not crazy?

Or alone. Listen, using satirical critique and portraiture as an interrogation of somebody's morality is fine. And, sure, examining a politician's corro-

DRAWING A POLITICIAN AS AN ASSHOLE AND THEN LABELING HIM AS ONE IS NOT A MEANINGFUL ACT OF DISSENT OR PROGRESSIVISM, NOR IS HAVING THE DRAWING PUBLISHED AND SEEN BY AN AUDIENCE WHO AGREES THAT THE POLITICIAN IS AN ASSHOLE. A MEANINGFUL ACT OF DISSENT AND PROGRESSIVISM WOULD BE TO GET EVERYBODY TO RECOGNIZE THE ASSHOLINESS OF THE POLITICIAN'S JOB SO THAT WE CAN ALL BEGIN THE FIRST POSITIVE STEPS TOWARD ERADICATING THE OCCUPATION, ITSELF, THEREBY PREVENTING MORE AND MORE QUALIFIED APPLICANTS FROM COMING ALONG TO MEET THE REQUIREMENTS AND TO FILL THE POSITION AND TO PERFORM IN IT WITH SUCH DIGNIFIED AND CHEERFUL EXPERTISE

MR.FISH

sive essence can be depressing as hell, but these fuckers are trying to take over the world, and that kind of thing really hurts my delicate sensibilities — it really does.

Let's talk about your Track 16 retrospective. What's going to be in it?

A lot of stuff that nobody's ever seen before — or that they've only seen as reproductions. The show is really about providing that one-to-one, con-templative art experience of being face to face with a real painting by a real person. That's how I received some of the greatest shocks and insights of my life — a tiny kid standing in front of *Guernica*. Reproductions are okay, but a real painting gives off some kind of narcotic effluvia that makes you unsure of how the rest of your day is going to go.

Sure — it's like the difference between live music and recorded. There's an emotional, visceral athleticism that's lost in reproduction.

There's nothing like looking at real paint that's been pushed around.

What is only hinted at by your posters is how thick and sculptural the actual paint is — an effect that really underscores the ultimate Robbie Conal experience. You have these giant political icons whose strength derives from how frightening and bullying their reputations are, and you've made them vulnerable. In fact, they're rendered almost like fruit, like rotting fruit — they're not even animal anymore.

That's great, man — that's success! I can only hope that's true.

Really, you render them harmless. Rembrandt ruined his career draining the significance out of the upper class, and you've made yours doing the same thing.

Good — I hate those fuckers. *

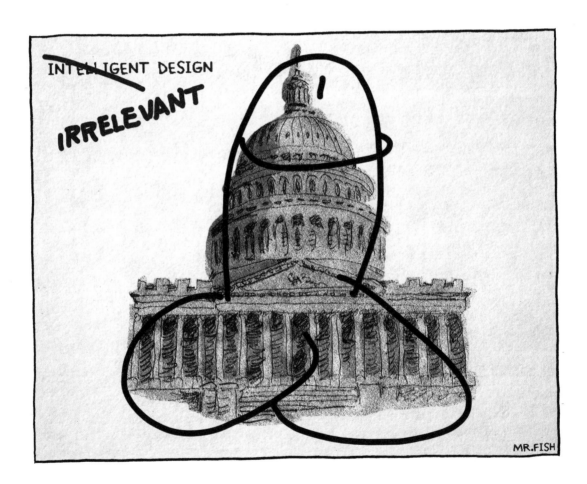

DEMOCRACY: ASSEMBLY REQUIRED (A CONVERSATION WITH TARIQ ALI)

"When it comes to the nitty-gritty, [the state] won't let the people have any power; they'll give [artists] all the rights to perform and to dance for [the king], but no real power."

—John Lennon to Tariq Ali in an interview published in *The Red Mole*, 1971

IT COULD BE SAID OF PORNOGRAPHY that dirty pictures aren't so much about sex as they are about masturbation, just as it could be said of politics that legislation isn't so much about the rule of law as it is about codifying the subjugation of freedom. If this is true, and every revolution and counter revolution in history has given us every indication that it absolutely is, then what is it about freedom that makes so many people supportive of such subjugation? Is it that freedom, because it diminishes the predictability of behavior regulated by propriety, suggest lawlessness—pandemonium, even? If so, when has a barrier to the free expression of our most basic impulses to exist cage-free and in contempt of prohibitive guidelines imposed by policy ever been built and policed by fiat and ritual not been breached by our natural instinct for emancipation? Is this a question of what distracts us from empathizing with the existential agony of our own personal circumstance, the heart or the head, and can a deep distrust of the head's ability to justify our surrender to a straightjacket of obedience to authority corrupt our willingness to forever distrust the yearning in our heart for liberation?

Who is supposed to ask these questions and who is supposed to answer them?

THANKS

FOR DYING
WHILE TRYING TO KILL
A SHITLOAD OF OTHER PEOPLE
BECAUSE WITHOUT YOU AND THE RICH
BIGOTED ASSHOLES WHO MADE YOU THE WEAPONIZED
AUTOMATONS OF THEIR GREED, PREJUDICE, PARANOIA AND COWARDICE
I WOULDN'T KNOW WHAT HEROISM IS!

I teach a course at the University of Pennsylvania about the history of art as commentary. I rely heavily on cartoons, illustrations and photography from the 1960s underground press because of the format's long history battling censorship and charges of indecency. Each semester I assign a paper designed to show how the concept of obscenity is a socialized construct rather than an intuitive reaction to an external phenomenon; real *eye of the beholder* stuff. For the assignment, I ask the students to search for a piece of art that is personally offensive to them and then to defend its right to exist. After the papers are turned in, I ask the students to tell me about the experience of searching for offensive art, and each semester they tell me that the task was nearly impossible when they searched alone because nothing was truly offensive to them. Only when they looked for images with other people around did they feel shock or shame. The exercise is analogous to reading, writing or saying a dirty word while alone versus engaging with so-called obscene language in a public space. The former inspires no reaction whatsoever and the latter causes real and genuine discomfort, proving that obscenity, like patriotism and acquiescence to authoritarian concepts of right and wrong, typically requires a herd mentality in order to be conjured.

I explain to my students that it is in that private space, in that state of aloneness, that most artists, poets, novelists, musicians, playwrights and satirists conceive their work, which is why some artwork can appear vulgar in its honesty or obscene beyond its intention when viewed in public. It is comparable to the inclination one feels when confronted with an itchy ass while walking down a crowded street. Similar to an irritable conflation of bogus ideas sloppily strung together in service of concepts conceived by propriety to ignore impulse in deference to decorum, an itchy ass insists on immediate attention and carries with it an innate understanding of exactly what to do for relief. That said, you are more likely to scratch your ass if you are alone than if you are in public, just as you are more likely to dismiss bullshit — political, religious or otherwise — if you are alone than if you are in public, and it is with that clarity of purpose and egoless confrontation with distress that artists of all sorts typically enunciate their utility most succinctly. And *that* is why art as both a language and a philosophy has great potential to enlighten, because it operates with fewer restrictions and fearlessly uses the blade of honesty more than other methods of communication that may be more publicly sanctioned.

Tariq Ali was born in British India at a time when the Paris Commune, the Russian Revolution and Revolutionary Catalonia were all still recent enough to exist within the living memories of his parents, grandparents and great-grandparents, all of whom had witnessed, endured and even participated in the early struggles waged by working class people to make government less an instrument of crowd control and more a full orchestra of balanced collaboration. It was when those who previously believed that their human rights were whatever the ruling class deemed appropriate to grant them suddenly realized that the privileges of personhood are not what an aristocracy gives to a population but rather what an aristocracy must recognize as a preexisting condition among those whom they've had trapped beneath their bejeweled slipper for centuries.

Key, of course, to this realization and its mass propagation throughout the world was the arts community and, by proxy, those most moved and motivated by the frankness, probity and courage of artists to simultaneously tell and question the truth.

I met with Tariq Ali in a hotel at the edge of Central Park in midtown Manhattan just as the 2008 election was coming to a close and Barack Obama was preparing to give the black portion of the skunk an opportunity to stink up the place. Having spent his 20s and 30s agitating for peace, labor rights, prisoners' rights, poor people's rights, women's rights, true democracy and free speech in the teargas-choked streets of London, allied with writers, readers, painters, poets, singers, satirists and public intellectuals all hoping to extend the still fledgling concept that one's destiny should be determined by the individual and not by bureaucratic committee, I had one simple question for Ali: What happened over the last 50 years to shift the question of how best to organize human tribes of various sizes into participatory co-ops designed to promote, preserve and protect the dignity and rights of free-thinking people away from *We the People* and back to the state, specifically the business sector and the politicians who serve as the PR goons for the world's multinational financial institutions?

Here's what he said.

❀ ❀ ❀

I've been interested in the crossover between culture and politics for a long time now and I'd say that there has been a very sharp decline over the last 15 years in how information is created and shared. The name I give this decline, and have for some time, is *market realism*. In Stalinist Russia all the crap produced by painters and writers was called *socialist realism*, but we don't have that anymore, it's all gone. Now we have market realism where the market determines and dominates, by and large, what the culture requires and what the culture is permitted. We have seen, since the years of Reagan and Thatcher, a big decline in, for instance, what public broadcasting is able to offer to an audience. [Consider] a Michael Moore documentary like *Bowling for Columbine* or *Fahrenheit 9/11*. In the old days, these films would have been shown on television — *mainstream* television at prime time! — and people would've said, "Well, that was interesting," and it would have set off a debate in the public. *That* is now not permitted. Moore has to make a documentary, fight to have it seen in movie theaters, and because he's Moore he can do this. [Of course,] there are equally gifted young filmmakers in their 20s and 30s who are not known at all but are very sharp and are making documentaries that are not being shown and are only seen among friends.

Or they circulate through the festival circuit where they're killed by distributors who only know how to sell entertainment and not information to an uninformed public.

Yeah — so when this happens, we need to ask ourselves what made this collapse so sudden. How do we have subsidized culture one day and then the next day it's gone? I think one of the major causes for this shift had to do with the collapse of the Soviet Union and of the whole communist world because as long as that world was around, capitalist states — and America in particular — felt obliged to say to that world, "Look, we have genuine liberties! We have dissidents whom we have given space in *The New York Times* and who have appeared on primetime television. We [also] have critical coverage of wars that we are waging ourselves — you cannot compete with us!" And there was no reply from the other side, and with the collapse of the other side [the capitalist states] no longer needed to present that argument, nor did

they need to prove their virtue by letting dissidents speak critically of the system. Why bother, why waste the money? Suddenly there was no need to allow the public to have a voice and that is a weakness of the system that it can no longer permit the previous level of free speech, limited as it was. For a long time, ideologically [America] controlled its own public by pointing to the [Soviet Union] and saying, "Look at them, they have nothing." And now that the [Soviet Union] is gone, [America has] to look for fake enemies.

And those enemies are us! Suddenly, the biggest threats to democracy are the black people and the immigrants and the poor people who already live here and who are [considered] *dissidents* because they refuse to be white and middleclass [and native-born].

Exactly! And that is one of the reasons why the internal situation has become so volatile.

Which [likely] plays into the notion that perhaps it isn't radicalism as an attitude that's been destroyed, but rather our confidence to express radicalism as a political idea in public [that's been subdued]. This is where the importance of art and the unique ability of the arts community to keep radicalism alive needs to be pointed out. Let's use you as an example. For you to write a nonfiction book that expresses your concerns about how the United States and the Western World see Islam purely as a religion of hate, you limit your audience to those who already agree with your point of view, or at least feel comfortable dealing with controversial subjects in a purely intellectual way. At the same time, you're also alienating those who already believe the anti-Islam propaganda that you're hoping to subvert, and [those people] don't even read a single sentence you write. On the other hand, when you use a novel that includes Islam as part of a fictitious narrative that explores human relationships [above and beyond political ones], you increase your chances of being able to talk about how those who live in the Middle East [as Muslims] are often victims of [U.S. and Israeli brutalities] and how no single religion should be seen as a source of universal misery. In that case, art is the most effective strategy we have for communicating truth over political opinion. To quote Picasso: "There are painters who transform the sun to a yellow spot, but there are others who,

with the help of their art and their intelligence, transform a yellow spot into sun."

You're 100% right about that.

So, then the plan of action becomes one of resuscitating the arts community over the [politically] dissident one, the idea being that art as a revolt against complacency helps create and sustain a curious and nonconformist worldview which, when threatened by [repressive state policies], will exhibit itself politically. That, I believe, is one of the leading reasons why progressive politics were so pervasive during the 1960s, because radicalism wasn't just a political movement but also a cultural one created by the arts community.

Look, I agree with you. I think the idea that collective action between all layers of society will get you gains has gone out of the world. The last big spasms of mass mobilization were the big demonstrations [organized] to stop the Iraq War. This was a time when millions of people came out onto the streets in North America and Europe to participate in the largest demonstrations in world history. The majority of these people had never participated in politics before, yet had an instinct of gut distrust of their elected leaders and what they were being told on television about weapons of mass destruction and they thought that if they came out and protested in large numbers that they'd be able to stop the war. When they [didn't stop the war], they didn't come out again

and the anti-war movement shrunk very quickly. Essentially, what happened to this movement is a reflection of what you were saying earlier, that the individualization and atomization of the community has gone very far and very deep and that the only political involvement available to us is the Jon Stewart show, which confines us all to tiny living rooms. I'm not saying Stewart is not good! Some of [his] shows are very funny, but the overall [purpose of entertainment television] is to make the individual feel good. [Stewart] is talking *for* me [when he criticizes the President], I agree with him, so then I don't need to do it myself and that is quite dangerous for democracy. I believe what has been happening since the Reagan/Thatcher boom years, especially in the Anglo-Saxon world, is that the combination of consumerism and celebrity has dominated politics and culture in the Western world so that wherever [Barack] Obama travels he's greeted like a rock star, because that's what he is. The Republicans then feel that they have to come up with an alternative celebrity, so they give us Sarah Palin. Politicians are no longer vetted, they're cast.

TO ASSUME THAT THE REST OF THE WORLD HATES US BECAUSE THEY'RE JEALOUS OF OUR FREEDOM TO DO WHATEVER THE FUCK WE WANT, TO WHOMEVER THE FUCK WE WANT, WHENEVER THE FUCK WE WANT, IS TO ASSUME THAT A VICTIM OF RAPE HATES BEING RAPED BECAUSE HE OR SHE IS JEALOUS OF THE RAPIST'S ORGASM

MR. FISH

To your point, it always amazes me how most Americans don't seem to understand that being President is a job and that a candidate is somebody who applies for that job [with a complete understanding of] what is expected of [him or her]. In other words, the Presidency is [the brain of] a machine that already exists and whoever ends up sitting in that chair has to learn how to work the machine—and it's a very brutal machine! Obama, because he isn't Bush and because he's black, has been cast as Nelson Mandela and when Nelson Mandela doesn't walk into the Oval Office in January everybody is going to be shocked and upset. Every election cycle it's the same thing! It's like hiring the Dalai Lama as the chief interrogator at Guantanamo Bay and then being pissed off when Guantanamo Bay doesn't become Yasgur's Farm.

Which is why when people vote for a President they are not really interested in the political or social issues that become waylaid by a [leader's] agenda. There are two ways to look at the Obama-mania. One is that there is a real desperation on the part of young people who are alienated from traditional politics to find somebody different. We now know that his slogan, *Yes We Can*, which was coined by his spin doctors, was something that Obama tried to resist using for a long time, but he was told that he had to have it. It's vapid, it's empty, it makes you feel good and it's bullshit. If you look at the way he started his campaign in the primaries, back when he had every reason to assume Hillary would win, he was more radical and then gradually, as it became more obvious to him that he might win, his positions began to alter and weasel words began to trickle out of his mouth and now you have him, with a big economic crisis in the country, demonstrating that there's very little that differentiates him from Bush. On the war with Afghanistan and expanding that war to Pakistan, he's far more aggressive than McCain was just a few weeks ago. It is very sad this development, but it's the world we live in.

How do you see the concept of misbehavior deterring political engagement on the part of the public?

How do you mean?

Well, dissent [will always] be seen as a form of misbehavior because it's typically rendered in opposition to whatever the dominant culture has [established] as the norm. When SNCC sat down at segregated lunch counters in Alabama, they were misbehaving according to the Jim Crow laws [that had been established] to determine what civilized living should look like. Same with the sit-ins for the Free Speech Movement and the sit-ins for ending the [Vietnam War] and the sit-ins for ending apartheid in South Africa. Whenever a person is arrested for anything, whether it's for political agitation or for drunk driving, [he or she] is being arrested for dissenting against a rule, for misbehaving, and rules are there to establish order, even when the order [like in the case of the segregated South] is wrong and immoral. Here's my question: because being impolite in an ostentatious way is [profoundly] difficult for most people, by removing the ostentatious language of both art and public protest and [limiting] our political engagement to more acceptable [modes of expression] like voting and virtual protests on [social media], are we making ourselves more and more vulnerable to passivity by only [grappling with] civil disobedience as a theory and never as an experience?**

This is all absolutely true that power has a way of subverting the meaning of dissent by obfuscating the language and, in a way, criminalizing resistance. What we also had in the '60s were very radical theater groups, where a playwright would write a play, rehearse it for three weeks and then find a public space and put it on for free. These public spaces have been narrowing and shrinking for the last 40 years and that is quite frightening. You're also right about art and artists and how they are linked with progressivism because both rely on human relationships over political ones. On our first really big demonstration against the Vietnam War we had Mick Jagger marching with us. In the 1970s we had John Lennon. There were also lots of lesser known artists who were part of our protests, lots of musicians and writers and playwrights, and there was this feeling that political activity was part of a broader culture movement. This also happened in the 1920s and '30s, this mix of politics and culture, before it disappeared through the Cold War period and then resurfaced again in the 1960s and then vanished again with the big [social justice] defeats of the late '70s and '80s. Will it reemerge again? These things are very hard to predict.

Part of the reason why I'm writing this book and talking to people like you is to provide eyewitness accounts to those who either don't have a reliable enough memory to comprehend that there's been a [marked] decline in participatory progressivism in this country or they're so young that they have no true concept of what it means to be a radical beyond whatever benign folklore the establishment [has deemed] appropriate [enough to share with them]. Specifically, so much of what ends up being the official version of American history runs contradictory to the direct experience of those who actually lived through events where power was corrupt and people were direct victims of that corruption, either physically or psychically.

History has become irrelevant. I remember watching Morley Safer when he was a correspondent in Vietnam, reporting on primetime CBS news, saying, "This is Morley Safer, *so many* miles outside of Saigon, I'm with a team of Marines…" then we were shown the Marines destroying a village with flamethrowers, killing women and children, and Safer had [this] throwaway remark: *This is the fight for freedom.* Vicious! He went there to report what he saw, he wasn't embedded, and there were many, many journalists like him. That is not happening with any of the wars we are currently fighting. It's not happening in Iraq or Afghanistan. [The government] learned from the Vietnam War that they can never allow reporting like that ever again because it demonstrated how such an important democratic institution as the press is indispensable when educating the public on such grave matters as war and peace.

And getting back to the importance of the arts community, without folk musicians like Woody Guthrie and Lead Belly and Pete Seeger and artists like Art Young and William Gropper and Robert Minor, or writers like John Steinbeck and Upton Sinclair and Theodore Dreiser, the story of the Labor Movement [in this country] would have been lost forever. Artists preserve the meaning and significance of struggle where state sponsored narratives negate the human perspective.

I've been invited to give a series of lectures in Flint, Michigan, next year and to teach and I said to the guy who asked me that I was dying to come because [the city] has such a rich history. He knew about it, but he said that most people don't. He said that nobody will talk to me about the sit-ins, the factory occupations [or] the militant workers because nobody knows about them, despite the fact that they're all grown up surrounded by the wreckage from that time period. There's evidence of that struggle everywhere in the United States. The Wobblies, for instance, were an amazing group that didn't exist anywhere else in the world! The songs they inspired, and the songwriters like Joe Hill, and the satirizing of the Salvation Army by calling them the *Starvation Army* — amazing! Sadly, this is increasingly the case with Western culture, this fear of history, as if knowledge of past events will frighten the children. We mustn't frighten the children.

These are the same idiots who thought we needed protection from bebop jazz and the *negro* influence on white culture. Of course, to comprehend John Coltrane is to comprehend what a revolution can be, which I guess is something to be afraid of if you're somebody who benefits from how the system is set up. To your point about Flint, the wreckage of jazz is all around us in the form of Kenny G and David Sanborn and fucking Chuck Mangione and nobody has any idea what musical adventurism even is anymore, so we've lost yet another [serviceable] model for how to question standardized codes of [conciliatory guidelines].

The greatest thing about jazz, and something that I've always loved about it, is the spontaneity — the extemporization that these guys used to do at jam sessions is really like politics from below. Finding comradery in improvising meaning out of a shared moment is all that we might hope for when considering how organic democracy could [feasibly] manifest. [Jazz] is proof somehow that free association as a form of open communication is possible.

That is, until we consider economics as a form of communication and free enterprise as a perverted example of *open* communication. Kurt Vonnegut has this terrific quote that says, "We could have saved the Earth, but we were too damn cheap." How do you see our inability to truly commit to saving the planet from environmental collapse until we can make our survival profitable as anything but lunacy — or at least it's proof that we are likely doomed because human consciousness seems incapable of recognizing that a budget is not the number one thing we should be worried about when trying to prevent our extinction as a species?

I'm not convinced that it's purely a question of consciousness. This question about the environment and its degradation has become very relevant over the last thirty years. I think it's linked to everything we've been talking about, specifically how we are blind to everything but the present. We have no concept of the past, so we cannot have an educated opinion about what the future might hold. A friend of mine in Germany wrote a two-volume book on the motor car, many years ago, explaining the evolution of the motor car and how that evolution led to the destruction of canals in Berlin, and led to the destruction of the railways in the United States and Britain and other parts of Europe, and how the car lobbies function. It's quite an amazing book. Anyway, he was invited to give a talk at Volkswagen — they were very interested that he'd written a book about their industry — so he went and he spoke to them and they were very polite. Then a guy said to him, "What you say is absolutely true, that by the end of the 21st century the motor car will have outlived its usefulness and by that time it will have destroyed this, that and the other, but have you forgotten what the great economist [John Maynard] Keynes said, that in the long run we're dead so we shouldn't think that far ahead. A totally cynical remark, *totally* cynical, but if you think seriously about the need to protect the environment you do need economic planning. You need to examine how your economy is run and whose interests are being served and if it's a system that's being totally dominated by profit and greed [then] it has to be changed.

But that's what I'm asking — so long as capital determines our ability to satisfy our most basic survival needs, like food and shelter and social acceptance, then how will we ever be able to look beyond economics for the solutions to all the problems that come from our reliance on capital to motivate our actions to save ourselves? See what I mean? In order to condemn the disease of capitalism and [to] warn against the commodification of absolutely everything, I need an income — I literally need to commodify the messaging that the commodification of everything is bad.

I follow what you mean. I've always believed that how people think is determined overwhelmingly by their experiences. The U.S. government will send a bunch of kids to fight in Iraq who will [then] experience absolute hell and they will be changed forever. Chances are they would never have been changed by reading anything I've written or by any cartoon you've drawn. It is personal experience that transforms a person, so that a veteran who is told by a civilian who has never known fighting that the war on terror is a great war he will know by experience that that is absolute bullshit. Similarly, those people who have experienced massive economic collapse will be haunted forever and understand hierarchy.

Does that mean the only meaningful teaching tool we have to warn people of catastrophe is catastrophe, itself?

It's an awful thing to say, but I think in some circumstances that's the case. I don't think people's consciousness shifts in a dramatic way on an individual basis.

For some people it does — for visionaries and crackpots it does.

Yes, for some it does, but really a very small minority. For it to shift in a collective way, in a way that changes the direction of a whole society, the impetus must first be recognized by more than just a minority of individuals. Take, for instance, the draft. During the Vietnam War, the draft democratized who went to fight and, because it was a lottery, it had the potential to involve every single family, regardless of its color or class, which is why the anti-war movement from that period was so massive, because it included every color and class and not just [the rank and file]. That's why we don't have a draft today, because the government saw what was possible through the mobilization of a mass consciousness and it frightened them.

So maybe there's a way to frighten [tyrannical governments] without relying on a catastrophe to create a mass consciousness that celebrates truth, beauty and justice. Maybe we should end our conversation with some more hopeful examples of seismic shifts in the culture that were bloodless and *non*-catastrophic. How about Sesame Street?

Very radical show!

It was *All You Need is Love* for kids! Of course, for the harder anti-authoritarian stuff you had to look to Bugs Bunny, who was the first version of Lenny Bruce I ever encountered, which led me to the real Lenny Bruce, who led me to Nichols and May and George Carlin, who let me to Abbie Hoffman, who led me to Angela Davis and Gloria Steinem, who led me to Susan Sontag, who led me to Vonnegut and Mailer and Vidal, who led me to the Beats and Roger Waters and Fritz Lang and Voltaire, who led me to Chomsky and Krassner, who led me to Picasso, Miles Davis, John Lennon, Bob Dylan and finally to this chair, in this hotel, at this moment on a beautiful fall day in midtown Manhattan talking to you, Mr. *Street Fightin' Man*, himself, about why giving a shit might or might not be a waste of time.

I like that.

That's all, folks! ✳

HEROISM IS IMPOSSIBLE
WHEN THE DANGER YOU FACE

COMES FROM THE VICTIMS OF YOUR OPPRESSION
ATTEMPTING TO RESIST YOUR TORTURE

WHEN WAS YOUR LAST MOVEMENT?

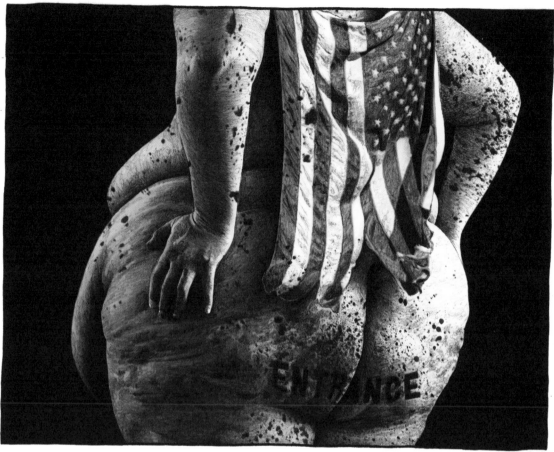

MR.FISH

THE MEETING, THE PURPOSE OF WHICH was to demonstrate to the world that there existed a progressive peace movement in America that was huge and organized and poised for revolution, began with the collapsing of all the empty chairs.

It happened at the community center in Korea Town on a Tuesday night in 2003 at one of the very first Los Angeles meetings of the A.N.S.W.E.R. (*Act Now to Stop War and End Racism*) Coalition. It was two weeks after the invasion of Iraq, five months before I would become a father of twin girls and eighteen months before I would begin receiving daily death threats in my email from people completely pissed off by the notion that a political cartoonist might sometimes use his cartooning to express an opinion contrary to that held by the Executive Branch.

Having spent the previous eighteen months since 9/11 closing myself off in my room every night so that I could freebase the near fatal cocktail of Noam Chomsky, John Coltrane and enough ferociously black coffee to convince my colon that it might actually possess the right muscles to become an accomplished yodeler, I decided that, for sanity's sake, I needed to follow the basic instruction of what I was reading and participate, with *real people*, in the communalizing of humanity; the idea being that a community, like a mass of cells comprising a living organism, able to remain aware of its own biology will tend to make decisions about its healthcare more likely to preserve it's cohesion.

The idea of collapsing the chairs came from one of the three A.N.S.W.E.R. event organizers, a woman so excruciatingly plain and bone crushingly sexless that one might've assumed that the only passion known to her loins must've come from whatever her vagina could glean from listening hard through the body of a cat to re-runs of *thirtysomething* and *Doctor Quinn, Medicine*

Woman. In fact, contrary to the stereotype, she appeared as likely to burn her bra in protest of the patriarch as she was to refuse a gift of lingerie from any member of the patriarch willing to do her the cruel favor of objectifying her.

Everybody pitched in with the chairs, *everybody* being a total of five sleepy people, everybody except for me and the other two event organizers who were busy walking around the room with a gigantic banner that read *Protest the REAL Axis of Evil — WAR, RACISM, POVERTY*. The banner was being held up in various locations in an attempt to find a spot that might provide maximum visibility to the audience, at one point ending up on the front portion of the table facing the dwindling graveyard of chairs. "No, not here," said one of the organizers, letting down his corner. "It'll be too hard for the people in the back to see." I turned around to see what he had failed to notice about *the back*, namely that it was presently being stacked loudly against the wall in clumsy rows. The banner ended up being suspended from the hot metal shade of one of the ceiling light fixtures behind the table, only to slowly unhinge itself steadily throughout the course of the meeting until finally, after hanging by a single piece of masking tape for ten minutes like a white surrender flag, it fell in a heap to the floor, the whole process as thrilling to watch as a

striptease choreographed to reveal the pornography of wasted time. It was Samuel Beckett at his best.

Meeting adjourned, I saw the lady organizer stand and, in her NIKE sneakers and FILA sweatshirt (two companies that I imagined any day would be announcing a new perfume line made from pheromones extracted from the perspiration produced cheaply and gleefully by their sweatshop workers) stretch her back and exhale the sigh of an exhausted champion and say to the other two organizers, "Not too shabby." The two organizers, still sitting on ass cracks whose significance they imagined rivaled the one set in the Liberty Bell, not to mention the trillions set through the logic of their wanting to be deputy Jesuses to the world's downtrodden when neither one of them appeared willing to sacrifice his armpits to a soapy sponge let alone his life to the spiritual problems of the wretched majority, looked at her inquisitively, refusing to verbalize even a monosyllabic *huh?*, having practiced all through their middle age a poker face suggesting that they had all the answers. "Not an empty seat in the house!" said the lady, gesturing to the room.

"Oh, right," they each said in turn, looking out at the fifteen people who eventually did show up and who were now clumped together like hyenas scavenging the final remnants of their own self-approbation. Standing back from the pack I watch them signing each other's petitions and buying each other's newsletters and realized that most of them already knew each other, either from previous meetings or from the hulls of any number of geek ingesting flying saucers where, while laying prone on examination tables to have their balls and ovaries drained, they talked with one another about upcoming Star Trek conventions and which cast members would be showing up drunk and indifferent to their costumes. I left wondering how soon it would be before *Klingonese* became the official language of the progressive left.

Indeed, what had attracted me to attend this particular meeting of purported likeminded nihilists and haters of what the United

States was turning into was an email I'd received announcing a march on Washington D.C., with a corresponding march to be held in San Francisco to accommodate West Coast complainers, primarily, I imagined, those in Los Angeles like me, to protest both the existing unjust wars that America the Beautiful was engaged in and the anticipated unjust wars that all her cowardice and paranoia would force her into fighting upon realizing more and more that the rest of the world was in terrified, yet unrepentant, opposition to her. In previous months my wife and I, in an effort to provide our political disgust with some constructive application, had agreed to host several meetings for the local chapter of the Green Party and, as a result, went from believing that if all the liberals across the United States organized at the local level then responsive pluralistic politics might have a real chance of affecting domestic and foreign policy in this country to believing that if all the liberals across the United States organized at the local level then we could see what happened to all the high school *Dungeons and Dragons* clubs after graduation disbanded them: they became anti-monarchists hell-

bent on toppling the thrones and laying waste to the immense armies of every Prom King and Queen this side of Tolkien's Middle-earth.

Following the removal of all the sofa pillows which, as discovered after the first meeting, only served as tepid referees officiating a dirty fist fight that went on inside the laps of some of the older revolutionaries between pee and perfume, our Green meetings would begin with the choosing of somebody to take the minutes, then somebody to keep the time as a way of preventing a fili-buster, and then the naming of all the topics of discussion in order of their importance and, spe-cifically, what political pressures we could affect on a local level through letter writing, leafleting, picketing, etcetera. Five minutes after setting our parameters we were ignoring them and, instead, talking about how Queen Elizabeth had Lady Di killed or how the FBI had murdered Martin Luther King because they wanted to steal the glory from the CIA who was planning to murder him themselves in May, around Memorial Day, when Fidel Castro would be unavailable to pose for any more assassination attempts because he would be too busy with the parade. There was even a time when the first 90 minutes of our night was taken up by a vote to determine who at the meeting would be allowed to vote on future proposals, which prompted a vote asking if democrats and republicans and independents should even be allowed at the meetings, forget about the voting part, which prompted a vote on whether the dues should be raised on non-Green participants. I then tried to get a vote started on how many water fountains my wife and I should have installed in our apartment and how we should label them. Nobody laughed.

Invariably, the meetings would end with announcements of upcoming demonstrations planned against mostly unprosecuted corporate malpractice suits going on in the area, with each demonstration usually talking place somewhere between the hours of 10 a.m. and 3 p.m., thereby excluding the participation of anybody who wasn't either retired, disabled, unemployed, or actually working at the location where the demonstration would be taking place. In other words, these were demonstrations that effectively marginalized absolutely everybody but the oddest and least respected 1% of the population who, by marching up and down on sidewalks in numbers not quite rivaling those of the Osmond Brothers, only ended up putting a face on a stereotype that nobody in their right mind — or, more precisely, that nobody interested in ever getting laid again in their lives — would want to emulate, much less support.

Now lest anybody think that my only concept of the left wing of the big dodo bird that makes up the political infrastructure of this country is one of utter contempt and apathetic folly, let me just say that when it comes to crediting any group with the overwhelming majority of all the social movements proven most beneficial to humanity as a whole over the last one hundred years the prize most definitely must go to the left wing, even when the left wing was more a feature of the northern Republican Party than the southern Democratic Party during the one hundred years before that, both iterations giving us an abolitionist movement, a civil rights movement, an environmental movement, a women's movement, a gay movement, a poor people's movement, a freedom of speech movement, a peace movement, an anti-globalization movement, and

a labor movement. Of course, what worries me is the speed in which the maintenance of such liberal attitudes seems to be losing momentum and how little the great majority of people, including most of the liberals themselves, seem to care. Then again, why should they care? What historical proof is there that anything but violent clashes and ugly confrontations between the ruling class and the proletariat can alter the political trajectory of a nation?

For the last twenty-five years all that would allow liberal attitudes to thrive, namely a culture able to provide a context for its free expression outside of politics (referred to cynically by previous generations as the *counterculture*), has almost disappeared entirely, partially by neglect of the liberal element yet largely by design of the actively *anti*-liberal element, otherwise known, particularly by members of the political elite and the corporate aristocracy, both of whom are jointly responsible for controlling the movement of capital in this country thereby determining the content of our collective perception of ourselves by seeing to it that only certain kinds of ideas, as they are propagated by advertising and books and television shows and art exhibits and movies and news outlets, receive funding and public exposure, as *Americans*. Even the liberal press has had to soften its critique of mainstream culture in order to maintain its readership, transforming such magazines as *Mother Jones*, at one time a true hell-raiser of political significance, into the MSNBC of progressive journalism and *The Nation* magazine into little more than a products catalogue for hemp hammocks and squatty potties.

And lest anybody think that my ability to make such a hackneyed and paranoid statement pigeonholing the political elite and corporate aristocracy as evil manipulators of our national identity is some indication that I believe that those in power are inexplicably subhuman, let me just say that, on the contrary, I believe that the opposite is true.

Considering the fact that a human being, rather than perceiving the world directly, is biologically predisposed to use the world to substantiate his or her abstract ideas *about* the world (the shortest distance between two points being an *imaginary* line), it is quintessentially human for there to be a value system self-imposed upon our consciousness which is configured to simplify our judgment of one another based upon a quantitative formula of numbers that we call our economic system. In fact, ever since the first coin was minted somewhere around 400 B.C., the worth of a human being, above and beyond all other discriminatory practices, has ultimately been based upon, not the content of his character, but rather upon his ability to generate an income either for himself or for somebody else. And in accordance with the rules of a quantitative value system, the more money a person has the more power and importance he has and the less money he has the less power and importance he has. Thus, the executive branch of a huge multinational corporation, for example, will always be considered a much more important group of people than say a group of farmers or teachers or, at the far end of the riffraff spectrum, sick or unemployed or homeless people, simply because those executive members of a huge multinational corporation are representative of a larger abstract number than the farmers are or the teachers are or the sick or unemployed or homeless are, who, by relying on the financial support of various social programs, are actually representative of negative numbers.

Or, consider this: because capital represents an accumulative value system — meaning that the more money you have, the more value is perceived, and the less money you have, the less value is perceived — and

human beings represent an intrinsic value system — meaning that all people, like all naturally occuring aggregates of biological cells that conspire to produce all living organisms, whether plant or animal, microscopic or macroscopic, maintain a bio-parity equal to one another — there will never exist adequation, parallelism or peace between men and money. Why? Because there will always be a scenario wherein capital, because it has the ability to increase in value, will supercede the fixed value of life, itself.

Therefore, given the morality of capitalism, which is nothing more *moral* than a hierarchy of ascending or descending numbers, depending upon your role as either exploiter or cheerful and unwitting consumer of exploitation, isn't it in the interest of the richest and most powerful members of society to do everything that they can to protect their wealth against those much poorer and much less important than themselves, especially when it's precisely poorness and unimportance that they must live contrary to in order to define themselves as wealthy and important? Answer: Yes. Is it fair? Answer, and here's the shocker: of course it is, as long as humanity continues to acknowledge any meaning whatsoever in a viable exchange rate between food and capital, shelter and capital, fuel and capital, medicine and capital, and dignity and capital. Under such circumstances life can be no

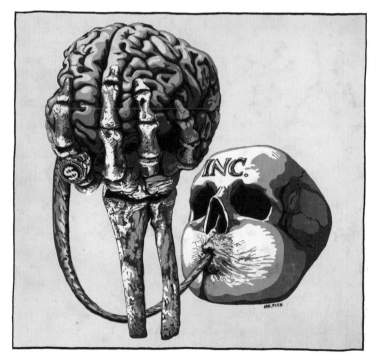

more meaningful than it is for a plastic game piece set around the squares of a game board by dice and an artificial urge implanted by the manufacturers of the game to collect and hoard as much play money as possible while trying to screw the other game pieces out of moving ahead and collecting and hoarding their own, all in the name of hoping to claim the bizarre victory of *most narcissistic* at the game's finale, which is a victory marked by the truly sinister joy of having attained as much play money as possible while showing the least amount of compassion to the other players.

After all, just as the inventors of God are the Chosen People, the inventors of the concept of wealth are the ruling class. And just as those fanatics sworn to protect the absolute power of every dominant religion throughout history have done, frequently to the point of literally banishing or murdering anyone with an opposing point of view until irreligious interpretations of the world eventually emerged as skepticism and atheism and replaced much of the superstitious buffoonery of religion with rational thought, thereby allowing for a lessening of prejudice between man and nature, so too does the ruling class wish to discourage the formation of a similar movement based on a rigorous disbelief of the value of capital, for such a movement would surely lessen the prejudice between man and man which is precisely the prejudice that keeps the ruling class in business, literally.

In the meantime, of course, while the promise (*threat?*) of a pro-humanitarian/anti-economic reformation comes and goes, given the frivolity of the idea that there could even exist a manmade currency invested potentially with enough conceptual value as to influence the way humanity arranges its principle code of ethics (frivolous for the simple reason that economics exist as a social philosophy merely because everyone collectively pretends that it has to, making its demise as easy as everyone suddenly choosing not to pretend anymore), it's important for those people with the most money to control all public discourse on the subject of privilege and the hierarchical power structure of the economic system — which, of course, is the very system that defines them as superhuman — so as to discourage the sort of critical thinking that might one day lead to actions by the growing number of people with the least amount of money of dismantling the current social paradigm that suggests an authentic inequality

between people by proving an inauthentic one based on income levels.

In fact, one of the most terrifying protections built into the design of corporate America (*corporate America*, of course, being a euphemism for the huge conglomerate of multinational money launderers established to bankroll political thuggery and elitist dominance over the consumer class worldwide) was established in an 1886 Supreme Court decision called *Santa Clara County v. Southern Pacific Railroad Co.*, which ruled that a corporation was a *person* and was free to enjoy all the protections offered by the Constitution. Of course, what this legislation ended up doing, besides legitimizing corporate propagation of private power into the public sector, which was simply a way of preventing the larger community from becoming self-sufficient and self determinate of their own futures, was to create a race of so-deemed *honorary people* who, by controlling the vast majority of the planet's wealth and effectively wielding not the power of only one vote but hundreds or even thousands, have been able to exercise their Constitutional rights, particularly their right to free speech, governmental representation, and their right to petition their golf buddies for a redress of grievances, at a level unavailable to the average citizen. Add to that, of course, the understanding that it is in the interest of every corporation to only invest money into a community that will return more money than was invested, which, besides being an effective way of guaranteeing that the poorest communities remain poor and that every other community has the potential to be bled dry, is an equation that only allows capital to flow in one direction and to only pool around the corporate class which has never represented more than 5% of the population nationally and never more than 2% internationally.

So, assuming that everything ever told to me about the virtues of American democracy was in the end nothing but a bureaucratic trick of misdirection designed to keep me from realizing that I was having my pocket picked, both financially and spiritually, by the recidivism of American capitalism, I went to the peace march in San Francisco on April 20th in 2002 and stood, much to my own surprise, with 50,000 other suckers and proclaimed both my awareness and my deep sadness at having to live in a country that considered pocket picking, because it was its most benign form of shaking down its own citizens to help pay for both the expanse of its operation into the rest of the world, which was an expanse that employed much less benign forms of shaking down people for their money and/or real estate and/or labor, and its future ability to pickpocket our children and our children's children and their children's children, to be something uniquely legible to the hearts and minds of freedom lovers, not to mention to the intellects of the staunchest defenders of our super-duper, highly evolved, envy of the goddamn universe western civilization. And although 50,000 critics of the U.S. government and the corporate imperialism that she and other governments like her encourage weren't considered significant enough to make the evening news — although I understand that we made the midday traffic report as "…an area that you'll want to avoid" — we certainly were significant enough, considering the additional

100,000 protesters demonstrating at the same time in Washington D.C., not to mention the hundreds of thousands who had participated in similar mass demonstrations in Seattle, Quebec City, Prague, Genoa, Qatar, Gothenburg, New York City, Rome, and Paris in recent months, to assume that a real revolution, bloodless or blood filled, was possible and perhaps even inevitable.

And despite the fact that most of the picket signs at the demonstration, then as now, contained the same clichéd *us vs. them* rhetoric that, rather than advancing the agenda of humanitarianism and progressive politics, only served to reinforce the reputation of liberalism as an overly simplistic expression of ill-informed nihilism, there were still enough of them there to fan the sky and, for a little while at least, to prevent it from falling on our repressors who might one day wish that they'd noticed and said thank you. ✳

WE ARE NOT ALONE

Blessed are the meek: for they shall inherit the earth.

— Anonymous

WHY DOES CELEBRITY FIGURE so prominently in what we're collectively willing to classify as wisdom and what does such a qualification do to diminish the viability of statements made by the faceless and the dispossessed? By attaching so much significance to the prominence of the people from which we draw our most celebrated quotes, are we not in danger of dismissing the opinions produced by the overwhelming majority of us and how might this cripple the stock exchange of ideas in a democracy made whole by its multiplicity? By exaggerating the relevance of the famous have we not gotten into the grotesque habit of permitting the megaphone of renown to silence the inconspicuous, the obscure and the ordinary? When we cast such a laudatory spotlight upon the quips and ruminations of well-known people because

the amplification of their voices is so much louder than the anonymity of our own, we run the risk of absolving the powerful of their mediocrity, their bullshit and their downright stupidity in deference to their social ranking — in other words, we allow attribution to matter above all else in the exchange of truly profound insights and inspiring observations, completely ignoring the fact that a keen proclamation is a keen proclamation regardless of the breath or pen from which it was articulated, likewise with asinine or insipid proclamations.

We have known for a long time that the better part of human knowledge is little more than our collective trust in hearsay, whether we're talking about our comprehension of gravity or politics or beauty. So much of what we assume to be fact is really secondhand information that we accept on faith from those with whom we identify as either experts in a particular field or authorities on a subject with which we lack sufficient curiosity, time, or patience to fully engage with. It is the opinions of other people and not direct experience that informs us that the Earth is round, for example, and that our breakfast cereal is wholly nutritious and that our telepathy is forever being eavesdropped upon by a broad-shouldered pro-American Caucasian Super Being who likes to set the ethereal nightgowns of angels on fire for committing the corporeal crime of talking back to their parents or being gay or eating clams, camels, armadillos, pigs or beavers. Indeed, whenever we relinquish ownership of anything to another person or institution, whether we're talking about information or goods and services, we are forfeiting full access to property, both intellectual and actual, and submitting ourselves to the regulatory constraints of a very often discriminatory barter system, which begs the question: What happens to the free and unfettered propagation of exquisite ideas and frank rationalism when strict ownership and distribution laws and traditions commodify knowledge and make it available only to those privileged enough to afford its purchase, not to mention the luxury of time to consume it?

Thusly, whether we're talking about incidental truths or the bedrock of our most treasured life philosophies or the moral laws upon which we rely most for structure and guidance, we have been conditioned to surrender our own rigorous interrogation of the world and how and why it functions as it does to the expertise and marketing strategies of those with whom we have no direct contact, nor personal relationship, nor reason to trust completely, in the comprehension of the vagaries of our own unique experiences. We have been encouraged to believe that our adulation of society's cultural, religious, political and artistic heroes is the best and perhaps the only way to commune with enlightenment, which, broadly speaking, has disburdened us from needing to confront, scrutinize and affect an influence on the trajectory of our own self-portrayal and, hence, on our participatory connection to the larger commonwealth.

If, for instance, my big brother, Jeff, said to me, while reaming the resin out of a pot pipe with the angry end of a broken wishbone, "You know, I was just thinking — we should start asking not what our country can do for us, but what we can do for our country," I wouldn't let the statement stall without asking him what a country was and why we should feel motivated to contribute to its perpetuation, one population's inspiring self-determination being another population's desperate struggle against extinction. Likewise, when Pope Francis was revered for saying, during his 2015 visit to the 9/11 Memorial in downtown Manhattan, with all the depth and sincerity of a Have a Nice Day smiley face, "For all our differences and disagreements, we can live in a world of peace," I wondered how a statement as cornball and platitudinous and contrary to the proof of the pontiff's literal surroundings could rise to the level of pansophy. For me, it was like watching someone in a bathing suit standing in a snowstorm and proclaiming that hypothermia is just a state of mind, or, more precisely, that the winter should get a fucking medal for swooping in just in time to save so many of us from drowning in our swimming pools.

And what sucks more than anything is we are not alone. *

BEING GAY

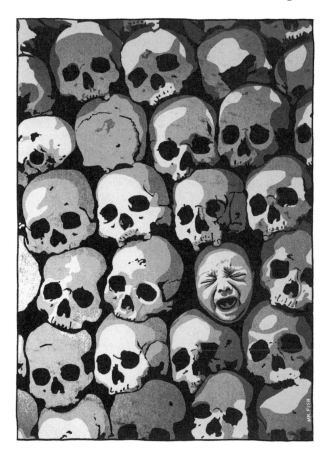

THERE'S A FAMOUS STORY about Truman Capote hanging out in a bar in the Florida Keys in the 1970s when a woman, set at a queer zigzag by booze and poor impulse control, approached his table, lifted up her shirt, held out an eyebrow pencil and asked him to sign her navel. Motivated by the desire to be left alone so that he could continue his conversation with Tennessee Williams, he acquiesced to the woman's request and spelled out his name in an ellipse around her bellybutton, writing all 12 letters as if they were numbers drawn on the face of a clock. Unaware that he had committed his autograph to flesh in clear view of the interloper's perturbed and equally inebriated husband, no sooner had Capote watched the woman walk away than he found himself looking up at her incensed spouse who had returned to the table with his wife's eyebrow pencil, his eyes full of venom and his body language replete with expletives.

There was, by now, complete silence in the bar, the man having made no secret of his outrage as he strutted across the room, his apparent jealousy inspiring the crowd to anticipate if not fisticuffs than at least the wretched sound of what passers-by outside might mistake for the skinning of an un-anesthetized chinchilla. "Since you're autographing things," the man growled while unzipping his fly, reaching in and hauling out his penis, "why don't you autograph this?"

Speaking slowly and turning the syllables over in his mouth as if to savor the flavor of his own tongue, Capote looked up at the guy and lisped lazily before a rapt audience, "I don't know if I can autograph it, but perhaps I can initial it."

✵ ✵ ✵

I first heard that story when I was 15, right around the time when I discovered that I was gay. At least I thought I was. This was back before I figured out that what I really was was just sexually convivial, self-obsessed and so contemptuous of propriety that I would've grown a middle finger out of the middle of my forehead had I been able to, just to avoid being like all the ticky-tacky robots surrounding me, smoothing their hair and testing the stench of their breath against the palm of their hand, all the while wondering whether Jesus wanted them as a moonbeam or a buttercup. Being gay was what my physiology chose to do instead of chain-smoking or shoplifting. It was an expression of nonconformity that had less to do with some deep-seated urge to suddenly proclaim my affection for one type of sex over another and more to do with my desire to lodge a formal protest against convention. I hated the idea that heterosexuality was perhaps the most widely relied upon yardstick with which society measured normalcy, as if comparing straight sex to gay sex was somehow dissimilar to comparing pancakes to waffles and that declaring a lifelong allegiance to the yumminess of one while simultaneously decrying the putridness of the other was somehow akin to a moral act.

Equally infuriating was the presumed courageousness with which straight society typically infused its anti-gay bigotry, as if courage, like allegiance, was not a morally neutral virtue. After all, it is seldom the courage to be principled and civilized that keeps you alive on the battlefield, but rather it is the courage to be ruthless and cutthroat and as far from your empathetic center as possible. Of course, if that is what courage is, then what does that say about cowardice, particularly the cowardice of those who wholeheartedly embrace a prejudice with all the incuriosity of any group that prefers to stay in line and follow the leader as compared to those who might prefer to question the wisdom of forming the line in the first place, and then confuse the sensation of moving forward with advancing? Doesn't the physics of human morality insist that below the neutrality of courage there exists something like purposeful wretchedness and willful ignorance?

I was determined to be gay, even if I had to sleep with other guys to do it, because, just as it was with racism and sexism, homophobia was not founded in reason so it could not be destroyed by logic. In fact, to merely talk about why it might be wrong to hate gay people made discrimination against homosexuals little more than a matter of opinion, no more substantive than announcing a dislike for argyle or Mexican food or dogs in sunglasses. It was for that reason that I believed homosexual affection had to be actively and deliberately demonstrated in venues where it was deemed most contemptible. Fags, I believed, needed to have the sensationalism of their lifestyle made mundane by the sort of repetitive and monotonous public display that straight society used to render gay relationships so full of voodoo in the first place.

Ironic that a mass movement predicated on the appeal of sodomy would be so incendiary to so many people who live their lives with their heads up their asses.

✵ ✵ ✵

What worried me most about suddenly wanting to have sex with other boys was not the emotional and physical abuse that decent society required I either experience or worry about experiencing,

MAYBE WE SHOULD WAIT UNTIL THE TINY GROUP OF BUREAUCRATIC WHITE HOMOPHOBIC MILLIONAIRES WHO CALL US MORAL DEGENERATES IN THE NAME OF A MAKE-PRETEND 2,000-YEAR-OLD VIRGIN LORD VOLDEMORT OF SANCTIMONIOUS INTOLERANCE SAY IT'S OKAY TO DO THIS.

MR. FISH

but rather it was the immediate acceptance that I predicted my mother would offer upon seeing me step out of the closet. After all, here was a woman who owned a three-legged dog named Bleu, a table lamp full of living sea horses, a green dwarf parrot that ate nothing but fried chicken and peanut butter, and a closet full of wigs, water pistols and rubber hands; plus, she had the largest collection of orphaned heads lifted from every puzzle in every pediatrician's office that she'd ever set foot into. How do you shock somebody like that and establish yourself as a rebellious personality? How do you not feel like just another benign eccentricity with all the cultural significance of a ceramic Easter Bunny that poops M&M's or a roll of black toilet paper or a set of plastic hillbilly teeth?

Here's how I imagined it going down:

INT. MR. FISH'S PARENTS' DINING ROOM — NIGHT

MR. FISH, his MOM and his STEPDAD are having dinner together at the family table. It is 1980 and the house is completely surrounded by hundreds and hundreds of miles of New Jersey. There is silence except for the sound of clinking silverware while everyone eats. MR. FISH stops eating.

FISH
Mom, Dad, I think I might be gay. Would you please pass the ketchup?

STEPDAD
(shocked)
You what?!

MOM
The ketchup, dear. He wants the ketchup.

STEPDAD
He said that he thinks he might be gay! Isn't that what you said?!

FISH
Give me the ketchup first and I'll tell you. My hot dog's getting cold.

STEPDAD
You would know, wouldn't you, you goddamn fruit! If I see you touch that hot dog again I'll slap your face!

MOM
Mrs. Leviticus has a gay nephew named Guy Saliva. She says that he's so oversexed that after he smokes a cigar he smokes a cigarette.

STEPDAD
How do you know that it's being gay, son, and not something like an iron deficiency?

FISH
I take a multivitamin.

STEPDAD
Maybe there isn't enough iron in it. Is it shaped like a cartoon character?

FISH
Leave me alone!

STEPDAD
Maybe you need less iron and a goddamn kick in the head!

FISH
Mom, will you please pass me the ketchup?

STEPDAD
When did all this gay nonsense first pop into your pea brain, anyway?

FISH
When I was old enough to lick men's underwear ads into soggy holes in the Sears catalog.

STEPDAD
Maybe you're really a stamp collector.

FISH

If you don't pass me the ketchup soon I'm going to have to sit on my hot dog to keep it warm.

STEPDAD

You'd love that, wouldn't you?

FISH

Pass me the goddamn ketchup!

MOM

Motherfucking, dear. Not *goddamn*. Remember the lesson of Jesus on the motherfucking cross.

FISH

I'm gay! Gay gay gay gay gay gay gay!

STEPDAD

I just don't see how you could be so sure.

FISH

I want a big hairy guy to fuck me up the ass and then I want to watch television with him afterward and play footsies while our balls reload.

STEPDAD

You're not gay. You just need a library card.

MOM

The c-a-t-s-u-p spelling of ketchup makes me think of cats. Isn't that weird?

STEPDAD

How could you be gay? You grew up wearing speedboat pajamas! I wanted you to be a Marine!

FISH

And there aren't any gay Marines? Come on, Pops — wake up!

MOM

Mrs. Leviticus' first husband was a Navy SEAL who got slaughtered for his pelt. She says that she wasn't surprised, that his pelt was why she married him. That and the fact that he could play "Pop Goes the Weasel" on a row of little horns using just his mouth.

STEPDAD

OK, if you plan on being welcome in this house and to keep drinking my root beer and eating my ketchup and being gay at the same time, I need you to do something for me.

FISH

What?

STEPDAD

It'll be for the good of the family.

FISH

What!

STEPDAD

Date Judy the Mustache.

FISH

Who?

STEPDAD

Judy. The Mustache. She's the shemale with the circus that comes through every summer.

FISH

You're crazy!

STEPDAD

For five bucks you get to watch her through a peephole while she makes an apple pie from scratch and then, after she sets it into the oven to bake, she holds nails in her mouth and builds a birdhouse. The whole time she's wearing nothing but a garter belt and a hard hat.

FISH

Mom, will you please pass me the ketchup?

MOM

Mee-owww! Cats-up! Get it?

STEPDAD

She's in the trailer way in the back behind all the tents, right next to the Unidentical Identical Twins. Damnedest things you ever saw, those twins. They look nothing alike!

FISH

I'm not dating Judy the Mustache!

STEPDAD

But she's got a penis! True, it's a little misshapen and definitely on the maroon side, but what do you expect with all the goddamn pies and birdhouses she has to make? She's working 12 hours a day, six days a week! Jesus frigging Christ, we should all work half as hard as she does!

MOM

Where's your hot dog, honey?

FISH

I'm sitting on it, Mom. Dad wouldn't give me the fucking ketchup and the goddamn thing was getting cold.

MOM

(offended)

Motherfucking thing, dear, please.

STEPDAD

He's sitting on it, woman! Now leave him alone! Son! Just consider it!

FISH

No!

STEPDAD

Why not? You get a penis and your mother and me get to see you holding hands with somebody with breasts and lipstick and her own toolbox.

FISH

No!

STEPDAD

She'll put beard burns on your tummy!

MOM

Mrs. Leviticus has such bad 5 o'clock shadows under her arms that whenever she bowls she catches fire.

STEPDAD

Why can't you just act normal for two seconds, you big sissy?!

FISH

Shut up old man and pass me the lousy ketchup!

STEPDAD

Just do it for your dear old dad!

FISH

NO!

STEPDAD

If you get married you'll be Fish the Mustache, you fucking little useless piece of no good dog shit! I thought I raised you better!

FISH

(pause)

All right, give me the ketchup bottle and I'll go down and suck her dick. But I'm not making any promises!

STEPDAD

That's my boy!

FISH

I love you, Dad.

STEPDAD

And I love you, Son.

MOM

Hey, that reminds me, honey. Do you remember that story that ran in the paper last Thanksgiving about Mr. Kirby, the widower over on Dudley who trained his cat to use a regular toilet instead of a litter box?

STEPDAD

No.

MOM

It turns out that the only reason he did it was so he could sneak into the cat's bedroom whenever the cat was taking a dump and try on its underwear.

As MOM speaks, the camera slowly pans over STEP-DAD and FISH and out of the dining room, coming to rest on a pot of hot dogs on the stove. A FLY buzzes in a manic circle upside down on the surface of the greasy water, hopelessly trapped and struggling hard against drowning.

MOM (CONT.)

The cat set up a video camera and got the whole thing on tape. Seems she started to suspect something was up when the dog began complaining that somebody was stealing money from his sock drawer every time he shaved.

❀ ❀ ❀

The thing about the Truman Capote story that so amazed me when I was 15 was how well it illustrated the ability of a good joke to recalibrate the politics of a dangerous situation and suddenly make it safe. Not only that, it demonstrated how jokes are uniquely capable of temporarily nullifying every prejudice within earshot of its telling in deference to both the high hilarity and camaraderie guaranteed by the levity of the moment. It didn't matter that Capote was gay, for example, any more than it mattered that a grown man had just exposed himself in a public place. The punch line had given justification to every detail of the story, as if the exposition could be substantiated by the pyrotechnics of the gag. Why was this? Was it because humor was escapism and that a joke provided a welcome interruption for people who felt as if their souls were being continuously ground down by a dastardly and unrelenting reality hellbent on telling it like it was without ceasing? Was comedy a lens through which reality was skewed and ultimately perverted into a fantasy that had no real relevance to what was commonly referred to as the truth?

Or was it the opposite?

Was it more likely that jokes actually provided insight into a reality rendered invisible by mainstream thinking and conventional wisdom? It was generally understood that civility destroyed humor, sure, just as being well mannered crippled candor and often encouraged subterfuge and duplicity. This certainly wasn't news to anybody. Still, I couldn't remember ever hearing anybody ask why the insincerity of decorum was prized over the bluntness so crucial to a sense of humor, which it was. Joke making, it seemed to me, was the human equivalent of what animals did when they play wrestled each other in nature. For instance, when tigers tackle each other and roll around pawing and gumming jugulars they are reinforcing their communal bonds and practicing how not to exercise lethal behavior. They are learning about the strengths and limitations of their physical bodies and demonstrating what it feels like to be free and alive in the world. Jokes, likewise, represent the intellectual play that reinforce communal bonds between people and demonstrate how they should not exercise lethal behavior with each other. They reveal what our behavioral limitations are and teach us the importance of dissent from a standard that seeks to indoctrinate us with intolerance and humorlessness and paranoia and prejudice.

Jokes teach us that while a fart may not be at all amusing to a pastor whose job it is to stand at the head of a church and celebrate humankind as the greatest miracle of God's creation, it is at least a reminder that a pastor and the antediluvian sales pitch that he preaches from the Bible are, minimally, not the whole story.

That's when it occurred to me that instead of hoisting myself upon the broad shoulders of outrage and announcing that I was gay because I wanted to express my contempt for the priggishness of the dominant culture and the dishonesty that would be the guaranteed result from succumbing to it, I should be like Truman Capote in a bar in the Florida Keys in the 1970s and set about saving the world by inspiring people to want to publicly expose the indecency of truth by beautifying the androgyny of its nudity one yuck at a time. *

MR.FISH

Noah finding out that his gay turtle, Jerry, needs to start liking pussy immediately.

EPILOGUE:
The Search Engine That Couldn't

SO, THERE I WAS getting ready to jerk off to some online pornography, my hands resting in the classic Frank Edward McGurrin home row position, when I suddenly realized that my interface with reality had been corrupted by a language that wasn't my own. Squinting hard through the swelling crescendo of cold brass that is the spontaneous horniness we all experience every now and again, I caught a glimpse of myself reflected in my monitor — an LCD screen, no doubt, that had been screwed into place by suicidal Asian youth many thousands of miles away in a towering concrete factory skirted by nets for falling bodies — just as I felt the angry muzzle of my boner press itself into my stomach and, in a voice I imagined to be a cross between SpongeBob SquarePants and Heath Ledger's Joker, order me to empty my vas deferens without making a sound. Instead of seeing myself reflected in the glass, I saw a lab rat that had been conditioned to trigger a chute to drop a single shelled peanut by nudging an electrically charged metal plate with its nose, figuring that the temporary jolt of pain and humiliation would be justified by the meager reward of salt and fat, the sun brought to you by halogen, the weather by freon, the existential woe and elation of the vast and outlandish cosmos by Verizon Wireless.

How did this happen?

As a metaphor, how had *these* particular words, these Crayola-grade adjectives and this misogynistic slanguage, come to reside so comfortably in my fingertips? They weren't always there. None of us are born knowing instinctually how to cut such cheap and slimy bait and then how to sling it into the empty shaft of a search bar behind a blinking cursor. There was a time when all I needed was the faintest memory of how paralyzing my last blast off was to want another one, nothing else. Similarly, I used to be able to drive from point A to point B without surrendering all of my cognitive faculties to the scentless network of flying robots circling the planet; when all I had was a paper map or the handwritten directions carefully curated by a friend or relative listing the landmarks and the names and numbers of roads and highways I'd need to pay attention to as if they were the ingredients and precise measurements for something my trip, itself, would bake and ultimately served to me as my destination.

I also used to watch all the Rankin/Bass Christmas specials every December when I was growing up and then I'd have to wait a whole year before I'd be given the opportunity to watch any of them again, which is different from today. Today our phones and laptops brag of their superiority to the real world, insisting that the raw, unedited footage of actual life is bloated and tedious and completely indifferent to the dynamic appetites of our everchanging moods. Our modern technologies encourage our impatience and treat us like we're all Caligula Jong-un, our arms forever crossed and our imperious eyes forever demanding immediate and complete satiation of every curiosity that drifts through the Swiss cheese of our tattered concentration.

If, for instance, in the middle of August I wanted to kill some time while finishing off a box of Apple Cinnamon Cheerios, having just finished a bowl of regular Cheerios as my main course and deciding that, yes, I'd earned a dessert, I might head over to YouTube to take a closer look at the public speeches of Burgermeister Meisterburger to see if his insane hatred and rabid intolerance of toys in *Santa Claus is Comin' to Town* ever showed any signs that it might spread into Austria, Czechoslovakia, Poland, East Prussia and Belarus. Then, of course, I'd need to look at the ghoulish pictures of dead German soldiers that the Red Army had robbed of their boots and set frozen in the snow like freakish scarecrows along the Eastern Front in the middle of the Second World War. Then I'd have to watch the Snow Miser dance number from *The Year Without a Santa Claus* to see if it still held up, at which point I'd discover that both Snow Miser and his brother were much queenier and inflexible than I'd remembered and I'd finally understand that catastrophic climate change would be inevitable so long as these assholes kept trying to out-diva each other. Then I'd remember how Hermey the homosexual dentist from *Rudolph the Red-Nosed Reindeer* oinked like a pig before ripping out all the teeth of the Abominable Snowmonster with pliers, the brutality of the act finally allowing him to embrace his inner Josef Mengele and, thankfully, to feel less like a misfit — happy fucking Christmas, everybody! Then I'd think of Ned Beatty. Then I'd think about environmentalism and sustainable agriculture. Then I'd think about suicide seeds and the dangers they posed to independent farmers and the biodiversity of all the native species of plants that conspire to create the global ecosystem. It wouldn't be long before I'd be watching a grown man fucking a pumpkin in his kitchen, the entire afternoon gone and my search history long enough to wrap around my neck a thousand times over.

Of course, then I'd worry that maybe I might be addicted to the internet. I'd think about buying a book to help me diagnose my problem. Maybe there'd be strategies in this book to help me maintain my sobriety and perhaps become an inspiration to others struggling with the same affliction. Then I'd say to myself, "Why buy a book when

click, *click*, click, click, click, *click*, *click*, click, click, click, click, click, click, click, click, *click*... a grown man fucking a pumpkin in his kitchen.

I found myself wondering if we'd finally convinced ourselves that reality didn't require our actual presence in the world and that by chop-

there's probably a perfectly good article about all this for free somewhere online?" Click, *click*, click, *click*, click, click, click, click, click, click, click, click, *click*, *click*, *click*, click, click, click, click, click, click, *click*, click, click, click, *click*, click, click, click, click, click, click, click, *click*, click, *click*, click, *click*, click, click, *click*, click, click, click, click, click, click, click, click, click, click, click, click, click, click, click, click, click, click,

ping up the remaining remnants of our authentic experiences, whether we're talking about orgasmic freefalls or genuine love and respect for each other, and hiding them in vending machines and great mountains of bullshit, we've succeeded in repackaging our lives into byte-sized portions requiring coins to access and the respectful handling of bunk and moonshine to uncover. Of course, previous to the invention of the internet, in order to test my comprehension of anything, ranging from history and science to art and philosophy, it was necessary for me to wander through my own memories, past everybody who I've ever met either directly or indirectly and amid the strewn puzzle pieces of former deliberations I'd done on both the meaning and meaninglessness of life, never feeling as if I was arriving at a truth but rather that I was navigating an inspiring and terrifying terrain in the company of others equally satiated by the simple act of walking, climbing, sliding, falling, rolling and standing again, the primary purpose of the journey being the sharing of the journey.

What had finally convinced us all that we were tired and needed to sit down?

❀ ❀ ❀

The man dressed as a pickle would not say a word. With his face completely hidden behind a mesh screen in the top part of his whopping full-body boomeranging shaft, he bruised the air around him by presenting as the al-Qaeda version of a street mime. When I asked him to explain what he was doing there at the Fourth of July "Salute to America" celebration on the National Mall, he would only answer by dancing. His incoherence was maddening. Most people maintained a wide berth when passing him on their way to the Reflecting Pool area to await the President's inspiring tank-flanked message to the nation, which promised to be no more inspiring than any of the other messages I'd seen him deliver as the leader of the Free™ World: *WATCH ME MAS-TURBATE INTO A MIRROR TO A SHITTY CRUISE SHIP ARRANGEMENT OF THE O'JAYS'* FOR THE LOVE OF MONEY *AND PRETEND IT'S JOHN PHILIP SOUSA*. Occasionally, still, someone would stop and attempt to take a selfie with the pickle man and, judging by their deflated look when they walked away from him, end up with a picture of themselves smiling and giving a thumbs up next to a confounding green blur, the pickle's karate vogueing as elusive to capture as the smudged and iridescent confetti that would be pulled from the night sky in a couple hours by hundreds of tourists overconfident about their iPhone's ability to capture and forever quarantine patriotism, itself.

The majority of the passersby were white and polite and dressed as flags and, because the pickle man was wearing a full body stocking that included gloves and green ballet shoes, there seemed to be little common ground upon which to begin, much less finish, a conversation about something, much less anything. Laying back on the grass next to my wife to close my eyes for a moment against a sky that had been swelling like a soggy diaper all afternoon, I, wondering where I'd misplaced my optimism for the day, retraced my steps back to 7 a.m. and the moment when I stood in my kitchen in Philadelphia with a cup of coffee in my hand and decided to give a shit about the country.

The original plan was for me to travel to D.C. alone with my drawing supplies so I could carry on the noble tradition begun by Civil War sketch artists 150 years ago. These were the first imbedded photojournalists sent by newspaper and magazine editors into camps and onto battlefields to depict the experiences of soldiers and civilians before cameras were sophisticated enough to arrest an active moment in time and to keep it legible. I had done this work before for a website called Truthdig during the Democratic National Convention in July 2016. Originally assigned the task of creating a series of political cartoons to comment on the macabre spectacle of the 4-day event, I ended up seeing greater virtue in looking beyond the circus and reporting on the vulnerability of the flesh hidden by the costumes. After all, it didn't take long for me to figure out how there existed an unsettling parallel between the kind of people who stand outside fast food restaurants dressed as hamburgers waving at cars, having zero comprehension of how profoundly grotesque the meat industry is and how their waving is contributing in some small way to the perpetuation of a bovine holocaust that can in no way be justified, and the kind of people who allow themselves to become clownish mascots for their political party during a national convention, having zero comprehension of how profoundly irresponsible it is to fall into the bad habit of thinking a candidate, *any* candidate, whose real power derives from private power that functions outside of the democratic process and oftentimes in contempt of it, will not first serve the moneymaking agenda of multinationals as President before even considering how detrimental decisions that favor profit over people are. After all, according to John Dewey, who said this through one of the most arresting mustaches in Western philosophy: "As long as politics is the shadow of big business, the attenuation of the shadow will not change the substance."

Here are some of the battlefield sketches I did in 2016, with the accompanying captions I'd originally provided for context.

THE MURAL OF THE STORY. FROM 10AM TO 2PM TODAY, VISITORS TO THE CITY HALL COURTYARD WERE INVITED TO EXPRESS THEMSELVES AND TO CREATE HUGE MURALS THAT DEMONSTRATED THE POWER AND SIGNIFICANCE OF ART. WITH ONLY RED, WHITE AND BLUE PAINT AVAILABLE AND WITH THE FOLDING TABLES OPEN TO THE MURDEROUS SUN, THE ENTIRE ACTIVITY ATTRACTED NO ONE, SEEMINGLY REFLECTING THE CURRENT ELECTION PROCESS WHERE ONE IS OFFERED A SIMPLISTIC PALETTE LIMITED TO PATRIOTIC CLICHES AND A WOEFULLY UNPLEASANT ARENA IN WHICH TO CELEBRATE THE MYTHOLOGY OF ABSOLUTE CREATIVE FREEDOM. ONLY ONE OF THE EVENT ORGANIZERS COULD BE SEEN WORKING, A DECOY HOPING TO ATTRACT OTHERS TO HIS APPARENT AGONY.

THIS IS WHAT A *POLICE SEDATE LOOKS LIKE!* HERE'S AN ILLUSTRATION OF POLICEMEN MOVING THROUGH FDR PARK, WHERE CONVENTION PROTESTORS ARE CAMPING JUST OUTSIDE THE WELLS FARGO CENTER. WHILE CERTAINLY A VISIBLE PRESENCE TO THOSE CAMPING, SINGING, CHANTING AND MAKING SIGNS AND T-SHIRTS DEMANDING THAT WE ALL ACKNOWLEDGE THE MORAL ILLEGITIMACY OF BOTH THE CURRENT DEMOCRATIC AND REPUBLICAN PARTIES, THERE APPEARS TO BE LITTLE VITRIOL AIMED AT THE COPS, PERHAPS BECAUSE NONE OF THEM SEEM TO BE IN PARTICULARLY GOOD SHAPE AND, MINUS THE GUNS, MIGHT BE MISTAKEN FOR A DROWSING CROSS BETWEEN MAILMEN AND EXHAUSTED PAPERBOYS AT THE END OF THEIR ROUTES.

PITY TO THE PEOPLE! HERE IS A RADICAL DNC POSTER THAT HAS BEEN CORRECTED BY A MORE RADICAL PERSONALITY WHO TRAVELS WITH A RED MAGIC MARKER.

THE FOUNTAINS AT DILWORTH PARK AT CITY HALL. THE BERNIE SANDERS AND HILLARY CLINTON SUPPORT-
ERS CRISSCROSSING NEARBY ARE NOT INCLUDED IN THE RENDERING. NOR ARE THE CONVENTION BALLOONS
OR PLACARDS MEGAPHONING THEIR TIN WHISTLE GLEE FOR DEMOCKRACY EVERYWHERE YOU LOOK. NOR
IS THE SMALL BAND OF RELIGIOUS ZEALOTS STANDING NOT 10 FEET AWAY WITH SIGNS AND A BULLHORN
RAGING AGAINST HOMOSEXUALS AND MUSLIMS WHILE TOURISTS TAKE PICTURES WITH THEIR CELLPHONES.
I WANTED TO PAUSE AND REMIND MYSELF PRECISELY WHAT IS POETIC AND NONPOLITICAL ABOUT WHO WE
ARE, AS PEOPLE, AS COMPARED TO WHAT WE PRETEND TO BE, AS PARTISANS.

After having my enthusiasm shot full of holes by the repeated warnings of torrential downpours during the 2019 Fourth of July festivities in D.C., I decided against traveling alone with my pencils and drawing pad into a completely waterlogged nation's capital and, instead, asked my wife, Diana, if she'd like to drive down with me to join the planned demonstrations featuring the world famous Trump Baby Balloon that she and I had been getting emails about for a month. *JOIN*

THE TRUMP IS A BIG BABY FESTIVAL! is how it was being advertised by CodePink, who had secured a permit from the National Park Service for a section of ground just north of the Washington Monument for the flying — which turned out to be more an uneventful folding, since helium was not permitted for inflation by the park officials — of the 20-foot balloon made in China for the purpose of pacifying our outrage over the catastrophic actions of the most dangerous president in the history of the republic with burlesque. Because she hadn't been to D.C. for a political rally since the March for Women's Lives in 1994, having been trapped for years at home to temper the hourly coup attempts by our twin daughters to dethrone the reigning *momarchy* while I periodically left to mansplain the barricades, she said sure. And while we vocalized the importance of making the three-hour trip to protest Trump's brand-new staging of *You're Either Narcissus or Against US,* a vaudevillian sellabration of military muscle and plutocratic balderdash that even Stalin would've seen as a bit excessive, we also wanted to go down to have certain beliefs about how the world was put together corroborated, the existential aching that we'd been waking up with every morning since November 8th 2016 needed confirmation that it wasn't in our heads, but in our hearts.

24-hours later, I would look back at the emailed itineraries from the various progressive groups shilling for the CodePink event with fresh eyes and wonder how I'd missed the warning signs that were there, written in the clearest language possible, attempting to shoo me away from attending: *Demonstrations will begin Thursday with a flag burning, a senior citizens' singalong and the unveiling of Baby Trump!* It was the singalong. Old people, with their lungs as robust as greasy paper bags, are unintelligible in crowds, *Puff the Magic Dragon* or no *Puff the Magic Dragon.*

Fuck.

❋ ❋ ❋

If it's true that life is whatever we pay attention to, and I think it is, then how much of who we are has to do with how willing we are to allow cheerful distractions to overwhelm our perception of the world with what we want to be true over what might actually be true? When Barack Obama was elected as the first black President in 2008, I sat back and watched in horror while members of the white community predicted catastrophe because of the color of his skin and members of the black community predicted salvation because of the color of his skin, both perspectives racist and neither cued into the fact that the only difference between an asshole and an anus is how the crossword puzzle designations are phrased for each.

Perhaps the more specific question is this: What is it about politics that encourages us to always comply with its myopic and puerile demeanor rather than stay true to our headier principles and more sober assessments of how and why we should interpret the multiplicity of our massive tribe as interwoven threads of an exquisitely colored tapestry instead of as ball bearings set on an unsteady mirror and told to see reality only in our isolated, individual reflections and to interpret the unavoidable collisions caused by those around us as willful acts of aggression? Who among us would ever think to tolerate the padded narratives and empty promises made by our mothers and fathers if, every four years, they had to campaign against each other for leadership of the family, Dad citing his dexterity with household finances and his prowess as a karate champion even though the only time his foot ever goes above his waist is when he lays in his hammock and Mom crowing about her expertise in stroking bruised egos into beautifully ripened fruit and easing the pain of those in existential crisis with love and understanding, or cookies? When there exists an authoritarian class that feels the need to play out the charade that those it resides over are,

in fact, the authoritarian class — something that the subordinate class needs to believe in order to remain complicit with the skewed power dynamic without actually seeing it for what it is — the theater will always adhere to the tenets of farce and parody rather than logic and reason.

How else to explain our refusal to recognize every public servant that we're forced to consider during every election cycle as junk food extolling the virtues of a balanced diet? How else to explain the feeling I got every time I tried to use my work to initiate a substantive conversation about our *real* political circumstance as a collapsing empire during a campaign season, when magazine and newspaper editors would treat me like I was a child they'd just rescued from Joseph Kony's Lord's Resistance Army, insisting that I abandon my memories of the battlefield so they could give me new sneakers and a bath and then take me to *Friendly's* for an *I Kid You Nut Sundae* where I might render a harsh but hilarious criticism of the whipped cream?

Even minus the Obama phenomenon, there's nothing like a presidential campaign to demonstrate just how profoundly detached we are as a nation from recognizing why ours is a functioning democracy in reputation alone. It happens every four years. Candidates emerge from the self-glorifying genius of their own private fortunes to thump their chests, swelled to near bursting with a megalomania so full of empty symbolism as to serve as the perfect echo chamber for those in love with the sound of their own voices made booming by the vacuity. I recently discovered an unpublished interview that I did with Joan Baez a week after Obama was elected that communicates this frustration with our system of self-gullibility perfectly. The title I'd given to the incomplete conversation was *Joan of Art — If I Had a Hummer meets If I Had a Hammer:*

There it sits every four years, Election Day, like a megaton turd of brain-gobbling kryptonite on the calendar, its intellectually deleterious effects emanating out from the Tuesday after the first Monday of November like moron radiation from a black hole of self-emulating *über* nationalism so devoid of meaningful content that not even irony can escape it. And there I typically sit, unable to set editorial cartooning pen to paper because the political discourse in this country has become so insular and platitudinous and bombastic that satire can only appear derivative of the reality it's attempting to exaggerate. What kind of joke, after all, can one write when it is literally true that the only reason why Doomsday hasn't arrived yet is because Best Buy hasn't figured out how to sell the post-apocalyptic markdown on *Final Fantasy XIII* and *Call of Duty* yet?

"Campaign promises are only good for one thing," I said to Joan Baez over the phone two hours before I'd see her reduce her audience to grateful tears at Royce Hall on the campus of UCLA. "They manure the ground for all the real political activity that must go on outside the Beltway. The real tragedy is that most people think political engagement begins and ends with voting, not knowing that voting alone has about as much to do with sustaining a healthy democracy as flossing your teeth on the morning of a dentist appointment has to do with staving off gum disease. How do we make people aware that their teeth are rotting out of their heads when the anesthesia of the American Dream seems to have made them numb to the pain?"

THE "DIVERSION"

❈ ❈ ❈

We stop feeding them baby food.

How has the culture changed over the last 40 years — or maybe the question should be how have *you* changed over the last 40 years? I assume that with an artist such as yourself, who is so politically and socially minded, that you've experienced both terrific camaraderie [with] and genuine disdain for American society as it succeeds and fails to maintain its most widely publicized virtues.

Well, I came from an era when there were a lot of causes and I was very active in many of them, particularly those that related to non-violence. Then I believe there came a very dry spell during which time we were taken backwards in many respects.

Was that during the '80s?

Yes, the '80s and part of the '90s.

The unholy mirage of Reaganomics and *Max Headroom*.

Right.

Well, let's be specific about your legacy just so we have a point of comparison from which to measure

the societal changes I'm talking about. All one needs to do is look at old footage from the 1960s of you performing *There But For Fortune* and *Oh, Freedom* and *We Shall Overcome* and one gets a real sense of how deeply you and your audience cared about how important it was to propagate peace, justice, community, etc. These were spiritual events and your dedication to humanitarian values was terribly authentic and there seemed to be a real reverence towards the enormity of that responsibility. These were *WE* events, not *ME* events. Are you able to find contemporary venues and audiences capable of recreating that sense of purpose and optimism and comradery?

Yeah, well, at the moment, I'm not trying to do a great deal with that, but I do know that when I walk onstage I either represent history or the anti-Christ to people. I prefer history.

But isn't that what's tragic, the fact that your commitment to non-violence and civil rights and activism looks like history to people? Shouldn't progressive political engagement be more prevalent in the culture, or at least in [the music industry]? When did muzzling popular culture as a viable megaphone for social justice become a good idea? When Howard Zinn or Alexander Cockburn or Noam Chomsky or Angela Davis or

TAMPER-PROOF

VOTING MACHINE

Gloria Steinem or Kurt Vonnegut walk onstage, they represent the present, not the past — so should you!

Well, that's nice, but it isn't really up to me, is it?

Is performing still a fresh experience for you?

In this atmosphere, with Barack Obama being elected President and becoming a real catalyst for change, yes, it's totally fresh. For instance, I'm doing songs now that I haven't done for many years because I thought they were just a nostalgia trip for people — songs like *[With] God on Our Side* — and I'm perfectly comfortable singing them now.

Well, I hope the socially conscious and liberally committed factions of society are ready to proceed with building a new progressive movement without [Obama] if he decides he doesn't want to undermine the opulent minority who all Presidents end up serving in the end.

I think we have to demand his participation. *We* have to be the ones he consults and not just the same old white guys with four stars on their shoulders. Unless we step up, generals and business leaders and special interest groups will be the only advice he seeks, and [they will provide] the only advice he gets. I think we have half a chance, but it will take some doing.

I worry about how willing [Obama] seems to be to play politics. Specifically, I'm bothered by his refusal to express an opinion about how [George W.] Bush is responding to the Gaza Massacre, saying that, "there can only be one President at a time." Seems like a cop out, as if responding to an obvious Israeli-led atrocity with criticism and concern that runs contrary to the jack ass still in the White House compromises our national security or something. He's being a coward, frankly.

You're right, and that refusal to comment made in support of the Israeli lobby doesn't help the struggling Middle East peace process. I've marched with IDF soldiers who have gone to jail because they refused to kill Palestinians — *these* are the people we should know about. *These* are the people who [Obama] needs to acknowledge.

I've often wondered about people like you, and Donovan and Harry Belafonte — people who have committed themselves to adopting a lifestyle that reflects their politics so precisely and whose resistance to conventionality has gone beyond street protest and has manifested [itself] in the clothes you buy and the lightbulbs you use and the tea you drink and the solar panels you install and the charities you support, and so on. How frustrating is it for you not to see a wider embrace of the values so integral to all that was spearheaded in the 1960s and '70s, not just politically but personally? In other words, part of encouraging more sustainable living practices is paying attention to what goes into both our bodies *and* our minds and I can't imagine you're happy about how polluted our domestic and foreign policies have become

cially now, I haven't expected very much from the human race, so it's been easier to [deal with] all the disastrous twists and turns [of America in the 21st Century]. It isn't about caring less, it's about gaining a perspective and caring about the process more than getting to the finish line.

How has modern technology affected how young people engage with the criminality of their own government? Is it even possible to build a resistance movement when the primary interface that people have with the outside world is less face-to-face and more face-to-screen, making universal misery and injustice something they can just turn off, or [more likely] swipe away from so they can return to the soap operatic drama promoted by their social media feeds?

Most of the interviews I do nowadays are with younger people who are really struggling to build a movement that has some meaning and that makes sense, but the problem is that the only tools the American culture has given them is a legacy of greed and a feeling of entitlement. Americans simply assume that they're better than everybody else and that they deserve whatever they want, whenever they want it, and nothing needs to be earned. Peace and love is a brand now.

That's what I was getting at with the question about lifestyle, how everybody acts like they're a carnivore

with the Patriot Act and the NSA and the War on Terror and police brutality and global warming.

You're 100% right and, trust me, I'm not the only one who's had to struggle hard to hang onto my Gandhian roots. It's very difficult sometimes — but as far as frustration goes, the more you expect and the less that happens the more frustrated you'll be, and the more frustrated you become the less effective you'll be, both politically and personally. For many years, and espe-

for saving the commonwealth from fascism but nobody has the stomach for hunting. So many people will put on a Shepard Fairey *HOPE* t-shirt and somehow think it compares to going into Birmingham as a Freedom Rider. They're like goth kids who are just as likely to become real vampires by wearing black lipstick as I would be to become Jesus Christ if I grew a beard.

I think the word *sacrifice* left our vocabulary a long time ago. Any serious social change doesn't happen without a person risking, at the very least, [his or her] peace of mind and oftentimes there's a lot more they're going to lose [in the process].

Well, your ex-husband [David Harris] went to jail for evading the draft.

He sure did, for twenty months.

And, of course, now there's no draft anymore, so one less way to protest against a government's criminality in a way that directly disrupts their crimes. A drone isn't suddenly going to have a crisis of faith and grow its hair.

That's why we have to look around and at least try to notice each other. I know it's a corny thing to say nowadays, but there's a difference between wanting to change the world and trying to *be* the world. One is [an act of aggression] and the other is [an act of] compromise and cooperation. Community is really what it's all about.

I agree — being [an integral] part of a community makes it almost impossible to live comfortably with indifference as a pragmatic act of self-preservation.

❀ ❀ ❀

On November 15th in 2011 the fledgling Occupy Wall Street movement had its gonads and ovaries yanked out and ground into the frozen New York City concrete when police literally turned on the lights in the middle of the night and tore nylon tents from the sleeping earth in Zuccotti Park as if they were unsightly scabs covering the self-inflicted wounds of way too many bleeding hearts. Laptops and cell-phones were confiscated, sleeping bags were upended, and the makeshift People's Library was pushed over and five-thousand books were taken away in garbage trucks with the official jus-

tification being that they presented a danger to public health and the environment. Having begun as a leaderless movement born from middleclass discontent and based largely on a kind of cooperative groping for a nationwide acknowledgement that the accumulative value system proposed by economics will always run contrary to the intrinsic worth of all people regardless of class and income stream, much of Occupy's inability to rebound from the dismantling of its primary encampment in Zuccotti Park had to do with how the young protestors grew up being conditioned to find prolonged exposure to physical discomfort and public humiliation intolerable. Additionally, when an entire generation is encouraged to download its humanity onto the mainframe of a social media platform controlled and surveilled by both the national security state and every retailer on the globe wishing to infect every potential customer with a sense of woeful incompleteness reparable by purchase, existence offline and in the real world may oftentimes feel akin to existing in very murky water while breathing through a very slender reed, nothing that anybody would care to embark upon for an extended amount of time.

Eight months after Zuccotti, the rogue elements of the fractured movement decided to name Philadelphia as the location for an Occupy rebirth, thus a national gathering was planned for the 4th of July in 2012. According to the press releases and jubilant invitations being circulated

by organizations such as MoveOn, the ANSWER Coalition, Occupy Guitarmy and CodePink, as many as 100,000 participants were predicted to overwhelm Franklin Square and Independence Hall on the 3rd, followed by a weeklong march to the New York Stock Exchange beginning on the morning of the 5th, the size of the caravan expected to double and maybe even triple like a scrappy, placard-encrusted snowball sent down a slope along the way. Thrilled by the opportunity to witness the miraculous rebirth of Occupy in my own hometown, I went with a buddy, Pablo, and his film camera to commune with the unarmed troops of the resistance, imagining that their massive and sprawling encampment would be polka dotted by campfires, that the nighttime air would be caressed into a kind of rapture by the darling sound of guitars and laughter, and that the whole blessed scene would be made holy by the combined scent of marijuana smoke, incense, sex and Sharpies.

After facing absolutely no traffic and parking with all the ease of slotting an empty fist into an empty pocket, the only gathering my friend and I were able to find in the city that night was at Independence Mall, where the Philly Pops Orchestra played a free concert of patriotic tunes before a vast and shallow ocean of white-haired people in lawn chairs.

Returning the next day to Center City wondering if the only reason why I hadn't seen any Occupiers the night before was because they had deliberately rendered themselves invisible like a guerilla army by sleeping in the many hundreds of alleys, nooks and underpasses around town, I was greeted by the depressing realization that, no, the bedraggled band of saintly riffraff I discovered squatting under the trees in Franklin Square was all there was. According to estimates reported over the subsequent week by newspapers, the number of committed activists I saw who had come to reignite the movement, if represented by dollar bills, would only have been enough to buy one-tenth of a small hot air balloon, and that's without the basket, the burners, the gas bottles, the inflation fan, the ropes and the Occupy logo, *just* the slack fabric completely empty of hot air. I would also learn later that, not wishing to admit defeat, a signup sheet was circulated among the rank and file who had come with backpacks for the march to Manhattan and that only 45 names had been collected. I never found out if those 45

ever left the following morning, nor if they found themselves on Wall Street several days later where they were outnumbered every time a school bus unloaded nearby.

It was all very heartbreaking.

After standing and watching a people's microphone ask 80 people if anybody had a Band-Aid, Pablo and I decided to move deeper into the city to see how flamboyantly militaristic the Independence Day Parade down Broad Street had become, not because we needed to see such a garish spectacle to confirm what we already knew about the country, but rather because we wished to find some other target for our savage disappointment other than the gloomy rabble scattered before us. It was if we'd started the day by typing "resistance" into a search bar and were presented with a full page of non-political options, mostly having to do with electronics, as in: *The electrical resistance of an object is a measure of its opposition to the flow of electric current.* Momentarily distressed that progressivism was dead in America, we decided to reframe what we were looking at and to skew the evidence in front of us and to see it as a metaphor for contrarianism. Onward!

It wasn't long before we caught up to a dozen or so CodePink hellraisers, led by the organization's cofounder, the most outraged Peter Pan in activism, Medea Benjamin, all of whom must've left Franklin Square only moments before we had. They, too, appeared destined for the star-spangled fanfare of the miles-long procession of jingoistic confectionary snaking its way through town, although, according to the expectant wording barking from their signs and the shouting that Benjamin was doing into an auxiliary microphone that was as big as a bar of soap and attached to a pink megaphone as she walked, their agenda was much more noble than ours. While I typically regard sloganeering to be as meaningful to political discourse as sending smoke signals would be to reciting Walt Whitman, I always found an activist's ability to look our bloated and fractured democracy square in the face and to tell her — on her birthday in this case! — that she is fat and ugly over and over again, amazing, ridiculous, courageous, petulant and well beyond my comfort level. My method of ridicule tended more in the direction of stealth, not because I believed it was a superior approach to revolution but rather because, in tandem with direct and overt confrontation, I felt like it was my job to weaken the resolve of those who kept themselves sequestered well behind the frontlines and who supported the brutality of the monarchy without ever questioning the gruesome hostilities necessary to maintain it.

Banks got bailed out! We got sold out! Banks got bailed out! We got sold out!

Simply put, my contribution to the cause was to sit quietly in the back of the classroom and to draw a picture that, yes, depicted America as being fat and ugly, but also implicated us, We the People, as being the ones manning the chow line with our shovels, too timid and uncertain of our ability to survive outside the system to breach the walls of our captivity.

All Day! All Week! Occupy Wall Street! All Day! All Week! Occupy Wall Street!

Wishing to lend our bodies to the CodePink megaphone if only to help augment the size of the inspiring but nearly inconspicuous mob of badass malcontents trailing behind Benjamin's booming voice, my friend and I quickened our pace so we could take up their rear flank, proud to demonstrate our public allegiance to their stated principles, which, according to their website, was to, "…[E]nd U.S. wars and militarism, support peace and human rights initiatives, and redirect our tax dollars into healthcare, education, green jobs and other life-affirming programs" *by any means of boondogglery necessary.* The addendum to their mission is my own and is not meant to demean the efforts and integrity of CodePink as much as remind us all how any organization hoping to win the hearts and minds of the undecided, whether we're talking about the NRA or the AFL, will sometimes behave beyond the probity of its charter. In fact, until we all recognize our own personal tendency to lean into petty dishonesty whenever we're faced with a circumstance that appears either dismissive of our altruism or contemptuous of our naked desire to alter the existing world in some way, we will never learn to embrace the grace of empathy when forgiving the fallibility of those we wish to understand, love and influence.

Such an acknowledgment is what endears us all to the poets and painters and playwrights who are forever accentuating our shortcomings and vulnerabilities, never in an effort to mock or condemn our failings but rather to normalize them and, at long last, to make pandemic their appeal.

MR. FISH

※ ※ ※

"Occupy masks, nine dollars — cash only!" shouted the kid marching next to me, his words fattened into cotton balls and emanating from behind a Guy Fawkes mask. "Nine fwucking dollars!" he continued, waving a stack of similar masks high about his head as if he were signaling to the speck of a ship on the horizon; one that was moving the other way. "What the fwuck is wrong with you fwucking people?!"

"Hey," I said to him, watching as scowling parents covered their children's ears as we walked past, "where were you last night?"

"Nine dollars!" he shrieked, completely unaware that I was talking to him. "Some other asshole is selling the same thing for twelve dollars — I'm selling them for nine! That's a three-dollar savings!" I looked over at Pablo to see if he was getting any of this, only to find him explaining to his marching partner, a bearded teenager who had painted his bare arms, back, neck and chest with pink acrylic paint, how the temperature was supposed to climb to 100° and that covering a human body with what amounted to hot plastic might end up being a really bad idea.

Turning back to the Guy Fawkes kid and touching him on the shoulder, again I said, "Hey!"

"What?" he said, pausing to look at me with eyes like tiny razorblades. His plastic lips didn't move.

"My buddy and I came down last night to hang out with you guys and we couldn't find you anywhere," I said. "I read somewhere that you were all going to sleep in Franklin Square."

"Fwranklin Square?" he said. "Fwuck that! Way too many fwucking bugs."

"Where did you sleep?" I asked.

"On the steps of Wells Fwargo," he said. "It was fwucking awesome! Super fwucking clean."

"How many of you were there?"

"About seven," he said. "I didn't know anybody else. I had to sleep with my wallet in my fwront pocket. A lot of assholes in this city."

Just then the blur of a panicked and bug-eyed pink teenager ran past me, his desire to make the world a better place threatening to drown him in his own perspiration, I gathered. Again, I looked at Pablo who just shrugged.

※ ※ ※

Every once in a while, I feel like I've finally figured something out, although the feeling never lasts very long. And why should it? It's been said that the truth only comes to a person at the moment when he or she tires of thinking, meaning that a belief is nothing but an expression of compromise between what a person doesn't know and what he or she hopes is true. Still, standing in the pouring rain on the 4th of July in 2019 and watching fewer than 20 drenched protestors huddled and laughing beneath a makeshift stage in Washington D.C. while Neil Young's *Ohio* blasted from a nearby speaker, I was absolutely convinced that the reason why the 1960s generation that grew up to occupy the current government had failed to humanize it was because civilization had finally become a contraption that was too complicated to have its reprehensibility excised from its moral fortitude. No, it wasn't the failure of the peaceniks and the protestors and the newly liberated women, blacks, browns, reds, greens and gays from that generation, but rather the fact that America, like every other modern society on the planet, at the end of the day is made up of a shit-ton of interdependent parts and symbiotic gears with interlocking teeth that all rely on one another for their continued functionality.

In 1964 at UC Berkeley, famed member of the campus Free Speech movement, Mario Savio, addressed an enormous crowd of fellow students at Sproul Hall condemning the university's ban on political expression and the dehumanizing classification made by school officials suggesting that the student body represented little more than the raw material purchasable by employers waiting at the other end of graduation, the totality of our human experience being no more meaningful than if we were all widgets in a business schematic, saying:

> *There is a time when the operation of the machine becomes so odious, makes you so sick at heart, that you can't take part; you can't even passively take part, and you've got to put your bodies upon the gears and upon the wheels, upon the levers, upon all the apparatus, and you've got to make it stop. And you've got to indicate to the people who run it, to the people who own it, that unless you're free, the machine will be prevented from working at all!*

It was a beautiful speech that helped give tuitioned college students—and *not* the groundskeepers, janitors, housekeeping staff, security team, secretaries or cafeteria personnel employed by the university—a bulldozed and manicured clearing wherein they might enjoy the intellectual equivalent of frisbee and sunbathing, but altered absolutely nothing as far as the bullshitting they'd still need to do at every job interview and board meeting and country club consultation and bank loan adjuration they'd be experiencing outside of school.

Indeed, the income stream that moves the turbines and generates the electricity that powers the outlet that turns the corroded fan on the crappy refrigerator that holds the rationed insulin of the underpaid and muzzled limousine driver for the CEO of Raytheon is the same income stream that powers the outlet that turns the corroded fan on the crappy refrigerator that holds the rationed insulin of the underpaid and muzzled limousine driver for the CEO of Amazon. And as long as remuneration remains as the primary motivation for both the creation of trash and the removal of trash, with the production end of the process always paying substantially more than the clean-up, the reciprocity reliant on the same bloodstream will persist. Likewise, in a society stacked like Jenga squares on the precarious notion proposed by our power institutions that human rights are something we gain rather than something we embody, and where we all have been caressed like magnetic shavings into muted rows of compliance with that demeaning idea, we will never be brave enough as a collective to demand, let alone expect, all that comes from being fully free.

Life for all of us will be an expression of normalized insanity; of being put into a cubicle and commanded to think outside the box.

❀ ❀ ❀

Although I failed to transcribe the detail into my notebook, I believe the break in the barricade was inspired by somebody's need to find a bathroom.

We had been skirting Broad Street for some time with no discernable destination in mind when Medea Benjamin suddenly made a right turn and led us straight into what amounted to a long row of slatted metal bike racks set up to keep spectators from spilling into the roadway during the parade. True to the physics of any long procession composed of unique segments moving at various speeds—one, in this particular case, involving toddlers dressed as hula dancers being moved along by mothers as if they were oranges being rolled by badminton rackets and another involving a squad of gay riflemen from Florida twirling their weapons and pausing on occasion to strike a delightfully campy cheesecake pose—after some time sizable gaps will naturally open up between the performers and honored guests. This is when onlookers will stop butterflying their tiny flags to rehydrate, chat and reapply sunscreen, momentarily returning to themselves like actors in between scenes.

Seeing the empty boulevard as the miraculous appearance of a temporary land bridge made visible in between tides, Benjamin, like Moses, announced to the group that this was where we were going to cross. She then shoved the barricade aside and sent the first few Pinkers into the street. Just as two more protestors readied themselves to exit through the ramparts, a policeman rolled up on a bicycle to see what was going on. "Excuse me," he said, as imposing as a chubby question in a light blue polo shirt, "the parade is still moving, and we can't allow anybody to cross."

At this, Medea Benjamin suddenly threw up her hands as if to ward off blows from an invisible billy club, shouting, "Hey! Hey!" The captive audience surrounding her fell silent, like they were watching a grown man fucking a pumpkin in his kitchen.

"Ma'am," said the officer calmly, "I need you to step back away from the barricade."

"But I need to be with my husband!" she shouted, gesturing in the direction of the escaped protestors who were now squeezing themselves through the barricades on the other side of the street.

"If I let your group through," he explained, "everybody will want to come through. I'm sorry, but you'll need to wait until the parade is over before you can cross."

"There is no parade!" said Benjamin, looking around for an *AMEN* that never came.

"Ma'am," said the officer.

"But my daughter!" interrupted Benjamin.

"Ma'am," said the officer.

"She has a medical condition!" said Benjamin, pausing for a moment as if she were pulling her thoughts from a Scrabble bag and assembling them in front of her mind's eye. "And she needs her medication!"

With that, a second policeman coasted over on a bicycle. "Is everything okay?" he asked, looking at his colleague.

"Whoa whoa whoa!" said Benjamin, taking a step back and activating the switch on her megaphone as if she were throwing the switch on a spotlight. "THIS IS WHAT A POLICE STATE LOOKS LIKE! THIS IS WHAT A POLICE STATE LOOKS LIKE!" she chanted, hoping to convince the crowd that she wasn't exemplifying the statement, but rather using it to warn of an impending and quite unavoidable tyranny. ✳

RADICAL AMERICA

One Summer Street
Somerville, Massachusetts 02143
(617) 628-6585

2/8/88

Dear Mr. Fish,

    I took the cartoon you submitted for publication in
<u>RA</u> to our board meeting. We decided not to publish it.

    The cartoon brought out strong reactions from most of
our members who reacted with disgust at your potrayal.
While I realize that the cartoon was intended as a satire,
I believe that the depiction of naked women crawling towards
a man who will or just did stick his arm up their vaginas into their
wombs is just not funny (even in the satirical sense). It's both
too close to home and too bizarre and painful of a concept.

    But thanks for thinking of us. . .

                   For the editors,

                   Kim Westheimer

mr. fish
893 Sandy Circle
Manahawkin, New Jersey
2/10/88

RADICAL AMERICA magazine
One Summer Street
Somerville, Massachusetts

To the editors:

I would like for you to understand my cartoon and myself.
There is nothing more dangerous than being misunderstood.

My cartoon is certainly a depiction of what you called a
close to home, bizarre and painful concept, but certainly
one that is a reflection of a bizarre and painful reality
—a very sad one, one of discrimination. Depictions of
such gross realities shouldn't try to be cute or funny
(even in a satirical sense) but should rather express the
pain and dangerous consequences of the circumstance it's
trying to spot-light.

Take rape for instance. You couldn't expect a clown to
portray an accurate depiction of rape because rape is bizarre
and painful and sad, a gross reality. Clowns are predominantly
silly, and at their best could only make rape entertaining,
in either an excessively sad or happy way—only rape isn't
entertainment. Nor could you expect a so-called artist to
portray an accurate depiction of rape because rape isn't art,
and for an artist to portray rape inside some artistic context
(that's what artists do) would be to distract attention away
from rape and direct it to the artist's interpretation of
rape. If the art depicting rape is good art then the art is
applauded, and if the art is bad then the art is criticized
and forgotten—either way nothing is said or done towards
understanding the problem of rape as RAPE, as opposed to rape
as ART, or even rape as ENTERTAINMENT. Rape must be depicted
as RAPE, just like war must be depicted as WAR, and love as
LOVE—or, as in the case of my cartoon, discrimination as
DISCRIMINATION, where the Moral Majority is attempting to
pass legislation which is both stupid and chaotic because it
refuses women the freedom of choice, the freedom to be equal
among men, to be equal under any God or none. My depiction
of vaginas and wombs is a depiction of what the Moral Majority
is attempting to violate—literally.

Unless WAR and RAPE and DISCRIMINATION are depicted as something disgusting and dangerous, then WAR and RAPE and
DISCRIMINATION won't be disgusting or dangerous enough to
prevent. They will continue as ART and ENTERTAINMENT.

I do not wish to make art or to entertain. My cartoon is
meant to disgust because there is no better inspiration for
change. When there's a fire you don't yell FIRE!, you yell FUCK!

PEACE

mr. fish

Mr. Fish lives in Philadelphia, PA. Occasionally, he laughs his head off. His mother has no idea what he's up to. She cries easily. For more information, date him.